The Beginner's Guide to Computer-Based Music Production

By Zack Price

Cherry Lane Music Company
Educational Director/Project Supervisor: Susan Poliniak
Director of Publications: Mark Phillips

ISBN 1-57560-564-3

Visit our website at
www.cherrylane.com

TABLE OF CONTENTS

INTRODUCTION

When I first mentioned to a colleague who manages a music store that I was writing a book on computer-based music production, his initial reaction was one of excitement. "People are always asking me what sort of computer they need, what type of audio hardware they should get, and which software they should buy to do multitrack recording on a computer. They're usually starting from scratch, so I spend an incredible amount of time providing them with the basic information they need before they're even ready to buy anything. My job would be so much easier if I could just hand them a book with all that information and tell them to come back when they're done reading it. Then I could help them get what they really need. Is that something your book plans to cover?" When I assured him that this information was indeed in the book, it pleased him so much that I think he was ready to pre-order a hundred copies right then and there!

After his initial enthusiasm, though, he raised a concern that probably many of you have. "How will you be able to keep this book timely? Computers change every year, so this book will have a pretty short shelf life, won't it?" I realize that one is still talking about a snapshot in time even when discussing the most current computer technology, so, in one sense, information is obsolete as soon as it's presented. In another sense, though, the same information can be looked at as a reference point for learning about future technological developments.

A few weeks after that discussion, I was reading through a copy of an article I had written over eight years ago that brought this point home. The article discussed setting up a Windows-based computer for multitrack digital audio recording, and, at first, I couldn't believe what I was reading. I was talking about using fast Intel 80486DX processors (or better yet, the newer, faster Pentium 90s!), the need for at least 16 MB (megabytes) of RAM (random access memory), graphics cards with 2 MB of video RAM, and whether Enhanced IDE (integrated drive electronics) hard drives or SCSI (small computer system interface) hard drives were a better choice. "How did we ever do any serious work on these slow systems?" I said to myself in wonder. Nonetheless, the truth is that we *did* do serious work, and did it amazingly well with that equipment at the time.

As I read on, I began to realize that computer specs may have changed, but the basic elements for computer-based music production haven't changed all that much. The computer still has to be fast enough and have enough RAM to run the intended software, and it still needs a good graphics card with the necessary RAM to smoothly redraw the constantly changing graphics that occur during the operation of any digital audio program. The computer also needs sufficiently fast hard drives, as well as the appropriate audio I/O (input/output) hardware, for recording and playing back the digital audio data.

Of course, computers are much faster now than they were then, and the kinds of components they can use are more varied, too. Even so, I'm confident that someone reading that article today would still be able to understand the basics of designing a computer-based music production system. Naturally, they would have to do some additional research into the latest computer hardware—as well as the most current music software and audio hardware—to bring them up to speed with regards to present requirements. Notwithstanding that, the fundamentals of computer-based multitrack recording are essentially the same as they were eight years ago.

Likewise, the *techniques* of computer-based multitrack digital audio recording remain the same. You still need to be able to record, edit, and eventually mix down your multitrack recordings to stereo format. Of course, eight years ago the highest level of audio quality for most systems was 16-bit/48kHz resolution. Now the highest possible digital audio resolution for most systems is 24-bit/96kHz, with 24-bit/192kHz starting to become available. Eight years ago, I was happy if I could get 12-track playback of 16-bit audio from my computer-based system. Now I can achieve 24-track playback of 24-bit digital audio with plenty of computer power to spare, and I'm not even using the fastest computer available!

Of course, the speed and power of today's computer-based music production systems give users additional capabilities that just weren't possible eight years ago. Back then, real-time software-based synthesizers were just beginning to come into their own. However, their sound quality was often mediocre, and usually required so much of the computer's resources that it was impossible to run digital audio recording software with them simultaneously. Now it's possible to run multiple high quality software synthesizers while playing back several digital audio tracks in a single production environment.

Also, loop-based audio production software that allows you to alter pitch and/or tempo in real-time was unheard of back then. Now it is a well-recognized and widely used audio production tool. Moreover, with the availability of affordable DVD authoring tools, some digital audio sequencing programs and multitrack digital audio software applications now offer video editing and surround sound mixing capabilities as part of their packages. That, too, was unheard of eight years ago.

In short, it's truly amazing when one thinks of what one can do with a computer now. Yet despite their vastly improved power, today's computer-based recording systems cost no more than they did eight years ago—in fact, they're often cheaper now. And as computer power continues to increase, you will be able to do even more at once with your computer or, equally likely, do many different things using multiple inexpensive computers simultaneously. Either way, you'll be able to improve the quality of what you currently do. And you'll be able to keep up with any changes that occur in the future—no matter what the future holds—once you understand the basics of computer-based music production.

One final note: Although this book is tailored for musicians who want to create demos or finished works of their music either for sale, promotional purposes, or personal enjoyment, it is still a beginner's guide. This book won't teach you everything you need to know about creating music using a personal computer—but then, no single book can do that properly. What this book can do for you is lay a foundation for building your skills regarding all the different aspects of computer-based music production. It's fun but challenging work, and you won't learn everything about this overnight. However, don't get discouraged by that. You didn't learn to play your favorite instrument overnight, either, but if you stop to think about it, part of the fun was just in learning to play. And I hope that you will embrace this same spirit of fun as you learn the material in this book.

Zack Price

CHAPTER 1

BEFORE WE BEGIN . . .

I know that you're eager to dive in and begin creating music with your computer. However, before you get into the hands-on material, you'll need to absorb some required technical information that will help you to properly buy, use, and maintain your computer-based music production system. I know that absorbing this technical info is not as exciting as learning how to record and produce a song, but you need to know this background material if you want to master your system and keep it in proper working order. So here's the overview.

Computer

Obviously, the centerpiece of any computer-based music production system is the computer itself. Chances are that you've already bought one, so for now I'll assume that you've purchased one that's fast enough to run the music programs you're interested in using. Even so, your brand-new computer may be missing a couple of extra features that can make your life much easier. (Note: If you haven't yet bought a computer, be sure to read "Chapter 2: Choosing the Right Computer" before you start shopping so you'll know how to choose the right one for music production.)

Second Hard Drive

A computer just bought off the shelf probably has only one hard drive in it. Even though that drive may have a large data storage capacity, a second hard drive dedicated to storing digital audio data is really a must for multitrack hard disk recording. If you want to know why it's so important to devote a second hard drive to multitrack digital audio data or what type of second hard drive you should get for your computer, we'll get into more information in the next chapter; you might also want to read "Appendix A: A Hard Disk Primer" for even more information. For now, though, consider getting a second hard drive a high-priority item for your computer if you don't already have one.

Extra RAM

The average computer user is usually able to work with the 256 MB of RAM that currently seems to come standard with many machines. However, computer-based musicians are not like the average users—their systems need more RAM in order to successfully run most music programs. 256MB RAM is really the bare minimum for computer-based music production systems; at least 512MB RAM is preferred. If you're using software-based samplers or dual-processor systems (and you'll read more about each later in this book), you should have between 640MB and 1GB (a gigabyte, which equals 1024 MB) of RAM in your system. And if your system can handle even more RAM and you can afford it, get it. Eventually, you'll use it.

CD-RW or DVD-RW Drive

Almost every computer sold now includes a *CD-RW* (CD-ReWritable) drive as part of its overall package. However, if you're one of those rare people whose computer doesn't have a CD-RW drive, I have two words of advice for you: Get one! This device lets you create permanent audio and data CD-Rs (recordable but *not* rewritable CDs), as well as CD-RWs (recordable *and* rewritable) to which you can write, erase, and rewrite data. Naturally, as a musician you'll need to make audio CDs of your work, but you should also make backups of your digital audio data and project files. You can use rewritable disks for temporary backups (say, after each recording session) and recordable disks for permanent backups once a project is finished. Then, you can erase those project files off your hard drive to make room for other projects.

On average, the disk storage capacity for a CD-R is 700MB and about 535MB for a CD-RW disk. How much content you can actually store may vary according to the CD-RW drive make and model, and the media (disks) you use. More expensive *DVD-RW* (Digital Versatile Disk ReWritable) drives are also available. They can make audio and data CDs and CD-RWs, as well as larger capacity data and video DVDs (you'll learn more about this in "Chapter 2: Choosing the Right Computer)". If you can't afford a DVD-RW drive, then at least get a DVD-ROM/CD-RW combination drive. You'll still be able to make CD backups of your data files, as well create audio and video CDs. Plus, you'll be able to read data DVDs, which are becoming a more common storage medium for programs and sound libraries. And don't forget that you'll be able to watch DVD movies on your computer, too!

Almost every CD-RW and DVD-RW drive includes CD or DVD burning software as part of its package. Likewise, an increasing number of music software applications include CD burning capabilities as well. Even so, you may want to consider purchasing a separate, more professional CD or DVD burning program, since a number of the programs bundled with music software write audio CDs in such a way that all songs on the CD have a preset gap of two seconds between them, and you may want more flexibility than that.

Software

Many of you will probably use one of the following four programs to produce music with your computer: Cakewalk's Sonar, Emagic's Logic Audio, Mark of the Unicorn's (a.k.a. MOTU) Digital Performer, or Steinberg's Cubase. Sonar is designed for the Windows platform, while Logic Audio and Digital Performer are written for the Mac OS. Cubase is the only program of the four that has a version for both the Mac and Windows operating systems. All four of these programs are *digital audio sequencers*; that is, they combine MIDI (musical instrument digital interface) sequencing (and you'll learn *much* more about this later in the book), the playing of *virtual instruments* (MIDI instruments that exist solely within software), and digital audio recording and playback in a single environment. Although I'll use each of these programs to illustrate examples of computer-based music production methods throughout the book, other types of programs will be discussed as well. Some of these programs provide alternative ways of creating music on a computer, others perform specialized tasks that digital audio sequencers don't do as well, and some handle non-musical but essential tasks that keep your system operating at peak performance.

Audio and MIDI Interfaces

You'll need a professional-quality audio interface to record and play back digital audio tracks—as well as hear virtual instruments—with your computer and software. While the built-in Mac audio capabilities and PC multimedia cards are pretty good, they usually don't have all of the features and *drivers* (little programs that allow the computer, its operating system, and the appropriate music software to interact with certain pieces of hardware) that are needed to work with professional digital audio sequencers and other music software. There are a wide variety of audio interface types that are suitable for the different types of computers. Many of you will probably use the MIDI features of your digital audio sequencer, and many audio interfaces have MIDI capabilities. If yours doesn't then you will need a separate MIDI interface. At any rate, all of these interfaces are discussed in "Chapter 3: Choosing the Right Audio and/or MIDI Interface."

Mixer

Many audio interfaces also function as audio mixers. If you use an audio interface that includes this capability, you may not need a separate mixer, provided that you limit yourself to recording digital audio and virtual instrument tracks. However, investing in a separate mixer may be required or even preferred in some circumstances. For instance, you need a mixer to combine the audio outputs of your hardware synths and samplers—as well as your digital audio tracks—if you want to hear all of them simultaneously. Also, you may want to use an *outboard* (i.e., a piece of hardware separate from your computer) mixer to monitor the separate audio channels of a multichannel audio interface. This can give you a little more flexibility in creating rough mixes on the fly, which is especially helpful during the recording phase of production.

An external mixer, such as the Mackie MS1202-VLZ pictured here, is needed to hear the combined outputs of your external MIDI instruments and digital audio tracks simultaneously.

Headphones and Monitors

You'll need headphones and *monitors* (essentially, speakers) to listen to the playback of all of your audio and MIDI tracks simultaneously, hear digital audio and MIDI parts as they're being recorded, and monitor your song mixes. Many audio interfaces that function as mixers also include a headphone jack, as well as stereo mix output jacks for routing to an external monitoring system. Even if you have to use a separate mixer, you'll still want to use headphones and a pair of external monitors with it.

Headphones

If you're on a limited budget, a good pair of professional-quality headphones is all you really need to monitor your music. In fact, I often use headphones exclusively during the production process. However, you have to be willing to take the time and spend the money to make sure that you buy a good set. So what do you look for when choosing a pair? First, make sure that the headphone design is *circumaural*—that is, the headphones surround your ears. This design offers some important advantages. For one thing, they're more comfortable than headphones that press up against the outer ear, which can make the difference between getting through a long session or having to quit early because your outer ears hurt too much. Also, the circumaural design reduces sound leakage, which is especially important when you're monitoring a mix through headphones while recording a vocal performance. You don't want to ruin a vocal take because audio leaked from the headphones into the microphone!

Also, it's important to make sure that your headphones have an accurate frequency response. Unfortunately, the manufacturer's specs are not always that helpful when it comes to judging this. Furthermore, audio accuracy is often in the ear of the beholder, so you'll need to test headphones before you buy them. When you go shopping, bring a CD of some material with which you are very familiar, and listen to it through several pairs. Choose a set that gives you a sound that most closely matches what you hear on external monitors.

Professional headphones such as the ones shown here are an excellent way to monitor your music if you're on a limited budget. Note the circumaural design.

This advice seems pretty simple, but it's actually difficult to follow. For one thing, the monitoring system at the store may not match up to your system at home. Also, you must take into account that you'll hear more pronounced reverb, panoramic differences, and fades through headphones (you'll learn more about these as you work through this book). You must listen critically, and make the mental adjustments that go along with testing equipment on other people's systems. The ultimate test, however, is what the headphones will do when they are hooked up to your system—so before you buy, make sure that the store has a good return policy and save your receipt.

There may be some optional design features you may want to consider as well. For instance, some manufacturers offer headphones that have increased bass response—if you like to hear kickin' bass and drums when you monitor a mix, you may want to select headphones with this feature. Also, your choice of headphones may depend on how much you need to have external noise blocked out during monitoring. Headphones with sealed speaker designs prevent a significant amount of external noise from being heard by the wearer. This is essential in high-noise environments, but may not be as important in quieter studio settings. Headphones with closed speaker designs prevent external noise intrusion to a lesser extent, while headphones with semi-open, open, and diffuse designs block progressively less noise. That's not always a bad thing if, for example, you need to listen for external sounds (like a timer or a telephone) while working.

Also, you may want to get a *headphone distribution amp* so that more than one person can listen to a mix via headphones. A headphone distribution amp connects to the stereo mix output of your audio interface or mixer. Instead of one headphone jack, a headphone distribution amp has several jacks, each with its own volume control. Obviously, this is a useful device when you're collaborating with other people while producing music. However, if you know that you'll be the only person monitoring your mixes, then you need not worry about getting one of these.

Monitors

If you can afford it right away, get a pair of good near-field monitors as well. *Near-field monitors*, as the name suggests, are speakers that can be positioned near the listener. Their main advantage is that they can be used in rooms that aren't acoustically treated, unlike studio control rooms that *are* acoustically treated to reduce noise and other audio problems. Because the listener is close to the monitors, room noise and acoustics are less of an influencing factor.

If you want to use near-field monitors, I recommend that you get a good pair of *self-powered* monitors. Self-powered monitors include built-in amplifiers and, obviously, the speakers themselves. They cost about the same as a pair of *passive* (non-powered) speakers and a good power amplifier, which you would need to power the passive speakers anyway. Self-powered monitors offer a couple of advantages over a separate speaker/amplifier package. First, there is less signal degradation from the amplifier to the speaker because the signal path between the two of them is very short. By contrast, connecting passive speakers to a separate amplifier can cause some signal degradation, depending on the length and impedance of the connecting cables between them. Second, good self-powered monitors are usually *biamplified* systems; that is, each speaker has two amplifiers. Because it takes more energy to amplify bass sounds, one amplifier drives the *woofer*, which is the larger speaker that reproduces the lower frequencies of the audio spectrum. The other amplifier powers the *driver*, which reproduces the higher frequencies. The result is a more efficient amplification system with more accurate monitoring.

Self-powered near-field monitors, such as the Event 20/20bas, are usually biamplified, which provides more accurate monitoring of audio sources.

As you may have guessed, the type of self-powered near-field monitors I'm talking about are *not* the tiny, inexpensive monitors you buy for your home computer. I'm referring to the larger, more powerful monitoring systems with at least 6.5-inch woofers (although 8-inch woofers are better for reproducing bass sounds) and a separate driver for the mid and upper frequencies. Prices for these types of monitors can run from $500 to $1500 per pair, and they're an important investment in your audio production system. As I said earlier, audio accuracy is in the ear of the beholder, so make sure you choose a pair that gives you the results you want. Test them out with some familiar reference material at the store, and then again in your own recording space. As always, make sure the store has a good return policy in case you have to bring them back. And don't forget to save the receipt!

Surface Controller

One of the things you'll begin to realize as you learn how to produce music with your computer is that its keyboard and mouse aren't always the best tools for interacting with your music software. You may want to consider acquiring a *surface controller* to work more effectively with your music software. Even though it isn't absolutely necessary to have one, they certainly make computer-based music production much easier. Surface controllers look and behave much like mixers in that they have sliders and knobs to control different software track parameters, such as volume, *pan* (which shifts the sound to a certain position—for example, a left or right speaker), and EQ (equalization). Depending on the controller

(and software) you use, it may be possible to perform other tasks, such as controlling effects *plug-ins* (software versions of signal processing equipment such as compressor/limiters and so forth), virtual instruments, and so on. In addition, they usually provide *transport controls* (play, stop, fast forward, reverse, and record) for the software you use, as well as allow you to *arm* (prepare for recording), *solo* (listen to only one track), and mute tracks.

All four of the digital audio sequencers mentioned previously can be controlled by a number of third-party hardware controllers. What's more, some surface controllers, such as the Tascam US-428 and the Event EZ-Bus, also act as audio/MIDI interfaces, which makes them extremely cost-effective multi-purpose devices.

The Emagic Logic Control has motorized faders, and connects to a computer via a USB port.

If you decide to go shopping for a surface controller, you'll find that they fall into two specific price groups: those that cost around $500–$600, and those that sell for $1000–$1800. The main difference between these two groups is that the latter includes motorized faders that automatically move to the same position as the corresponding faders on the software's mixer screen during playback so you can get constant visual feedback on your song's audio levels. The less expensive surface controllers don't have motorized faders, so their positions may not always reflect the software audio mixer's settings. In fact, moving a fader will cause the software parameter it controls to jump to the value represented by the fader position if there is a difference between them! To avoid that, most surface controllers with non-motorized faders have a "null" button you can press when moving the surface controller so that the mixer levels won't change until the fader "catches" at the same level as the software's onscreen mixer. This allows the less expensive hardware controllers to perform level changes that can be recorded by the software's mixer automation.

Cables

You'll also need audio and MIDI cables which, oddly enough, most people forget to buy until they're ready to start making music. While buying cables is a simple process, there are a couple of things you need to consider. For one, make sure that you buy cables that are long enough to connect to the proper devices without causing strain on either the cable or the device. Likewise, remember that you'll probably have to route those cables around other devices or studio furniture, so allow for more length than just the direct distance between the two connecting devices. By the same token, however, don't buy cables that are far too long. The last thing you need to worry about is coiled bunches that can tangle or cause someone to trip.

Also, make sure that you buy cables with the proper connections *on each end!* For instance, if you're connecting a device with RCA jacks to a device with unbalanced phono jacks, get cables with RCA connectors on one end and phono jacks on the other. Avoid using audio plug adapters that convert one type of plug into another. Adapters are an extra expense, and the weight of an attached adapter can potentially damage a device's audio connection as well. (You'll read more about different types of cable connections in "Chapter 4: Hardware and Software Setup.")

Microphones

You'll need at least one good microphone to record vocals and/or acoustic instruments. The most commonly used type of mic for this purpose is a condenser mic, but there are also other types of microphones—such as dynamic and ribbon mics—that are useful for a variety of recording situations. If you're fortunate enough to be able to record real drum kits, you'll need a variety of mics to capture the sounds of the various components. However, rather than go into great detail at this time, I suggest that you read "Appendix B: Microphone Basics" to learn more about microphones types and their uses.

If you use a condenser mic, you'll need to make sure that your audio interface or mixer also includes a *mic preamp* and a *phantom power supply*. Condenser mics are very sensitive mics that can detect extremely small levels of change in sound pressure. In order to hear those small changes, a mic preamp is required to *boost* (increase) the mic's output level. Additionally, condenser mics need a power source in order to operate properly. Some condenser mics use batteries, but most need an external power supply. Many mixers—and some audio interfaces—can supply power to a condenser mic through the mic cable's wiring. That power source is called a phantom power supply.

Microphone preamps such as the ART MPA Gold have phantom power supplies for condenser mics.

It's important to remember that just because an audio interface or mixer has a microphone jack, it does not follow that it also has a mic preamp or phantom power supply—read its manual or spec sheet to be sure! (By the way, many audio manufacturers offer downloadable versions of their product manuals in Adobe Acrobat format [PDF], and almost all provide production specifications online. Take advantage of these resources when you shop for any audio equipment!) Sometimes a mixer or audio interface will be able to boost a condenser mic's signal, as long as it has an external phantom power supply source. More often, though, you'll need to get a mic preamp with phantom power included if your mixer or audio interface doesn't have this capability.

Miscellaneous Equipment

I've listed what I believe are the essential elements of a good computer-based music production system. However, you'll find that you may want or need a variety of other equipment as well, depending on the type of work you'll wish to do. For instance, perhaps you'll have a use for a guitar effects processor. You could get an outboard effects processor, an effects processor that connects directly to your computer, or even a computer-based virtual guitar effects processor. The main thing to remember is that you have options, so choose the equipmet that is the best for your purposes.

CHAPTER 2
CHOOSING THE RIGHT COMPUTER

Choosing the right computer for music production is a subject rife with confusion and partisan passion for beginners and experienced users alike. Furthermore, the personal computer industry has changed dramatically over the last several years, offering consumers a wider variety of computer and peripheral configurations. Some types of computers are ideal for music production, while others are less suited to the task. One fact is certain, though: there's no longer such a thing as a "one size fits all" computer.

The Great Mac vs. PC Debate

Invariably, the first question I'm asked by those who are taking the computer music production plunge is, "Which is better, Mac or PC?" My half-serious answer is, "It depends on who you ask." Both platforms have their ardent supporters. But despite partisan claims to the contrary, the truth is that both Macs and Windows PCs function well enough to be viable platforms for computer-based music production. In fact, I use both Macs *and* Windows computers myself. Each type of computer has its strengths and weaknesses, but, on balance, Windows and Mac systems both get the job done. Besides, the real issue these days isn't "which computer is better?"—it's "which Macs and which PCs are best suited to the task?" Part of the answer to that question depends on what type of user you are. The other part of that answer lies in knowing what types of computers are capable of music production.

Desktop, Laptop, and Tabletop Computers

When most people hear the word "computer," they visualize a tower or mid-tower system that sits on the floor next to a desk, with a computer monitor, keyboard, and mouse sitting on the desk itself. However, there are other types of computers that employ technologies that are easy to use and offer *hot-swappable interconnectivity*—that is, they use devices that you can plug into or unplug from a computer while it's still running. For instance, less expensive and often quieter *tabletop* (i.e., small enough to fit entirely on a desktop without taking up a lot of real estate) models connected to *USB* (Universal Serial Bus) and FireWire devices usually perform well enough to meet many musicians' needs. Laptops can be as powerful as many desktop systems, and offer the extra advantage of portability. Combine them with USB, FireWire, and PC Card (PCMCIA) devices, and you often have the functional equivalent of many desktop systems. All three types of computers have their strengths and weaknesses.

Desktop Systems

There was a time when high-end personal computers were housed in horizontal cases that actually sat on a desktop, hence the term *desktop computer*. Even today, there are still a few systems like that, but now most systems that we call desktops are actually encased in vertical "towers" or "mid-towers" that usually sit on the floor. I also include rackmount computers in this category because they have the same basic features of desktop systems, except that they're housed in cases that can be installed horizontally in rackmount furniture.

Desktop computers offer several advantages to the computer-based musician. They are by far the most expandable in terms of devices and interfacing formats. For example, users can install PCI (peripheral component interconnect) cards for a variety of purposes, such as digital audio and SCSI interfacing. Furthermore, every system nowadays includes USB 2.0 ports as a matter of course, and often FireWire ports, too. Even if a desktop computer doesn't have FireWire ports, one can easily install a PCI card to add in this option.

Additionally, desktop systems are housed in cases that contain and power internal *peripherals* (items that are not part of the actual, original computer, per se, such as printers, drives, scanners, etc.), including hard drives, CD-RW drives, and DVD drives. This makes desktop systems the least expensive option in terms of expansion. Within the actual case that houses your computer, you can incorporate and power devices that often cost an extra $100 *each* on average if purchased as an external unit.

Desktops are usually the only systems that can provide the potential for dual monitor support, which allows one to view multiple program windows or extend screen information across two monitors. This is not to be confused with duplicating what is viewed on a main monitor with a secondary monitor, which is what some laptop and tabletop computers are limited to doing (you should note that some laptops now include dual monitor support, too—you need to connect an external monitor to the laptop's monitor port in order to take advantage of this capability, of course). Desktops are also the only systems that offer the potential for dual processor support. This is important to computer-based musicians who use high-end software that takes advantage of dual processors for increased performance.

On the other hand, desktop systems have some major disadvantages. Their expandability is as much a minus as it is a plus for those afflicted with computer phobia. Some people just get anxious when it's time to open the case and install a new hardware component, such as an audio card, a second hard drive, or extra RAM. Even though installing an internal component is very easy, the mere thought of opening a computer's case to do so just scares some people. These are exactly the people for whom laptops and tabletop computers were made.

Desktop systems can also be notoriously noisy, and that's not good in music production environments. Minimizing system noise can sometimes be a difficult and/or expensive venture. It may involve doing something as simple as positioning the system under the desk in such a way that the noise is at least tolerable, but sometimes more drastic action is called for, such as housing the computer in an equipment closet or a specially built cabinet.

Fortunately, some companies understand that this is an important problem, and are designing their computers for studio use. For instance, Carillon Audio Systems builds PC systems that are designed to be extremely quiet for studio work and yet durable enough for roadwork. The systems are enclosed in heavy rackmount cases, and their components are selected both for their performance and

Carillon Audio Systems manufactures low-noise rackmount PC systems that are designed for studio use.

quietness. There are also other companies that offer products and components designed to reduce computer noise, such as low-noise computer fans, hard disk sleeves that muffle hard drive noise, and padding to dampen computer case vibration.

In terms of being mobile while you work, however, desktop systems are not easily transportable. They are heavy and bulky, even when housed in rackmount cases. Furthermore, there's the extra burden of taking along a monitor, which usually has no rackmount housing of any kind, as well as a keyboard, a mouse, and a mouse pad. This lack of transportability used to make it more difficult to employ a powerful computer in a remote recording or performance situation, but now there are options besides desktop systems that can be used in these circumstances.

Laptop Systems

Laptop systems are rapidly becoming the primary computer of choice for many general users, as well as computer-based musicians. Their share of the computer market has been steadily increasing because they offer some unique advantages. First, and most obviously, they are extremely portable and, to a large degree, self-contained systems. There's no need to worry about external keyboards,

pointing devices, or even a monitor when one has a laptop—it's all built-in! What's more, laptops can run on batteries for a limited amount of time, or run on AC power just like desktop and tabletop systems. Best of all, laptops are extremely quiet!

Laptop systems are rapidly becoming the standard for many computer-based musicians.

The expansion capabilities of laptop systems are constantly improving as well. Every laptop sold today has at least one USB 2.0 port, but more often they have two. Also, Apple iBooks and PowerBooks, Sony VAIO, and some other laptops include FireWire ports as well. Nearly every laptop computer contains at least one PC Card slot, and many models contain two. For all intents and purposes, this offers many laptop users the same type of expansion capabilities found in desktop systems. For example, one can easily add a PC Card multichannel audio interface to a laptop system. If a laptop doesn't have a FireWire port, one can easily add on a PC Card–to–FireWire adapter.

Laptops do have some disadvantages, though. First, they can be the most expensive of all computer types in terms of the initial purchase. However, price corresponds to size: Smaller laptops, as a rule, are more expensive than bigger laptops, all features being equal. Luckily, most laptop musicians don't need or even want small laptops with tiny screens; their preference is for the larger, less expensive laptops that act as powerful replacements for desktop systems. Fortunately, these larger laptops—especially PC laptops—can cost roughly the same as a good desktop system.

Second, expanding a laptop's memory or upgrading its internal hard drive often costs up to twice as much as it would to similarly upgrade desktop system components. To make matters worse, there is no way to upgrade the processor or provide for internal expansion other than what may have been initially designed for the laptop in question.

Also, a laptop monitor display is often half the replacement cost of a laptop itself. That's all the more troubling because the monitor is often the weakest link in a laptop system. This is due to the risk of *flexing*, which is the process of bending and warping a monitor through improper handling. The risk is serious enough that separate laptop monitor insurance policies are now being marketed.

Laptop monitors often have smaller display areas compared to desktop systems. However, there are three things to keep in mind. First, people usually sit closer to laptop monitors than they do to desktop or tabletop monitors—this can offset the discrepancy in size. Second, laptop screens are in reality flat panel LCD displays, which have the advantages of no wasted screen space or RF (radio frequency) interference. Third, laptop monitors are often larger in size these days, with most systems sporting screens with at least a 15-inch viewing area, and it's becoming increasingly common for many laptops to have 16-inch and even 17-inch monitors. Apple has PowerBook laptops with 17-inch monitors, and likewise some Hewlett Packard, Sony, and Toshiba models include them as well. However, the 17-inch monitors of these laptop systems have "theater" screens that are more rectangular than the average, more square-shaped computer monitors of most desktop systems.

Tabletop Systems

Tabletop systems, as the name suggests, are computers in compact housing units that take up generally much less space than a desktop system; in short, they can sit on top of a table (or desktop) with room to spare. Tabletop systems such as those in the newer Apple iMac and eMac, and Gateway Profile lines include built-in monitors, while computers in other lines such as the IBM ThinkCentre require a separate monitor.

Tabletop computers offer some unique advantages. In many cases, they are the least expensive of all computer types. Many of them generate no noise, or just a small amount, depending on the system. Furthermore, many tabletop systems

Tabletop systems such as the Apple iMac G4 combine power, compact housing, and hot-swappable peripheral expansion in a single computer system.

often use the same CPUs found in single-processor desktop systems, so you don't have to necessarily sacrifice power for compactness.

On the other hand, tabletop systems are not as internally expandable as desktop or even laptop systems. However, this is not as big an issue these days since FireWire and USB devices have begun to dominate all aspects of the peripherals market. Even so, external peripherals come with two important disadvantages: many are more expensive because the case and power supply add to their cost, and (of more concern to the computer-based musician) there is the potential for noise issues which could negate the advantage of the noiseless operation that is part of a tabletop system's appeal. On the positive side, though, it may be easier to house the offending external devices in a small, enclosed environment rather than segregate a whole noisy desktop computer in some sort of larger noise-muffling housing.

PC users may find it more difficult to get the right kind of tabletop system because so many tabletop PC makers configure different types of these systems for low-cost markets. Unfortunately, this often means that system design is compromised because too many manufacturers don't incorporate the best new technology features. As of this writing, many PC tabletop manufacturers don't use FireWire at all, and have only recently begun to use USB 2.0. Furthermore, PC manufacturers sometimes employ technologies that computer-based musicians can't take advantage of. For instance, some PC tabletop systems have PCI card slots, but the computer case is often too small for full-height PCI cards to be used in the system. Unfortunately, almost all PCI audio cards are full-height cards.

However, there is a new type of tabletop: the small form factor computer. This type of computer is small enough to sit on a desktop, although users may prefer to set it on a shelf under the computer desk. Due to their liquid cooling systems, they don't require the large noisy fans that are the bane of most desktop systems. More importantly, they usually come equipped with room for two internal hard drives, an optical drive (CD-RW or DVD-RW), and a slot for an AGP graphics card, plus a full-height PCI card. In addition, they often offer several USB 2.0 and FireWire ports for easy peripheral expansion. These systems are viable alternatives to large and potentially noisy desktop systems.

Who Uses What?

The type of computer you should buy depends on what your music-making goals are. For example, if you want to run digital audio sequencing programs with a large number of host-based effects *plug-ins* (little programs that run within the sequencing software) and virtual instruments, a desktop system with dual processors may be your best choice. Likewise, those wishing to use hardware-based audio systems such as Digidesign's Pro Tools, or even DSP-based effects processing and software synth PCI cards such as CreamWare Audio's Pulsar will want to stay with desktop systems. And if you want dual processor support, a desktop system is your only choice.

However, not everyone needs, wants, or even has the budget for that kind of power. Tabletop systems are ideally suited for those who don't need top-of-the-line systems, but still want a computer that can handle their particular production needs. What's more, the right tabletop won't break your piggy bank. That's why tabletop systems also make good secondary computers. After all, sometimes it's easier and more cost-effective to divide music production tasks between two computers of moderate power rather make a single high-powered system do all the work.

Laptops are the ideal option for those who don't need megabuck power systems, but do need powerful portability. They can also work with high-end desktop systems, and if both systems are configured properly, they can even share devices—that can more than offset a laptop's initially higher price. Increasingly, they can act as complete workstations in their own right. For not much extra money, they can easily compete with tabletop systems, and even many desktop systems.

The Need for Speed

No matter what type of computer you get, you first must make sure that the computer is fast enough to run whatever programs you want to use. To that I would add that you should buy the fastest computer you can afford that exceeds those program requirements. Still, this begs the question, "How can I determine what is the fastest computer available?" Well, there's no simple answer to that question.

For example, many people believe that processor speed is the most important indicator of computer speed. Until recently, processor speed was actually a good (though not perfect) benchmark for determining computer performance. For instance, one could be confident that a computer with a processor speed of 800 MHz (megahertz) was much faster than a computer with a 500 MHz CPU, but only a little faster than a 750 MHz computer. Besides, we like our answers to be easy, and having one simple measurement with which to compare computers makes things simple.

However, processor speed no longer tells the whole story. For example, if I were to ask you, "Which is faster, an Intel Pentium 4 processor running at 2 GHz (gigahertz) or a Mac G4 Motorola processor operating at 1 GHz?" what would your answer be? If you were to compare the relative speed of each processor, it would seem obvious that the 2 GHz Pentium 4 runs twice as fast as the 1 GHz Mac G4. However, this is comparing Apples to . . . well, PCs! The truth is that the two processors perform their instructions in different ways, so a pure speed comparison is impossible. Besides, there are a whole host of other factors that affect computer performance.

For instance, the efficiency of the motherboard's *chipset* also affects computer performance. The chipset, which is a series of chips attached directly to the motherboard, controls the entire computer system and its capabilities. Actually, chipsets now usually consist of two or three VLSI (very large-scale instruction) chips that do all of the work that dozens of smaller chips used to do. All components (memory, PCI cards, hard disks, etc.) communicate with the processor through the chipset, which is the hub for all data transfers and the organizer and controller of the data flow. It doesn't matter how fast the processor is if the motherboard's chipset doesn't efficiently communicate with all of the components in a computer system.

Bus speed, which is a measure of how fast data can be sent to and from the CPU by the computer's peripheral components (such as RAM, sound cards, and hard drives), is another important factor in determining overall computer performance. For instance, a computer with an 800 MHz processor whose bus speed is 100 MHz will probably be a little slower than an 800 MHz processor whose bus speed is 133 MHz. In most cases, however, the average user wouldn't notice a significant difference in performance between the two.

Likewise, the efficiency of an operating system determines how effectively programs interact with a computer. In a similar vein, how well a program is written also determines how efficiently it functions under a particular operating system. In short, well-written operating systems and programs mean that computers function more efficiently and quickly, all things being equal.

What Really Matters

However, it should be obvious by now that all things *aren't* equal, especially when it comes to comparing computers. So, if that's the case, how do you go about buying the computer that's right for you? Well, my first rule is this: *If you want to buy a Mac, buy a Mac. If you want to buy a PC, buy a PC.* Don't worry about which one is better because, as I mentioned earlier, both are viable platforms for computer-based music production. They're both just about as easy to use, although that doesn't mean that both are easy to use *all of the time.*

I know—and, to a certain extent, agree with—the conventional wisdom that you should select the software you wish to use, and *then* base your choice of computer on that. On the other hand, there are so many software packages that have corresponding versions available for both Macs and PCs that, at some point, it just boils down to the type of computer (and its corresponding operating system) that you personally prefer. The only thing you need to make sure of is that the computer you want is powerful enough to run the software you wish to use. Once that requirement is met, all that remains is to be happy with what you've got!

That being said, there are some key components to look for when buying *any* computer for music production. Furthermore, always remember that what really matters is the quality of the *interaction* among the various computer components. Focusing on an individual component to the exclusion of overall computer performance is a waste of time—especially when you consider that no computer in existence can claim to have every feature fully optimized for ideal performance.

Processor

If you want to buy a Mac, then you should know that, as of this writing, Apple uses one of two processor families in their computers: the G4 or the G5. G4 processors are fast enough for multitrack digital audio production and software synthesis use. For high-end music production, however, the G5 is the better processor due to its faster speed and ability to process more instructions per second than the G4.

If you want to buy a PC, though, you'll find that selecting one based on the processor is a little more complicated. First, there are different processor makers, of which Intel and Advanced Micro Devices (AMD) are the two best-known companies. Like Apple, these two companies produce different processors within their own product line. AMD produces the Athlon and Opteron series, while Intel produces the Celeron, Centrino, and Pentium series; each of these processors is geared towards different market segments. For instance, many inexpensive home-based systems—as well as many basic business systems that use several low-cost computers connected to a server—employ Celeron or Athlon processors.

Pentium III and Athlon processors are previous-generation offerings from Intel and AMD, respectively, but they are still considered to be powerful, and their comparatively low costs make them highly useful in certain systems. For example, some laptops use these processors because they don't consume as much battery power as more powerful processors. However, laptops that are designed to run for a long time on battery power now tend to use the Centrino processor. Remember, though, that these processors sacrifice speed for extended battery operation, so laptops that use them aren't always the best choices for computer-based music production.

On the other hand, Pentium III and the Athlon processors can be used in dual processor motherboards. Even so, the latest generation of Pentium 4 and Opteron processors can often outperform these dual processor systems. In the case of the Pentium 4 processor, it has a feature called *hyperthreading*. Essentially, this allows the processor to perform faster by processing multiple predictive streams of data simultaneously. To explain the processor architecture that allows the Pentium 4 to do this is beyond the scope of this book—all you need to know is that if you want to buy a system with a Pentium 4 processor, make sure that it has hyperthreading.

The Pentium 4 and the Opteron as of this writing represent the apex of their respective companies' product lines for the general consumer (Intel and AMD make other high-speed processors designed for the network server market). They are their companies' most powerful processors, which makes them ideally suited to high-end applications such as music and video production.

Motherboard/Chipset

The best processor in the world will function poorly if it sits in a motherboard whose chipset is not up to par. Unfortunately, finding the right motherboard can be confusing for PC users because there are many motherboard and chipset manufacturers in the marketplace. (Apple users don't face this dilemma because only one company manufactures its motherboards and the accompanying chipsets. So, if you're planning to buy a Mac, you can skip ahead to the next section—*Bus Speed*.) This becomes more of a problem once you realize that the most crucial element of a motherboard is its chipset. After all, it controls the entire computer system and its capabilities. Also, chipsets aren't replaceable because they are soldered onto the motherboard, so it's impossible to discuss one without referring to the other.

The key to matching a motherboard/chipset to a processor is to get a motherboard with a chipset geared *specifically* to that processor. For instance, if you want to buy an Intel Pentium 4 processor, get a motherboard with the Intel chipset designed for that processor. Naturally, Intel makes their own motherboards, but there are also respected third-party motherboard manufacturers, such as Abit and Asus. There are third-party motherboard makers for AMD processors as well, and that company manufactures motherboards and chipsets for its Athlon XP and Opteron processors, too.

It's possible to get motherboards with other chipsets that are compatible with Intel and/or AMD processors, but be very careful about using these motherboard/chipset combinations. Some audio interfaces, especially PCI audio cards, don't work properly with certain chipsets. Likewise, some software manufacturers advise against using their programs with computers that have specific chipsets or processors. Check first with the manufacturers of the programs and audio interfaces you plan to use to find out if they are compatible with the specific chipset and CPU that are in the computer you want to purchase.

Bus Speed

Bus speed determines how fast data can be sent to and from the CPU by the computer's components, such as the RAM and hard drives. (By the way, bus speed is not to be confused with *frontside bus speed* or *backside bus speed*, each of which refer to a specialized form of high-speed memory known as a *cache*, which is where data is copied to when it is retrieved from RAM.) Currently, typical bus speeds are 100 MHz and 133 MHz. Some processor and motherboard manufacturers have developed ways of increasing *apparent* bus speed; however, the *true* bus speed is still important. For now, the most important thing to remember is that bus speed is an important factor in determining overall computer performance. To reference the example I gave earlier, a computer with an 800 MHz processor whose bus speed is 100 MHz will probably be a little slower in overall operation than an 800 MHz processor whose bus speed is 133 MHz.

Regardless of your motherboard's bus speed, you'll need to match components that operate up to the bus's capabilities. For example, installing an Ultra-ATA 66 MHz hard drive in a computer whose bus speed is 133 MHz won't hurt the computer, but the drive won't work any faster than 66 MHz, which is a waste of the bus's speed capacity. That can significantly affect, for example, how many tracks a digital audio recording program can play back at once on a computer.

RAM

In this day and age, many users know that RAM is used for storing data and programs currently being processed. However, not everyone knows that there are a few different types of RAM currently in use. For instance, until 2003 the most common type of RAM was *SDRAM* (synchronous dynamic random access memory), which came in two speeds: 100 MHz and 133 MHz, to coincide with the system bus speeds mentioned earlier.

However, SDRAM has been phased out in favor of another type of memory: *DDR-SDRAM* (double data rate SDRAM). This type of RAM effectively doubles the memory chip's data throughput. DDR-SDRAM also consumes less power, which makes it ideal for notebook computers. The first generation of DDR-SDRAM had speeds of 266 MHz, which is exactly double the speed of 133 MHz, but later generations of DDR-SDRAM are even faster.

Remember when I mentioned earlier that some processor and motherboard manufacturers have developed ways of increasing the *apparent* bus speed? Using DDR-SDRAM is one of them. In reality, a motherboard's bus speed may still be 133 MHz, but the apparent speed is double this figure because this type of RAM transfers data twice (or more) in a computer's clock cycle instead of once in a cycle (don't worry about the details regarding clock cycles—you only need to know that faster is better in this department). Note, however, that a motherboard's chipset has to be able to support DDR-SDRAM use. You can't just install this type of RAM into any motherboard and expect it to work.

RDRAM (Rambus dynamic random access memory) is another type of RAM currently in use. It's a form of high-speed asynchronous memory designed by Rambus to achieve high effective bandwidth processing speeds. RDRAM scales its performance and capacity by using multiple data channels in parallel. In simple terms, this type of RAM divides up its memory to tailor its performance to the tasks at hand. Although the cost of RDRAM can be higher than other forms of RAM, it has the potential to be ideal for use in computers for music and audio, so its development bears watching.

No matter which type of RAM your new computer requires, make sure that there is enough of it in your system for it to effectively operate any music software you want to use. As of this writing, I would recommend that every new computer used for music production have at least 512 MB RAM installed. If you plan on using software-based *samplers* (software that creates sounds with recordings of instruments) such as Steinberg's HALion or Bitheadz' Unity Session with sequencing software, I would recommend installing even more RAM—1 GB is a good idea. In fact, make sure that your new computer can support at least 1 GB of installed RAM if you have a dual processor system or plan on using software samplers in the future. That's because many software samplers—even streaming samplers—need to use a significant portion of the computer's RAM to function properly.

Computer Options

In addition to the computer requirements just mentioned, there are other features you may want to consider as well. For some people, these options are necessities, and for others, these additional features simply add to their quality of use. In any event, carefully consider whether these additional features are right for you before you buy a computer for music production.

Dual Processors

If you're planning to buy a desktop or rackmount system, you may want to choose one with dual processors; a number of Mac and PC configurations contain them.

No matter which dual processor system you choose, there are certain facts that you need to know about dual processor systems in general. First, you have to make sure that both processors are identical. That's not a problem on Mac systems, because that's how their dual processor systems are sold. However, some PC users who build their own systems may not be aware of this fact (albeit if you are capable of putting your own system together, you *should* know this already!). Second, you need to make sure that the operating system supports dual processor capability. As of this writing, Apple's OS X supports dual processors, but only Windows 2000 and Windows XP Professional support dual processors; Windows XP Home does not.

However, don't assume that having dual processors means your computer will run twice as fast. Usually, you'll experience at least a 10-percent increase in processing capability, and more likely up to as much as 50 percent or more. However, the key to improved performance is whether the *software* has been optimized for dual processor support. Fortunately, all of the major digital audio sequencers have been designed to work with dual processors, as have a number of related applications.

On the other hand, it may be more cost-effective or resource-efficient to run two separate computers instead. For example, the newer versions of Steinberg's Cubase and Nuendo include VST (virtual studio technology) System Link, which allows Cubase and Nuendo users to link and sync one computer with another computer running any of these programs via a single digital audio channel. For instance, one computer could handle all of the digital audio tracks and effects plug-ins for those tracks, while the other computer could run all of the software synthesizers and samplers. Each computer in this "dual processor" system would be able to concentrate on one or two specific tasks, making full use of both independent processors. This is sometimes preferable to wasting part of a dual processor system's power on the overhead involved to operate both processors in the same system simultaneously.

Dual Monitor Support

Desktop and rackmount computer users may also want to consider employing dual monitors. Many programs have different windows for different functions. For example, a program might have separate mixer, multitrack waveform, and plug-in windows. Sometimes it's fine just to switch among the various views, but at other times it would be much better to have several windows open simultaneously. After all, it's not always possible to adequately view all windows on a single monitor, even with the biggest models. Why not spread out all of the various windows or views you need between two separate monitors? (By the way, you can also spread one window across two monitors for one large view as well.) Obviously, the computer will need a graphics card that provides dual monitor support, but they're readily available. Also, the software in question needs to support dual monitor capability, but a large percentage of software supports this function because it's such a handy feature.

Monitors—CRT vs. LCD

Even if you buy only one monitor for your system, the *type* of monitor you choose is also important. Basically, there are two types of monitors: CRT (cathode ray tube) and LCD (liquid crystal display). CRT monitors are the big, heavy, traditional monitors we've used for years. LCD monitors, also often called *flat-panel displays*, are the newer monitors that are becoming far more commonplace. As an older form of technology, CRT displays are now much lower in cost than their LCD counterparts. Those of you who are trying to keep system costs down may be tempted to purchase CRTs for your digital audio setup; however, LCD displays have several advantages that can more than compensate for their initially higher prices.

First, there's viewing area. A CRT monitor always has a smaller viewing area than its stated screen size. For instance, a 17-inch CRT monitor may have only a 15.9-inch diagonal viewing area. By contrast, a 17-inch LCD display really does have a 17-inch diagonal display. To get the equivalent viewing area on a CRT display, you would likely need a more expensive 19-inch monitor. Furthermore, there is no black space around the edges of the viewing area, as there sometimes is with CRTs, so basically there's no wasted screen space. Also, because the display is flat, the image is not distorted.

Second, there's overall size. Flat-panel displays take up less desktop real estate than CRT monitors. Also, because flat-panel displays don't have the bulky "butts" that jut out from the back of CRT monitors, you can more easily place them in spots where you need them. For instance, you can mount a flat-panel display on a wall or on a small shelf near a second computer located away from your workstation. That's pretty handy when you just want to look over and see what's happening on another computer.

Third, LCD displays are more energy efficient than CRT displays. Not only do they lower operating costs for your system, but they're more environmentally friendly as well.

Finally, CRTs can generate RF interference, which can often be a problem in recording situations. For instance, if you happen to be sitting too close to a CRT computer monitor while recording an electric guitar part, its RF noise can be detected and amplified by the guitar's pick-ups. This noise can also get recorded into a digital audio track, which is obviously something you don't want. Speakers can also pick up RF interference, and the magnets in speakers can distort a CRT's screen image or cause it to jitter if they sit too close to each other. None of these are issues with LCD displays.

Second Hard Drive

Having a large hard drive dedicated to digital audio data is a must, in my opinion. However, there are now a variety of hard drive choices for the computer-based musician. For instance, ATA drives (sometimes referred to as IDE drives) are inexpensive, reliable choices for computer music production. As of this writing, faster serial ATA drives are also becoming available. They differ from ATA drives in this important respect: ATA drives transfer data *in parallel* (more than one bit at once) while serial ATA drives transfer data *serially* (one bit at a time). When data is transferred in parallel, more data is transferred at once. The problem, though, is that there are waiting periods in the cycle until the next batch of data is ready to be transferred. Serial ATA drives may send data serially, but the stream of data is constant, so the information is actually transferred more quickly. To use an analogy, an ATA drive is like an electronic billboard that can flash only one word at a time, while a serial ATA drive is like an electronic billboard that streams its text until the message is finished. If you've ever noticed, it's easier to read and understand information from the latter than the former.

SCSI drives have been a mainstay of digital audio systems for many years, too. As of this writing, the latest generation of SCSI drives is SCSI 320, which can transfer data faster than the fastest ATA drive. On the other hand, they are much more expensive than other types of drives, and require an appropriate SCSI card interface, which can also be expensive.

FireWire hard drives are also a good choice for digital audio work, and now there is the option of using FireWire 800 drives which can transfer data even faster. However, the computer needs to have a FireWire 800 port in order to get the maximum performance from this type of drive. As of this writing, the new Mac G5 systems have FireWire 800 ports, as do the top-of-the-line PowerBooks. PCs don't have built-in FireWire 800 ports yet, although some add-in FireWire 800 cards are becoming available for desktop systems.

The newer USB 2.0 drives can also be a good choice for PC and Mac users. USB 2.0 drives, like FireWire drives, are hot-swappable, so you can plug or unplug them while your computer or hard drive is on. However, FireWire and USB 2.0 devices follow different technical standards, so it's not possible to attach a FireWire drive to a USB 2.0 port or vice versa. (Note: Some hard drive manufacturers offer combination FireWire/USB 2.0 drives that feature both types of connectors.)

This is all a basic overview. If you'd like more detailed information on hard drives, just turn to the back of the book and read "Appendix A: A Hard Disk Primer."

Duplication/Back-Up Hardware

You may not have thought about it yet, but at some point it's going to dawn on you that your hard drive will eventually run out of space. If you are particularly paranoid (and you should be!) you may even realize that you need to make backups of existing digital audio data as you go along, just in case your hard drive ever fails. Fortunately, there's a perfect solution to this problem: Install a CD-RW drive in your system. It burns audio CDs, CD-ROMs that can be permanent archives of your digital audio files, and rewritable CD-ROMs that can be temporary backups of an ongoing project. CD-RW drives can also play back CDs and read CD-ROMs, so there's no reason to purchase a separate CD-ROM drive for audio and data CD playback.

If you want to store even larger amounts of digital audio data on one disk, you may want to opt for a DVD-R or DVD-RW drive instead. Depending on the type of drive and media, you can store from 2.6 GB all the way up to 9.4 GB on one disk. The prices for DVD burners are higher than for CD-RWs, and the media for them is likewise more costly. On the other hand, they aren't any more expensive than what CD-R drives and disks were when they first started gaining acceptance—if history is any guide, DVD-R drives and disks will eventually become as cheap as CD-R drives and disks are now. Also, DVD-Rs can create audio and data CD-ROMs, so they maintain compatibility with currently accepted optical storage technology. Some can also burn video DVDs that can be played on DVD decks!

Unfortunately, though, there are three competing families of recordable DVD drive: DVD-RAM, DVD-R/DVD-RW, and DVD+R/DVD+RW. DVD-RAM is the oldest standard, and is designed only for data applications such as creating backups; the disks are available in various capacities, including 2.6 and 4.7 GB single-sided disks, and 5.2 and 9.4 GB double-sided disks, and are enclosed in cartridges that look similar to older magneto-optical disks. However, the newer disks can be removed from their cases to be used in DVD-ROM drives.

DVD-R/DVD-RW drives have the ability to burn DVDs of movies that can be viewed on standard DVD players. If you plan to do any digital video work, you may want to consider this option. On the other hand, the DVD+R/DVD+RW family is seeing a lot of industry support from manufacturers such as Sony and Hewlett-Packard. Even Microsoft has voiced its support for this technology, which can also burn DVDs that can be viewed on DVD players. Still, it is important to note that not all DVD+RW writers can handle DVD+R disks. If you do plan to buy a DVD+RW drive, make sure beforehand that it will support both DVD+R and DVD+RW media.

Final Considerations

As I've stated before, both Macs and Windows PCs are equally viable platforms for computer-based music production. Neither platform is inherently superior to the other, despite what supporters on either side may say. However, remember that not all Macs and PCs are created equal, nor are they even created in the same way. That's also going to influence how you buy a computer for music production.

An Apple a Day

In some respects, buying a Mac is extremely easy—partially because only Apple makes Macs. This confers upon Apple several advantages and disadvantages. For instance, the product line is smaller, which makes choosing the Mac you want easier and less confusing. However, if you want to custom configure components, your options are more limited than what they would be on the PC side.

Also, because Apple is the only maker of Macs, prices for their systems are often a little higher than PC systems. Part of this may have to do with economics of scale (Macs make up a smaller share of the computer market than do PCs), and part of this may be because they have no hardware competitors, although that didn't seem to matter when there were Mac clone manufacturers some years ago.

Moreover, as the only maker of Macs, Apple has total quality control over the computers it sells. That's why they can often be so easy to use right out of the box (although they aren't always so). Likewise, Apple has total control over the operating system for its own computers, which makes it possible to tailor their computers for their operating system and vice versa. Microsoft, on the other hand, has to write the Windows operating system for a variety of processors and hardware from different manufacturers over which they may exercise influence but not actual control.

PC Puzzles

While Apple is the only maker of Macs, there are literally thousands of PC systems and component makers. Unfortunately, finding the right PC for music production is more difficult because many off-the-shelf PC desktop systems—even those from the major companies—aren't always suitable for music production. In order to be economically competitive, some PC vendors cut corners in crucial areas. For example, they might install slower or smaller drives than what may be needed for digital audio production. Furthermore, they may use processors that are fine for general tasks, but are not the best choices for music or audio production.

Getting a custom-built PC from a local vendor may not be a good option either, especially if you (and they) don't fully know what components you need installed. Some vendors just don't understand the specific needs of computer-based music production, so they may not know which parts are ideally suited for digital audio systems. Moreover, their idea of digital audio may be geared more towards gaming or making MP3 files than serious multitrack audio work.

Turnkey Systems

On the other hand, a *turnkey* (i.e., designed for a specific purpose) system from a computer supplier that specializes in digital audio production can be a godsend to both PC and Mac users. You don't have to go through the headache of designing a system because the vendor has already done that for you, and these vendors test their systems to make sure that everything from sound cards to software works together without a glitch. This is especially comforting if all of this information about processors, motherboards, and chipsets intimidates you—and even the most experienced users can get frazzled trying to determine what components ideally go together.

While turnkey systems may seem to cost more than off-the-shelf or other custom-built systems, you have to remember that the cost of an entire turnkey system usually includes the cost of the appropriate software and audio/MIDI hardware. Once those costs are factored in, you often end up paying about as much for a turnkey system as you would if you were to acquire a custom-built system and purchase the separate audio software and hardware.

On the other hand, if you want to buy your own audio hardware and software, most turnkey vendors can also supply you with a competitively priced barebones system. This type of system usually comes with just the processor, RAM, and computer case, to which you add your own hard drives, operating system, audio interfaces, and so on. The advantage of a barebones system is that you can tailor your system to your exact preferences. The disadvantage is that you have to be experienced with computer design and components.

If your heart is set on building your own system, you should still closely examine what turnkey vendors offer in their systems so you have a better idea of what works. It might just be best to let an experienced vendor put a system together for you so you won't have to deal with all of the potential headaches that come with designing your own computer.

CHAPTER 3
CHOOSING THE RIGHT AUDIO AND/OR MIDI INTERFACE

Even if you're new to computer-based digital audio production, you probably know that you need some type of audio interface to record and play back digital audio. In fact, it goes without saying that your computer needs to have a sound card, right? Wrong! There are actually four basic kinds of audio interfaces that are categorized by their type of connection to the computer: PCI audio cards, USB, FireWire/iLink, and PC Card (PCMCIA) audio interfaces. Every computer has at least one of these types of connections, and most computers these days have two.

For example, desktop systems have PCI card slots for installing PCI audio cards, as well as USB ports for connecting USB audio interfaces. Desktop Macs have FireWire ports for connecting FireWire audio interfaces, and PC users can install PCI-to-FireWire adapter cards if their computers don't have those connections. Tabletop units such as the eMac, iMac G4, and the Gateway Profile 4 have USB and FireWire connections and, increasingly, many PC and Mac laptops have both types of connections as well. In addition, many Mac and PC laptops have at least one PC Card slot, providing yet another option for audio interfacing. So, as you can see, you're not limited to using traditional sound cards when you want to record and play back digital audio from your computer!

PCI Cards

The most common and time-tested type of audio interface is the PCI card. It installs into a PCI card slot, which can be found in virtually every Mac and PC desktop system. Interestingly, they're the only audio interfaces that are installed *inside* a computer. Even so, nearly every PCI audio card is part of a component setup consisting of the card itself, an external audio/MIDI I/O box, and a cable that connects the card to that box. As you will see later, PCI audio interface systems come in a variety of configurations and options.

USB

USB audio interfaces have achieved widespread popularity because they're so easy to use. They were designed to be used with the older USB 1.1 ports, which were commonly found on virtually all computers until mid-2003. These devices transfer data at a rate of 12 Mbps or about 1.5 MB per second—the maximum speed of a USB 1.1 port. Although this transfer speed is slow compared to those available on other interface connections, it's still fast enough to play back at least two channels of 24-bit/44.1kHz digital audio while simultaneously recording two channels of digital audio information at the same rate.

USB 2.0, which transfers data at a rate of 480 Mbps (or 60 MB per second) was designed by a consortium of PC manufacturers as an alternative to FireWire, which was first developed by Apple. Now, though, Apple includes USB 2.0 ports on their computers as well.

For a while after USB 2.0 was introduced, there were no USB 2.0 audio interfaces on the market. However, Roland has produced a multichannel USB 2.0 audio interface, and other companies have hinted that they may be developing interfaces as well, so I'm sure we'll be seeing plenty of them in the future.

The Edirol UA-1000 USB 2.0 audio interface can transfer audio at a much faster rate than a standard USB 1.1 interface.

For those who think that connecting a USB 1.1 audio interface into a USB 2.0 port will result in faster transfer speeds for the audio device, I have some disappointing news for you: It won't.

However, USB 2.0 is *backwards compatible* with USB 1.1 devices—i.e., you can plug a USB 1.1 device into a 2.0 port and it'll work fine (just not any faster than it was originally designed to—the most you'll ever get are "1.1 speeds").

FireWire/iLink

A third type of audio interface connection is FireWire, also known as IEEE-1394 or iLink on some PCs. FireWire transfers data at a rate of 400 Mbps (50 MB/sec), but raw transfer rates don't tell the

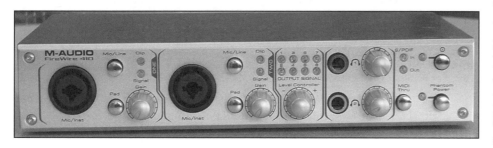

The M-Audio FireWire 410 audio/MIDI interface

whole story. For one thing, you can transfer data between FireWire devices without a computer. For instance, if you have a digital video camera with a FireWire port, and a FireWire hard drive, you can connect the two devices together and download the digital video data from the camera directly to the hard drive without the need for a computer to control the transfer. By contrast, this is not (yet) possible via USB—you need a computer to act as the hub for moving data between USB devices.

Because Apple developed FireWire, it shouldn't come as a surprise that FireWire ports are available on all newer Macs. Some PCs, especially laptops, have built-in FireWire ports, but many still require PCI-to-FireWire adapters in desktop systems or PC Card-to-FireWire adapters for laptop systems.

There are only a few PC tabletop systems with onboard FireWire ports. Furthermore, those systems rarely possess the capability for adding any sort of FireWire adapter, simply by virtue of their design.

Some PC systems have iLink ports, which are four-pin IEEE 1394 ports as opposed to the standard six-pin FireWire ports found on Macs and in FireWire adapters. The only difference between the two connections is that the four-pin ports don't carry power to other FireWire devices. For most FireWire device users, this isn't really an issue because most devices—including audio interfaces—have their own power supplies. However, you need a 4-to-6-pin FireWire cable to use iLink ports with 6-pin FireWire ports. Again, this is not a problem because computers with iLink ports almost always come with these cables included.

There is one issue of which PC FireWire users should be aware: Not all FireWire devices are compatible with the FireWire ports used in certain PCs because the devices and controllers may be using different and incompatible chipsets. Texas Instruments (TI) and NEC are the two main chip controller makers for most FireWire devices, and they are mutually incompatible. This incompatibility can lead to frustration for PC users, as the following example illustrates.

My Toshiba laptop has a built-in four-pin FireWire port controlled by a TI chip. The Western Digital external FireWire drive I bought to use with my laptop didn't work properly with my Toshiba laptop at first. I later discovered the reason for this: The Western Digital drive used an NEC chip for its controller. To correct the problem, I had two choices: either get a hard drive with a TI controller, or get a PC Card FireWire adapter with an NEC controller. I prefer Western Digital drives, and I wanted to be sure that I wouldn't have FireWire incompatibilities again, so I got an Adaptec PC Card FireWire adapter that also uses a NEC controller chip.

Keep in mind that FireWire audio interfaces are vulnerable to this PC problem, too. For instance, Mark of the Unicorn's FireWire audio interfaces are designed to work via connections using chipsets from Texas Instruments. Find out beforehand what chipset your computer's FireWire connections use before purchasing any FireWire devices for your PC. Also, try to find out what chipset a FireWire device uses before purchasing it. It may take a little effort, but it's worth it if you want to have a smooth-running FireWire-based digital audio production system.

As mentioned earlier, some Apple systems now have FireWire 800 ports, which allow for data transfer speeds up to 800 Mbps, or 100 MB per second. Devices that operate at current FireWire speeds are compatible with this new interface protocol, but will experience no increase in performance. Just like USB 2.0, the new FireWire connections will not improve the performance of any earlier-format FireWire devices—they will just provide more data bandwidth for any FireWire product connected to them.

PC (PCMCIA) Cards

The fourth type of audio interface connection is a PCMCIA card, now called simply a PC Card—a thin, flat card that can be inserted into a laptop computer, although desktop systems with PC Card reader/writers can use them, too. There are three types of PC Cards, labeled (logically enough) Type I, Type II, and Type III. Type I cards are the oldest kind of PC Card, and aren't used often these days.

Type II cards are the most commonly used, and are the ones in which we are most interested. Most laptops have at least one Type II slot, and some have two. Laptops with two slots can often accommodate Type III PC Cards, which take up two Type II slots. However, Type III cards aren't used often, either. All current audio PC Cards are Type II cards.

A Digigram VX Pocket 440 PC Card recording interface

PC Cards for digital audio come in two varieties; those with dedicated audio interfaces, and those that offer *breakout boxes* (external boxes to which the card connects) that are swappable with desktop PCI cards. Digigram and ESI (Ego Systems Inc.) make the former, while Echo Digital Audio and RME manufacture the latter.

Audio Interface Considerations

The choice of an audio interface depends partly on the type of computer you want to use for your audio work. PC desktop systems can use PCI cards or USB audio devices right out of the box. Desktop Mac users can use these audio devices, as well as FireWire audio interfaces. If a PC has no *native* (built-in) FireWire ports, a PCI-to-FireWire adapter card can be installed to provide that option.

Mac tabletop systems can be used with USB and FireWire audio interfaces. Most PC tabletops, on the other hand, may be limited to USB audio devices only. Still, a few PC tabletops do have FireWire, usually in the form of four-pin iLink ports. Similarly, a few PC tabletops may have one or two PCI slots, so you might be able to install a PCI audio card or a PCI-to-FireWire adapter card to use with a FireWire audio device. That, however, is a low-probability option, so don't count on being able to do that with many PC tabletop systems.

At this stage, all laptop systems have USB ports, so you can easily use USB audio devices with them. Mac laptops also have six-pin FireWire ports, and some new PC laptops also have these six-pin ports, although four-pin iLink ports are more common. Also, nearly every laptop system has at least one Type II PC Card slot, and some even have two. PC Card audio interfaces are a viable option for these systems. However, if you have a PC laptop with no FireWire ports and only one PC Card slot, I recommend that you invest in a PC Card-to-FireWire adapter—you'll be able to connect a FireWire audio interface and a FireWire hard drive for digital audio data storage with just one PC Card.

Audio Interface Features

Once you know what type of computer you'll use and the interface options available for it, then you can start looking at the features of the possible audio interfaces. Conversely, examining your audio interface options may lead you to reconsider what type of computer you really need. As I said earlier, there's no such thing as a "one size fits all" computer anymore. If you're thinking of buying a powerful desktop system to do a modest amount of digital audio work, you might find that a more affordable tabletop system with a USB or FireWire audio interface might be all you will ever need. Of course, a good way to determine whether or not this is the case is to examine the different audio interface features and decide what's important to you.

Audio I/O Channels

The first feature you need to consider is how many audio input and output channels your audio interface should have. You may find that an audio interface with two channels of input and two channels of output is sufficient for your purposes—after all, as an individual user, you can record only one or two tracks at a time. Moreover, all you need to do is monitor your recordings in stereo, right? Well, that may be so, but there is more to consider.

First, there may be occasions when you're recording with a friend and you both want to create stereo tracks of your respective parts. Perhaps you may want to record external MIDI tracks to digital audio, or play a guitar or piano while you sing your part. These circumstances may require you to have at least four input channels on your audio interface. Even if you need only two-channel input capability, you still may want to have at least four-channel output capability, which is what I always recommend.

If you're recording groups of performers in one pass, an 8-in/8-out audio interface is a must. That pretty well eliminates USB 1.1 audio interfaces altogether. However, there are plenty of USB 2.0 interfaces, PCI cards, FireWire interfaces, and PC Cards that offer multichannel audio I/O. Most of these are eight-channel devices, which is really ideal for personal users. However, what if you need to record more than eight channels of audio simultaneously?

Well, there are two approaches to that problem. The first is to select an audio interface that can support more than eight channels of audio. Most devices that do this have multiple *ADAT* optical connections, which carry eight channels of audio on each port. (ADAT stands for Alesis Digital Audio Tape, by the way, albeit you don't necessarily have to be recording to tape to use the connections!). For instance, Frontier Designs' Dakota PCI card has 16-channel I/O capability using two sets of ADAT ports. These can be expanded to 32 channels using the Montana expansion card, which has two more sets of ADAT ports. Similarly, RME's PCI and PC Card interfaces have ADAT ports as well. In each case, though, the user has to buy breakout boxes to connect them to these interfaces. Frontier Designs and RME market their own breakout boxes, but third-party ADAT-compatible I/O boxes can be used as well.

By the way, using ADAT-compatible audio interfaces has additional benefits. ADAT-compatible devices connect to each other with optical cables. These make the connections optically isolated, which means that they don't create or pass along any RF noise that can be generated by the breakout boxes. Another benefit is that you can set up ADAT breakout boxes up to 33 feet away from the computer containing the audio interface, which gives you more flexibility in the design of your studio. By contrast, most audio interfaces with breakout boxes use multi-pin cables that are between six to eight feet in length, which means that you have to set the breakout box close to the computer.

The other approach to achieving more than eight channels of audio I/O is to simply add more audio interfaces! However, there are a few important factors to consider before doing this. First, the ideal solution is to use yet another of the same audio interface that already exists on the system, especially one whose drivers have been written to allow multiple instances of the same sound card in the system. Aardvark, for example, makes PCI audio interfaces whose drivers support multiple Aardvark cards in one system. MOTU also has drivers that support two or more MOTU FireWire audio interfaces on one system. If you add an extra FireWire audio interface, make sure that the entire FireWire device chain doesn't exceed 12 feet in total length. Otherwise, you'll probably experience FireWire audio and hard disk performance problems.

Second, you can make sure you have a spare PCI slot to install a second or third audio card, if that's what you're using (you'd be surprised how often people don't think about this!).

Although I don't recommend this, you can also use audio interfaces from different manufacturers simultaneously. The problem with doing this is that each audio interface uses its own internal timing system when working with a computer. We'll discuss this further a little later on, but for now, suffice it to say that, unfortunately, no two interfaces can run perfectly in sync with each other, so eventually they'll drift apart in terms of their timing. Because of this drift, digital audio tracks will not be properly aligned. On the other hand, if there is some sort of common timing system (*clock*) to which these devices can be synchronized, you can avoid this problem. For instance, both audio cards may be able to synchronize to *word clock*, which is a type of synchronization protocol that ensures that digital audio devices stay continuously synchronized to each other with single sample accuracy. You just connect the word clock output of one device to the word clock input of the other device using the appropriate cable. Set the first device as the *master clock* (i.e., the one who issues the orders, so to speak), and the second device as the *slave* (i.e., the one who obeys the orders). This setup prevents the timing errors that can occur when each audio device uses its own internal clock as the timing source.

Audio Connection Types

The *number* of audio connections may be important, but so are the *types* of audio connections an audio interface provides. Most audio interfaces have *unbalanced* (includes one signal wire and one ground) quarter-inch inputs, and some have quarter-inch inputs that can act as *balanced* (includes two signal wires and one ground wire—the two signal wires have the same impedance as the ground, ergo the name) or unbalanced connections. Some audio interfaces even have Neutrik connectors that can accommodate both XLR and quarter-inch jacks. (To learn more about audio connections and cables, see "Chapter 4: Hardware and Software Setup.")

The previously mentioned types of audio connections are classified as *analog* I/O. Likewise, there are different types of *digital* I/O. The eight-channel ADAT connection mentioned earlier is one form of *multichannel digital I/O*. TDIF (Tascam Digital Interface Format) is another type of eight-channel digital I/O, but it's not as widely used as ADAT I/O. There are also other types of multichannel digital I/O connections that are not widely used, such as Roland's R-BUS and Yamaha's YGDAI. As you might guess, these digital I/O connections are used almost exclusively with the respective companies' products.

There are also different types of stereo digital audio I/O as well. The most commonly used type is S/PDIF (Sony/Philips Digital Interface Format), which comes in two flavors: electrical and optical.

Electrical S/PDIF uses an RCA-type connection for stereo digital input, and another for stereo digital output. However, it's better to use a 75-ohm coaxial cable than a standard RCA audio cable when transferring digital audio over electrical S/PDIF because regular audio cables are more susceptible to digital audio data *dropouts* (literally, missing sound data).

Optical S/PDIF, sometimes called Toslink, looks just like an ADAT connection, and can even use ADAT optical cables to transfer digital audio data. The only difference is that the data carried over the optical cables is in stereo only. Although you can't directly exchange digital audio data between Toslink and ADAT devices, most audio interfaces with optical connectors let you choose whether the optical jack will function as an ADAT or an S/PDIF connection.

The other type of stereo digital audio interface format is AES/EBU, the standard developed by the Audio Engineering Society and the European Broadcast Union. This format uses XLR jacks for its connections, to which you should attach well-shielded XLR cables that are ten feet or less in length. This helps to ensure that there are no digital audio data dropouts during transfers.

In the past, people used S/PDIF or AES/EBU connections mainly for transferring digital audio between computers and DAT (digital audio tape) decks. Nowadays, it's just as easy to mix down audio in a computer and then burn this to a CD, which means that most users just don't need DAT decks anymore. However, these digital audio connections still have some useful functions. For example, these ports can be used to input signals from mic preamps and effects processors with digital outputs into a digital audio recording system. Furthermore, you can often synchronize multiple audio interfaces by setting one interface as the master and another as a slave by connecting the digital audio out of the first device to the digital audio in of the second device (digital audio outputs and inputs can also act as sync ports, just like word clock ports do).

MIDI I/O Ports

Most audio interfaces, but not all, also include at least one set of MIDI I/O ports. Try to select an audio interface that has at least one set of MIDI I/O, even if you think that you won't need to use MIDI. For one thing, there may be occasions when you need to use *MIDI time code* (or MTC—simply put, a MIDI version of the time code used to sync audio to video) to synchronize external devices or systems with your computer. Likewise, you may need to sync to other sequencers or audio programs on other computers with *MIDI clock* (a sort of pulse transmitted from one device to another to keep them in sync), which is not the same as MIDI time code. Also, at some point you may collaborate with a friend or colleague who is going to use a MIDI instrument in a recording. Besides, you never know when you might finally decide to use one of those software synthesizers that came with your digital audio sequencer. An audio interface with built-in MIDI I/O is the ideal solution for using software-based synthesizers and samplers, because often it helps reduce *latency* (a type of unwanted delay—more on this in a moment).

If you're planning to use external MIDI equipment such as synthesizers and samplers, and MIDI-controlled effects processing devices, mixers, and control surfaces, you'll probably want an interface with multiple MIDI I/O ports. Frontier Designs' Dakota card, for example, offers two sets of MIDI I/O as a standard feature, and you can upgrade that to eight sets of MIDI I/O with the optional Sierra

MIDI interface unit. But if the audio interface you require doesn't have enough MIDI ports (or has none), you can buy a separate MIDI interface (more on this later in this chapter).

Sampling Frequencies and Resolutions

How well an audio interface digitally records and plays back audio is determined by its sampling frequency (expressed in kHz) and its resolution, or bit rate. For instance, if an audio interface samples at 24-bit/96kHz, it takes 96,000 "snapshots" (or "samples") of an audio waveform every second. Its bit rate refers to how precisely its digital audio converter can measure the changes between the audio levels of each sample. A 24-bit audio interface can detect 16,777,216 discrete levels of change (quantization intervals) in an audio signal. That's a lot!

So, if you need to buy an audio interface, select one that at least samples at 24-bit/44.1kHz resolution. Usually, these audio interfaces also support 48 kHz sampling rates as well, even though you probably won't use that sample rate (these audio interfaces can also usually support 16-bit resolution, should you wish to use it). If you have a fast enough system, or know that you won't generate a large number of digital audio tracks, select an audio interface that is capable of sampling at 24-bit/96kHz resolution. These audio interfaces, as a rule, also support 88.2, 48, and 44.1 kHz sample rates as well, which can be important, as you'll see later.

If you just have to have the latest in audio interfaces, then select one with 24-bit/192kHz resolution. This type of audio interface is geared more towards mastering than multitrack recording, but you can still do multitrack recording with a device like this. Remember, though, that recording digital audio at this sampling rate generates a huge amount of data that the computer has to process and store—make sure that the digital audio software you use is able to support this sample rate.

Zero-Latency Monitoring

To *overdub* audio tracks (that is, record new tracks alongside previously recorded audio tracks), you need to be able to hear them in sync with each other. In other words, you have to be able to hear the previously recorded tracks being played in time with the track(s) you're recording. In the old days of analog tape, overdubbing tracks was made possible with a multitrack deck's *selective synchronization* feature. Basically, the previously recorded tracks were monitored through the tape deck's record head while the new track was being recorded, which was also being monitored through the record head (the playback head, logically enough, was used just for multitrack playback). Without this feature, users would have heard a delay between the overdubbed and previously recorded tracks because the playback head was positioned after the record head.

Digital audio and computer technology make recording new tracks in sync with previously recorded tracks more difficult because of *audio latency* issues. Audio latency occurs because of a delay between the time it takes to record an audio signal into a digital audio system and the time it takes to hear the recorded signal played back. Audio latency comes from several different sources. For example, an audio interface's A/D (analog-to-digital) converter, which samples the audio, usually introduces a slight delay into the recording process. Converting the audio back to analog produces yet another small delay. To complicate matters, an audio interface stores audio data in a buffer before it alerts the operating system that it's ready to hand off the data. As a result, the oldest sample in the buffer is delayed by the duration of the buffer size. The system then has to get the audio data, but how quickly it does that depends on the operating system. Next, it has to process the digital audio information, which depends on how fast the computer processor is. Finally, the hard drive heads can only read or write (i.e., play back or record) data, and it always takes longer to write data than read it—which introduces even more delays! Before you know it, all of these slight delays here and there add up to significant delays that affect timing during overdubs.

Fortunately, most audio interface drivers can report the amount of audio latency to the digital audio program so that it can simply move the recorded data to the proper position on its audio timeline to compensate during overdubs. Also, some audio programs offer direct monitoring of audio input for both overdubbing and punch-in/punch-out recording (more details on these techniques later in the book). Even so, that depends on whether the audio interface has a driver that has been written to work with the program's direct monitoring feature.

To work around this problem of audio latency, many newer audio interfaces now feature *zero-latency monitoring*, which routes a copy of the incoming signal directly to the interface's output. Because the signal you're monitoring doesn't pass through the computer, you hear it instantly. On the positive side, you don't need to have a special driver and the proper digital audio program in order to use zero-latency monitoring. The negative side is that you won't be able to hear any software-based effects processing of inputted signals either. However, keep in mind that you'll often want to record tracks *dry* (with no effects) and then add effects later.

Software Mixer/Signal Router

Some of the newer audio interfaces have physical knobs or sliders that function as mixer controls. However, some audio interfaces use software mixers to control audio and, in a few instances, provide certain types of digital signal processing such as EQ or reverb. For instance, all of the Aardvark PCI audio cards contain a digital signal processing chip that allows a user to monitor signals with reverb. Furthermore, the user can choose whether the inputted signals monitored through the card's onboard reverb should be recorded dry or with the added reverb.

At the very least, multichannel audio interfaces include signal routing, which allows a user to determine which inputs will be monitored by what outputs. Software-based signal routing is helpful when you want to choose which ports will monitor recorded tracks, which ports will be the input ports, and which ports will be selected for zero-latency monitoring.

Most of the time, the digital audio software you use will control most of these features, so it may seem that software mixers and signal routers are unnecessary complications to digital audio work. However, when you consider that in many cases a software mixer replaces a physical mixer, these "complications" can actually work to your advantage. This is especially true for audio interfaces with onboard digital signal processing.

Virtual Instrument MIDI Latency

Those who work with software synthesizers and samplers need audio interfaces with MIDI I/O in order to work successfully with these virtual instruments. Part of that requires that the audio interface have the right driver for the software you want to use. For example, using virtual instruments within Cubase and other VST-compatible (VST being a software format of sorts) programs requires that the audio interface have an ASIO (audio stream input/output) driver installed in the computer. Likewise, a user implementing Sonar's DXi virtual instruments will need DirectX installed in the operating system, as well as an audio interface with a WDM (Windows Direct Media) driver, which is the new standard driver type for Windows. Emagic's Logic and MOTU's Digital Performer 4.0 for OS X use an even newer instrument and plug-in driver standard: Audio Units.

However, it's not enough that an audio interface has a driver that is compatible with the programs you plan to use—the driver has to be well written so that there is a minimal amount of delay between the time a note is played from the external keyboard and the time that the note is heard. This delay is also called latency, but in this specific case, it refers to how quickly a virtual instrument can respond to incoming MIDI note messages. The smaller the latency period, the faster the virtual instrument responds to incoming MIDI data. Note that virtual instrument latency is not an issue once the software synth/sampler MIDI tracks have been recorded.

Latency is also affected by the computer's processor speed and memory size, but ultimately the quality of the audio interface driver is more important. To find out how well a specific audio interface handles latency, go to the web site of the program you plan to use and get the latency specs for the audio interface in question. Similarly, you can go to the audio interface's web site to obtain latency and driver specs. There are also third-party sites, such as K-v-R Audio Plug-in Resources (www.kvr-vst.com), that provide latency specs for audio interfaces used with specific programs, especially VST host applications.

Control Surface Capabilities

Some audio interfaces, especially certain USB audio devices, aren't just audio interfaces. They also act as control surfaces for digital audio programs. For example, the Tascam US-428 and the Event EZbus USB audio interfaces also have knobs and sliders that can be mapped to a digital audio program's pan and volume controls. Similarly, these same knobs and sliders can be used to control various software synthesizer and sampler parameters by

The Tascam US-428 USB Audio/MIDI Computer Interface & Control Surface acts as a USB audio/MIDI interface and surface controller for a variety of digital audio programs.

The M-Audio Oxygen8 25-Key Mobile USB MIDI Controller

sending the appropriate control change messages (more on this in "Chapter 5: MIDI Basics") from these outboard units. Increasingly, these types of devices are being used less for digital audio than they are as control surfaces. Still, it can be cost-effective if these units perform both digital audio and control surface functions.

MIDI Interface Types and Features

If your audio interface does not have MIDI I/O, or doesn't have enough MIDI I/O ports for connecting your outboard synths, you will need to buy a dedicated MIDI interface as well. In the past, there were a variety of MIDI interfaces available for various types of connections (parallel ports, serial ports, etc.). Now, though, USB MIDI interfaces are almost exclusively the only type available. That's not a bad thing—MIDI produces much less data than digital audio, so USB is more than capable of handling multiple streams of MIDI data at once.

Just like audio interfaces, MIDI interfaces have a variety of features that the potential buyer needs to consider. First, and most importantly, how many I/O ports (and corresponding sets of MIDI channels) does the MIDI interface have? You can get a single I/O, 16-channel interface (i.e., one MIDI In port carrying 16 channels of data in, and one MIDI Out port carrying 16 channels of data out), all the way up to an eight I/O (eight "ins," eight "outs"), 128-channel interface. It just depends on how extensive your outboard MIDI system is.

You should also find out if the MIDI interface is capable of acting as a MIDI router when not connected to a computer. In other words, will your individual components be able to talk to each other when the computer is off? This is important if you want to be able to, for instance, play your keyboard and have the information go through the interface so that it's received and interpreted by a sound module—so you can "play" your notes through the sounds of that module. For some people (particularly those who work in "live" settings), this may be an important consideration; for others, it's not a big issue.

You'll also need to determine if you'll need to be able to synchronize your MIDI gear and your digital audio programs to an outboard multichannel tape deck or MDM (modular digital multitrack). Also, will you want to be able to sync up your audio to video of some sort? Most certainly, then, you'll also want your MIDI interface to be able to synchronize to SMPTE (Society of Motion Picture and Television Engineers) code (code that is embedded in video for the purpose of synchronizing audio to it, among other things) to do that.

However, what do you do if your audio interface doesn't have MIDI I/O, and you were planning to use only software synths and samplers? Do you have to buy a separate keyboard and a MIDI interface? The answer is "not anymore." There are a number of manufacturers that offer USB keyboards; that is, keyboard controllers that send MIDI information via a USB port. For many software synth users, that's all they need.

CHAPTER 4
HARDWARE AND SOFTWARE SETUP

Now that you've bought your computer, software, and audio/MIDI interface, you need to set up these components so that they will all work together properly. How you do this will depend on whether you're using a Mac or a Windows computer.

Driver and software installation isn't terribly difficult as long as you follow the manufacturers' instructions. Likewise, setting up MIDI and audio cabling isn't difficult, although it can be time-consuming. However, because it can be a lengthy process, the potential for making wiring mistakes can be great. Keeping a record of your cabling setup will help you to de-bug any errors that occur during this process.

The most difficult aspect of hardware and software setup is configuring your digital audio sequencer so that it can help you to organize and manage your recording, editing, and mixdown sessions in a way that's most efficient for you. It may take a few tries before you design a configuration that you like. In the meantime, though, don't become overly concerned about getting this right before doing *any* work. Digital audio sequencers have default settings and various template files that make good starting points. Additionally, your setup preferences will become self-evident the more you work with and alter these initial settings and templates.

Driver Installation Basics

The first step in setting up your system is to install the drivers for your audio/MIDI interface before installing the music software you plan to use. If you have separate audio and MIDI interfaces, you will need to install the drivers for each of them. As I mentioned earlier, drivers are little programs that allow the computer, its operating system, and, by extension, the appropriate music software to interact with your audio and MIDI hardware. Installing the drivers first makes it easier for your music software to find your interface(s) more or less automatically during program installation.

Installing a driver for an interface is actually easy as long as you follow the manufacturer's directions. However, make sure that you thoroughly read them *before* you begin the installation so you'll be sure to understand what you need to do before you actually have to do it. Also, make sure that you have the most current driver version for your interface. Because the interface manufacturers supply the drivers, check their web sites for the latest versions or updates. If a later version than what was included in your hardware package exists, simply download the latest driver from the site and install it. Don't install the old version unless specifically told to do so.

For Macs Only: OS X Driver and Software Setup

Those of you who have just bought a new Mac have already come face-to-face with OS X, Apple's sleek new operating system. For you computer purists out there, this new operating system is actually based on a different operating system (UNIX) that's even older than Microsoft's MS-DOS. Ironically, Apple is doing the same thing that Microsoft was criticized for doing with Windows for the last several years—namely, overlaying a graphic user interface on what is basically a command-line oriented operating system. Even so, OS X is a trimmed-down, better-running operating system than OS 9, Apple's previous system. And its graphics certainly are pretty!

Because OS X is a radical departure from previous Mac operating systems, making the switch over to software that runs on OS X has been difficult for developers, and the transition has been a long process in some cases. However, as of this writing, it looks as though this is more or less complete, which is a good thing, because Apple no longer offers the OS 9 operating system with their new computers.

Admittedly, there are still a few applications and devices that run only in OS 9. Fortunately, OS X is able to run OS 9 software in what is called the *Classic* environment, which is basically a program "shell" that runs in OS X, emulating the OS 9 operating system so that OS 9 software can function. Unfortunately, the Classic environment doesn't always allow programs to access the FireWire and USB ports, which means that Mac-based computer musicians who use USB and FireWire devices can't necessarily use older OS 9 music software.

OS X is still a better, easier-to-use operating system all around. For instance, there are new driver standards for digital audio and MIDI devices, called Core Audio and Core MIDI, respectively. Installing drivers and software in OS X is a breeze, because they automatically go into the Extensions folder. Moreover, there's no need to use additional special drivers in OS X. All audio and MIDI drivers that are OS X compatible support only Core Audio and/or Core MIDI.

Once the Core drivers have been installed, the applications can automatically detect their presence on the system.

Core MIDI Setup

Many years ago, Mac operating systems had their own MIDI manager called, logically enough, MIDI Manager. However, as MIDI hardware for Macs became more elaborate, and Mac MIDI applications became more complex, the limitations of Apple's MIDI Manager became more apparent. The final straw came when PowerBook users in the early 1990s experienced MIDI data flow problems when trying to use MIDI Manager with their sequencing applications. Opcode, whose Open Music System (OMS) added extensive MIDI support to the Mac operating system, stepped in with a free upgrade that solved this problem immediately. Mark of the Unicorn (MOTU) also presented their own solution to the problem by offering FreeMIDI, which worked in a similar fashion to OMS. By the time Apple presented their solution several months later, OMS was already the de facto standard for handling MIDI data on the Mac, and Apple didn't develop MIDI Manager further.

With the advent of OS X and Core MIDI, however, Apple is reclaiming control over the MIDI capabilities of its operating system. It shouldn't come as a surprise, then, that OMS and FreeMIDI do not operate in OS X. However, the more robust MIDI processing capabilities of Core MIDI make the elimination of OMS and FreeMIDI in OS X easier to take. Even so, the transition to Core MIDI has occurred with the loss of a few features that Mac users have come to rely on.

For instance, OMS and FreeMIDI allowed all MIDI applications access to the user's MIDI setup information. To that end, OMS and FreeMIDI each included lists of manufacturers and models to choose from so that users could quickly configure their MIDI setups simply by telling either program what hardware would be used. Moreover, OMS and FreeMIDI provided the factory *patch lists* of those devices so that the correct *patch* names would appear within a MIDI-based application (patches are essentially sounds that a piece of hardware or software is capable of making—more on them later).

With OS X, Apple currently includes a piece of utility software called Audio MIDI Setup (in the Utilities subfolder of the Applications folder). It lets you manually configure your MIDI setup, but it doesn't provide a pre-existing list of MIDI devices from which to choose. There are also no associated patch lists for any MIDI device you designate in your setup; in fact, there isn't any way to create a patch list from within the software. There is also no documentation bundled with this particular utility; however, it is very simple to use, and new users should have little trouble setting up their systems with this program.

Audio MIDI Setup Instructions

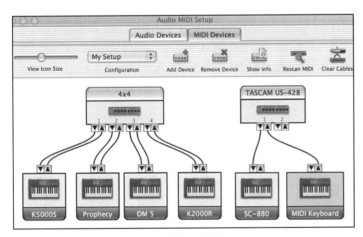

MIDI set-up in OS X—Initial Parameters

When you first start Audio MIDI Setup, the application scans your system for any connected audio and MIDI interfaces. As long as the devices have properly written Core Audio and/or Core MIDI drivers, the program will be able to detect them. When you select the Audio tab, you'll see the audio system settings for your Mac. Most of the time, though, you won't bother with these settings because this is not where you decide what device is to be used by a professional audio application—that is still done within the selected application itself. However, if you wish to route your Mac's audio output to a specific device other than its built-in audio interface, this is the place to do it. Most likely, you'll want to do this to listen to DVD sound output through another device.

On the other hand, you'll want to adjust the settings in the MIDI Devices tab so that it reflects your MIDI setup. While Apple has hinted that the automatic identification of any attached MIDI instruments and devices will be a feature of Audio MIDI Setup in the future, as of this writing, it isn't. If you want to indicate what MIDI devices are attached to your MIDI interface ports, you must do this manually. Here's how.

Click on the Add Device icon and a new device icon will appear below. Click on the new device icon to highlight it, and then click on Show Info. A small dialog box will appear with blank boxes for Device Name, Manufacturer, and Model. In the Device Name box, you can input your preferred name for the device. I usually use the model name, but you can call it whatever name you like (like "Fred" or "Wilma"). Next, enter the Manufacturer and Model names. Even though there is a drop-down box for each of these two entries, there's no list of manufacturers and models to choose from. You'll have to type in this information as well.

Selecting the More Properties arrow expands the dialog box, which reveals two more tab settings: Basic and Expert. From the Basic tab, you select the MIDI channels on which your new device transmits and receives. There are also other options indicated, such as whether the device can transmit or receive MIDI Clock or MIDI Time Code. Likewise, there are boxes to indicate whether the device is a General MIDI instrument or works with MIDI Machine Control (MMC). However, these options don't actually control any aspects of your MIDI devices. According to Apple, all of the parameters set in Audio MIDI Setup are for informational purposes only. The software doesn't program devices; rather, it describes them in a system-wide "document" that's available to all Core MIDI compatible applications. In other words, the information is there just to remind users about some of the MIDI features of the devices in question.

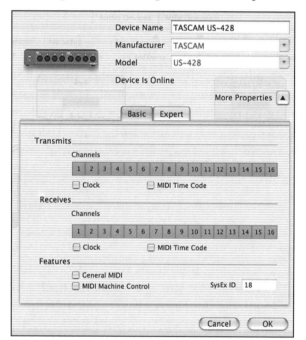

MIDI setup in Basic settings window

As you can see in the lower right-hand corner, there is also a SysEx ID box. However, there's no point entering the SysEx ID numbers of your MIDI devices because Audio and MIDI Setup does nothing with this information. Furthermore, end users can do nothing with this setting—only MIDI interface manufacturers can use it. Of course, this may change in the future, but for now, ignore the options. Likewise, don't bother to examine the information contained in the Expert tab unless you just want to satisfy your curiosity.

Once you've created a new device and have entered its information as previously described, connect it to the MIDI port of your choice. Back in the MIDI Devices window of Audio MIDI Setup, click and hold on the MIDI Out or In port of the interface or device. A line will appear as you drag the cursor to the appropriate MIDI port of the other device, which can be identified by the arrow that's oriented in the same direction on the other device. Don't worry about improperly wiring MIDI connections: Audio MIDI Setup won't connect mismatched MIDI ports between devices, so there's no way to make a mistake. However, if you want to change your MIDI devices' virtual cabling, just select Clear Cables and start again. Once you've done this for every device in your system, save the setup and exit the program.

Software Setup

Installing software in a Mac is simple. Just insert the CD-ROM and either follow the directions that pop up, or click on the CD icon when it appears on the desktop. A window will open, and you will see the file for installing the program. Just click on the installation program to begin the process. You will probably have to type in your administrator password, which acts a safety feature that prevents other users from adding or removing programs and updates. Once the password has been authenticated, the installation process will occur more or less automatically. Afterwards, you may have to restart your computer in order to run the newly installed software.

For PCs Only: Windows Driver and Software Setup

Installing drivers in Windows used to be an often-arduous process. Users had to make sure that there was a unique IRQ address available, the right available port address, and sometimes the right DMA and upper memory block addresses, too. However, with the advent of Windows Plug and Play, and the fact that devices can now share some of these previously mentioned resources, users no longer have to concern themselves with learning all of the ins and outs of driver installation. Nowadays, if you follow the manufacturer's instructions, driver installation is often an "automatic" and relatively stress-free process.

Even so, it's sometimes less automatic than it could be. That's because some manufacturers supply different drivers for different Windows operating systems, and they put those different drivers into separate folders on their installation CD-ROMs or floppy disks. This can throw off Windows' automatic driver search procedure, which just looks for the drivers at the top level of the file table—in other words, it doesn't search inside folders for any drivers that might be located there. However, you can always click on the Browse button in the Driver Setup dialog box to find and open the folder of the driver you want. Then, the driver setup can usually proceed automatically and without further fuss.

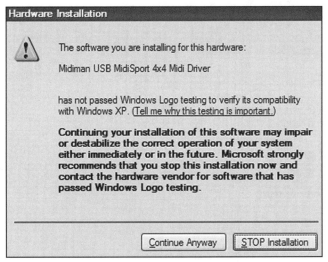

Windows Driver Warning dialog box

When installing drivers in Windows XP, you may see a dialog box with the message (in **bold** text) shown in the screenshot, left, where you are given the choice of stopping or continuing on with the installation. Despite the dire warning in the dialog box, you really should continue with the installation as instructed by the manufacturer. Microsoft is just attempting to ensure that all drivers follow the Windows Logo standard; the system will issue this warning whenever drivers that haven't been submitted to Microsoft for testing are being installed. For most audio and MIDI interface manufacturers, submitting drivers to Microsoft for testing and approval is not worth their time or money. However, they will work just fine, with or without the Windows Logo distinction.

Software Setup

Installing software in Windows is usually a breeze; just insert the CD-ROM and the setup automatically begins. If for some reason that doesn't happen, you simply go to the My Computer icon (located in the Start menu in Windows XP) and click on the CD-ROM drive icon. Doing this will display the contents of the CD-ROM. Select and open the Setup program, and the installation process will begin from there. Once you have installed the program, you will probably have to restart your computer before you can use the application.

Initially, setting up the audio and MIDI devices you intend to work with will differ depending on which audio sequencing software you use. Cubase, for example, uses ASIO drivers, so you need to make sure that the software for your audio interface includes an ASIO driver. Most do, so this shouldn't be a problem. In any event, it's a good idea to check if an audio interface is ASIO-compatible before you buy it. Sonar, on the other hand, works best with WDM drivers. The program can use the older Windows MME (Microsoft Multimedia Extension) drivers, but there will be noticeable virtual instrument latency delays in Sonar if you try to play them in real-time. However, most audio interfaces include WDM drivers as well. Likewise, though, you should make sure that an audio interface has WDM drivers before you buy it.

Cubase Setup

When you open Cubase for the very first time, you will be greeted with a dialog box that offers to test the ASIO capabilities of your audio interface. If your audio interface has an ASIO driver, don't attempt to use this utility to test it. Select "No" even though you will get a warning dialog box afterwards informing you that the MIDI to audio sync could be unstable.

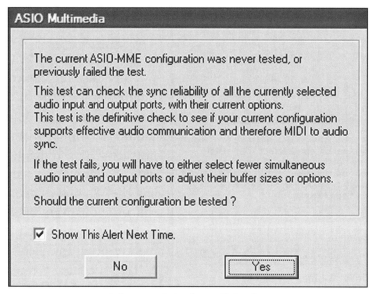

Cubase ASIO Card Test dialog box

Finally, you will see a dialog box of presets for different audio interfaces. Once again, click on Cancel, because your audio interface is unlikely to be in that list.

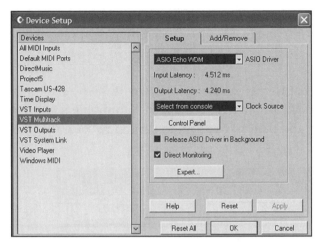

Cubase VST Multitrack Device Setup window

Instead, open Cubase and select Device Setup from the Device menu. Click on VST Multitrack, and the Setup menu will appear next to it. Select your audio interface from the ASIO Driver dropdown menu. The ideal settings for that device (Buffers, Buffer Size, Direct Monitoring, etc.) will be automatically configured when you select the ASIO driver for your audio interface from this location.

Likewise, you can select which MIDI ports will be active by selecting All MIDI Inputs in the Device Setup dialog box. To the right, you will see a list of all the MIDI ports your system can use. By clicking on the MIDI port in the Active column, you can toggle between activating and deactivating it. Similarly, you can choose which will be the default MIDI port when you click on the Default MIDI Ports setting.

Sonar Setup

Sonar runs a little utility called the Wave Profiler when you first install the program. It scans all audio devices connected to your system and creates a profile of their properties and the appropriate settings for these devices.

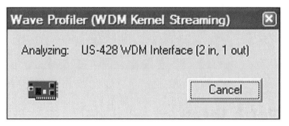

Wave Profiler Analyzer

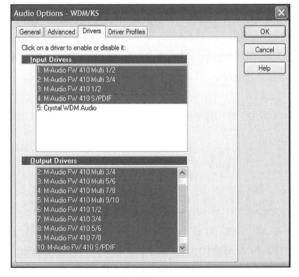

Sonar Audio Options dialog box

However, the first audio device it lists in the Audio Options dialog box may not be the device you want to use. For instance, it lists the Crystal WDM Audio device built into my laptop as the first device. However, I prefer to use the connected Tascam US-428 as my primary audio device. To do that, I have to open the Audio Options dialog box, select the Drivers tab, and deactivate the Crystal WDM Audio input and output drivers, and then highlight the Tascam US-428 input and output drivers to activate them. That way, I can be certain that the US-428 is the primary audio device.

When you open Sonar for the very first time, you will be informed that no MIDI input or output devices have been selected. Although you can continue to run the program without selecting any MIDI input or output ports, obviously you won't be able to work with any external MIDI devices. Also, you will continue to receive this message until you finally select the desired MIDI input and output ports anyway, so you might as well set up everything right at the beginning. You can always change things later if you need to.

Sonar lists all of the MIDI devices that are connected to the computer, plus any *virtual* (existing as software, not hardware) MIDI devices such as the Microsoft MIDI Mapper. Simply highlight the MIDI input and output ports that you wish to use, and then move them to the top to place them in the desired order.

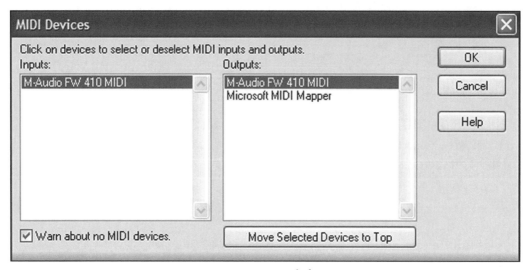

Sonar MIDI Setup window

Patch Setup

Each patch (i.e., instrument or sound) in a piece of MIDI hardware corresponds to a number determined by the hardware itself. The ideal situation is when the software you are using automatically knows which numbers correspond to which patches, but sometimes this sort of setup is not the case. In other words, the software you are using may not understand that patch 14 is a xylophone on a certain piece of equipment. To further complicate matters, even the numbering system can differ among software and hardware components. For instance, most *banks* (groups of patches) contain 128 patches. Often, these are numbered 1–128, but certain pieces of equipment instead number them as 0–127!

While you can select patches for the different devices in your MIDI setup by sending numerical values, this can be a tedious process. After all, wouldn't you rather know the name of the patch you're selecting, rather than try to remember which patch goes with which patch number? Fortunately, sequencing software often provides patch lists of many common (and even not so common) MIDI devices so that you can set up your program to actually show the name of the patch you're selecting. In many cases, all you need to do is associate the MIDI device and patch list with the MIDI port to which the device is attached.

As I mentioned earlier, some of the valuable features of OMS and FreeMIDI were the abilities to associate MIDI devices with MIDI ports and to provide a list of the patches for those MIDI devices. However, as of this writing, Core MIDI in OS X doesn't yet support this capability. Even so, you can still set up patches in, for instance, Logic through the use of the Environment window, which provides access to much more than just a way to associate MIDI devices and patch lists with MIDI ports—however this is not the place to go into its many features. Logic users should go through the corresponding information in the Logic manual to understand its multiple functions.

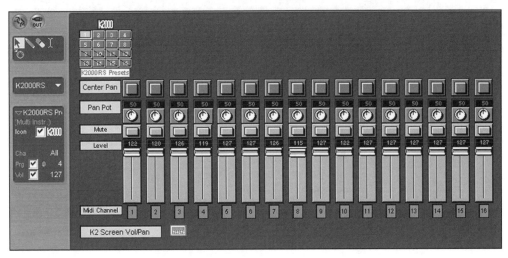

Logic's Environment window lets users customize their audio and MIDI setups, and offers extensive control over the hardware accessed by Logic.

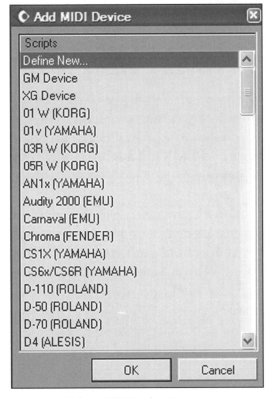

Cubase MIDI Device Manager

Patch setup in Cubase is much simpler. Just go to the Devices menu and select MIDI Device Manager. A dialog box will appear, whereupon you select Install Device. Another box will appear, listing the available MIDI devices. Select the desired device from this list and click OK. Make sure that you associate the installed MIDI device with the desired MIDI port before you close the MIDI Device Manager dialog box. Now, when you select the desired port in a MIDI sequence, the MIDI device name will appear and the associated patch names will be available for selection, too.

Setting up patches in Sonar is also simple. Just go to the Options menu and select Instruments. A dialog box will appear, showing all of the output channels of each MIDI port on one side, and an instrument list on the other side. Just highlight the port and channels you want to associate with a particular MIDI device. If you don't see the name of the device you want to use, click on the Define button to import additional device names. Once you define which MIDI device goes with which MIDI port and channel(s), click OK and your assignments will be saved.

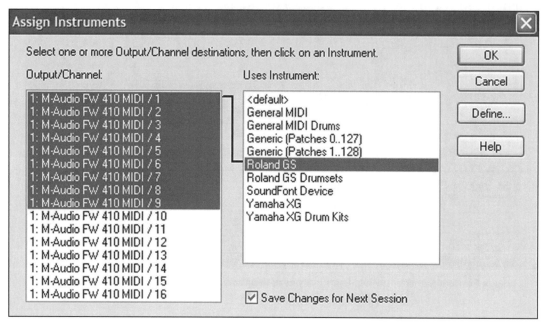

Sonar Assign Instruments dialog box

Unlisted MIDI Devices

Of course, you may have a particular MIDI device that doesn't have a pre-existing patch list. If that's the case, first try to find a patch list file that you can use with your digital audio sequencer. You can usually find these lists at the digital audio sequencer developer's web site, the MIDI device manufacturer's web site, and third-party web sites for either the program or the MIDI hardware. Synth Zone (www.synthzone.com) is also an excellent resource for this sort of thing.

Another option is to create a patch list for your device from within the program itself. All of the four major sequencer programs allow you to do this to varying degrees. It's time-consuming, but once it's done, it's done for good. An additional option is to import patch lists from a universal editor/librarian program, if it supports your devices. Users of Sonar and the PC version of Cubase can import patch lists from Sound Quest's MIDI Quest editor/librarian software. For Logic, you can use Emagic's SoundDiver, and for Digital Performer, there's MOTU's UniSyn.

Surface Controller Setup

Each of the four digital audio sequencers supports the use of a surface controller, which can greatly enhance your music production experience. Setting up a surface controller to use with a digital audio sequencer is extremely simple for all four programs. After you've hooked up the controller and installed its drivers, just go to the proper menu item in each sequencing program and choose your surface controller from the list of supported controllers. It's just that easy!

In fact, sometimes you don't even have to bother with surface controller selection. For instance, Logic automatically recognizes the presence of the Logic Control if it is attached to the system, and Cubase works automatically with Steinberg's Houston surface controller. The four major software packages also support third-party controllers, however, not every digital audio sequencer supports every controller, so be sure to check with the software manufacturer.

Template Setup

When you first start any of the four digital audio sequencers, you will see a default work area that loads automatically. Sometimes this work area is dependent on the type of audio and MIDI interface that's attached to your computer. Often, though, the work area is configured to work with a basic layout, such as eight digital audio tracks and 16 MIDI tracks. However, these programs also include different work area templates besides the default. For example, if you want to work with MIDI tracks exclusively in a particular song, there may be a MIDI-only template that you can load.

Over time, though, you'll probably have a few setups that you use exclusively. Most likely, there won't be pre-existing templates for those setups, so you'll have to make them yourself. The process in most cases is pretty simple: just set up the number of audio tracks you want, as well as their routing assignments if you use a multichannel audio interface. Likewise, set up the number of MIDI tracks you want, as well as the proper port and channel for each MIDI track. When you're finished, save it as a template file or just as an empty file that you can copy and load whenever you need to use that particular setup.

Cabling

Once you've installed the drivers and software, and have connected your audio and MIDI interfaces to the computer, the final step is to physically connect those interfaces with the appropriate outboard devices, such as synthesizers and mixers. In some cases, physical setups are simple. For instance, you may have just one MIDI keyboard and a two-channel audio interface. Some setups may be more complex, involving several external MIDI devices, multichannel audio interfaces, and outboard mixers. No matter how simple or complex your setup may be, there are a few easy rules to follow that will make setting up much easier.

First, make sure all of the audio and MIDI cables you use are long enough to connect to the proper devices without stretching or straining. Using cables that are too short is not only hard on the cables themselves, but can be hard on connection ports as well. And while a cable can be easily replaced, fixing a MIDI port or an audio jack is much more costly.

By that same token, don't use cables that are too long, either. Undue MIDI cable length can affect MIDI timing and can cause signal degradation. In the case of unbalanced connections, overly long cables can even introduce RF noise or hum into the signal.

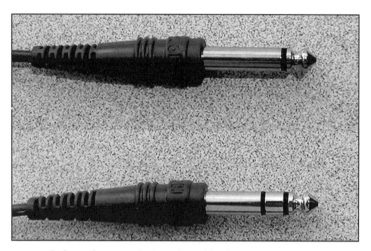

An unbalanced quarter-inch audio cable plug (top) and a balanced quarter-inch plug (bottom)

Also, make sure that you use the right type of audio cable with the proper connections at each end. Basically, there are two types of audio cables: balanced and unbalanced, which have the designations of 4 dBu and –10 dBu (which refer to voltage levels). If a manual lists an audio connection as –10 dBu, for instance, then it's referring to an unbalanced connection, which requires an unbalanced cable.

So how do you tell the difference between a balanced and an unbalanced plug (and, ergo, cable)? Actually, it's pretty easy to see the difference—unbalanced quarter-inch plugs have a tip and one ring, whereas balanced plugs have a tip and *two* rings. There are also other types of balanced and unbalanced audio jacks, however. For example, RCA jacks (which are commonly used to connect components in many stereo systems) are unbalanced plugs, while XLR jacks (which are commonly used for microphones) are balanced plugs.

RCA audio cable plugs (left) and XLR audio cable plugs (right)

So which type of cable and jack should you use? This depends partly on the audio devices being connected. For instance, most outboard synths and samplers use unbalanced connections, so you'll need to have unbalanced cables to connect them to an outboard mixer. Just make sure that the mixer accepts unbalanced signals, otherwise you'll have what's called an *impedance mismatch* (i.e., the audio jack expects one type of voltage reference with a cable designed to work with another). Most mixers, like Mackie mixers, accept both balanced and unbalanced signals. A few mixers, though, accept only one type of connection, so find out if this is the case before you purchase this type of mixer. For the sake of flexibility and usability, it's best to purchase a mixer that accepts both types.

On the other hand, some audio interfaces can use either balanced or unbalanced connections. If that's so, then use balanced audio cables if the recording source can use balanced audio cables, too. Balanced cables reject noise better than unbalanced cables, plus you can use longer cables safely. However, using unbalanced cables, while not preferable, is acceptable.

No matter what type of cabling you use, make sure to keep a record or diagram of all of the audio connections. Likewise, keep a record or diagram of your MIDI setup, especially if you're using a multiport MIDI interface and several outboard MIDI devices. Not only are they helpful references, but they also can help you to troubleshoot any signal flow problems that can occur when you first start using digital audio sequencing software.

Test Run

Now that everything is installed and connected, the last step is to take everything on a test run to make sure that it all works properly. Load the demo file that came with the program (all of the four major sequencing programs come with demo material), which will often have a small number of audio and MIDI tracks. Most of the time, they'll play just fine. If not, check the audio and MIDI cabling again. Likewise, make sure that the devices are properly powered up and the mixer faders and output levels are properly set (i.e., volume settings are turned up sufficiently).

If you've checked everything and have made sure that all connections are properly configured (and that the devices are on) but are still having problems, it's time to check with the software manufacturers for assistance. Part of the purchase price of your hardware and software goes toward product support, and most companies are glad to provide it. In fact, you'll find that certain problems appear regularly enough that their solutions can be found in the FAQ (frequently asked questions) pages on their web sites. Consult your manual first, and then a FAQ or two—if neither of these give you the information that you need to solve the problem, e-mail or call the technical support staff of the relevant hardware or software manufacturer.

CHAPTER 5
MIDI BASICS

Part of what a digital audio sequencer does is record and play back MIDI *sequences* (i.e., of data). It's probable that most of you have at least heard the term "MIDI," and some of you may even have a vague idea that it has something to do with synthesizers. In fact, many of you guitarists (or you other non-keyboardists) might be tempted to skip this chapter altogether because you don't think you need to know anything about MIDI to make music with your computer.

However, there's more to MIDI than just using it to sequence synthesizer and sampler parts. For instance, MIDI can be used to control various features of your audio tracks when used with surface controller hardware. Besides, you don't even need to be a keyboard player—or even *own* a keyboard— to create MIDI tracks with your digital audio sequencer. So, if you think that making music with MIDI isn't a necessary music production skill, think again! MIDI is a tool you should learn to use, no matter what your main instrument is.

What's MIDI?

One of the most common questions that newcomers to MIDI ask is "What's a MIDI?" Well, there's no such thing as *a* MIDI. There are products that employ MIDI features in their functions, but there's no package that you can open up and joyfully exclaim, "Oh, look! There's a MIDI inside!" Likewise, sequenced music files are sometimes referred to as MIDIs. This term is frequently used on web sites to denote MIDI sequence files that are available in Standard MIDI Format (See "Appendix C: General MIDI and Standard MIDI Files").

Anyway, the proper question is "*What's* MIDI?" The brief answer is that MIDI is the acronym for "musical instrument digital interface." But what the heck does *that* mean? Well, let's break that term down. I'm sure all of you know what a musical instrument is. Guitars, pianos, drums, and trumpets are all examples of musical instruments. However, the word *digital* indicates that we're talking about a special kind of instrument; that is, an electronic instrument (or at least one that is capable of producing digital tones of a certain type) with a digital microprocessor.

Even so, not all electronic instruments can be used with MIDI. As the final term *interface* indicates, there's a special way that these electronic musical instruments are connected so that they can "talk" with each other and/or a computer. Of course, if they have a special physical connection that lets them exchange information with each other, that also implies that the information they share is in a common language.

So in a nutshell, MIDI is both a hardware and a software *protocol* (a set of standards) that allows electronic musical instruments with microprocessors, other equipment, and computers to connect with each other and exchange information in a common data format.

The most common MIDI instruments are, of course, keyboard-based synthesizers. Likewise, there are MIDI-equipped sound-making devices called *modules* that are really just synthesizers without a keyboard attached. These modules generally don't transmit MIDI information—they only receive and interpret it.

What's more, there are also non-keyboard instruments that are MIDI-capable, or potentially so. For instance, you can modify a guitar with a guitar-to-MIDI converter so that it can send MIDI information. There are also custom devices like MIDI wind controllers (i.e., wind instruments) and percussion controllers that can send MIDI information as well. *MIDI controllers,* by the way, are devices that generate MIDI information but no sound.

However, electronic instruments aren't the only devices that are MIDI capable. With the right software and a MIDI interface, a computer can become a MIDI device. Outboard signal processors such as reverb units and multi-effects processors can use MIDI to select effects setups and control their various parameters (more details on this later). Even digital mixers can use MIDI to control various mixer functions such as volume level (more on this later, too). So, as you can see, MIDI isn't just for musical instruments, per se, and it's definitely not for just keyboard players.

MIDI Connections

As I mentioned earlier, the "interface" portion of the MIDI acronym indicates that there's a specific type of physical connection these electronic musical instruments use to exchange information with each other. That connection is called a *MIDI port,* which is a five-pin port that takes a special cable (called, logically enough, a *MIDI cable*) for connecting MIDI devices together. Most MIDI devices have two MIDI ports—*MIDI In* and *MIDI Out*—and some have a third type of MIDI port: *MIDI Thru.* As you can probably deduce from their names, MIDI In ports receive information from other

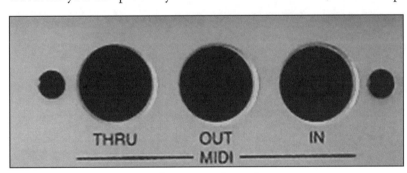

MIDI devices, while MIDI Out ports transmit information to other MIDI devices. MIDI Thru ports pass a copy of the MIDI data received via a MIDI In port through to its MIDI Out port— I'll explain this function more fully in a moment.

MIDI Thru, Out, and In and Ports

The names of the MIDI ports indicate that MIDI data flow is directional; in other words, MIDI Outs connect to MIDI Ins. For example, to send MIDI information from Device 1 to Device 2, connect one end of a MIDI cable to the MIDI Out of Device 1, and then connect the other end of the MIDI cable to the MIDI In of Device 2. You've now just set up a very simple MIDI network!

But what if you want to control a third device from the first? You've already got the MIDI Out from the first device going to the MIDI In of the second device, so you can't directly connect Device 1 to Device 3. However, you can connect one end of another MIDI cable to the MIDI Thru port of

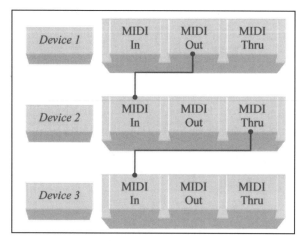

Diagram of a MIDI daisy chain network

Device 2 to the MIDI In port of Device 3. As I mentioned earlier, the MIDI Thru port passes along a copy of whatever MIDI data is received via the MIDI In port. As you can see, this MIDI network (called a *daisy chain*) is slightly more complex, though still relatively simple. You can add more devices to a daisy-chained MIDI network by connecting the MIDI Thru of Device 3 to the MIDI In of Device 4, the MIDI Thru of Device 4 to the MIDI In of Device 5, and so on.

However, there are a couple of good reasons why you don't want to create a daisy-chained MIDI network, especially if you have several MIDI devices.

First, you want your MIDI devices to be able to easily transmit or receive MIDI information as a situation dictates. That's why you'll probably have your MIDI hardware connected to a *multiport* MIDI interface, or at the very least, a MIDI *patch bay*. A multiport MIDI interface will let you individually connect several MIDI devices to your computer, which is a feature that has some distinct advantages, as we'll see later. A MIDI patch bay will also let you individually connect the various MIDI Ins

and Outs of your hardware—it's essentially a device designed for routing MIDI data flow to various combinations of MIDI devices hooked up to it.

Also, when a daisy-chained network is too long, you can experience MIDI timing delays. MIDI data travels serially at a rate of 31,250 bits per second, which is a little over half the speed of a 56K phone modem. These days, in computer terms, that's not very fast. Even so, that's fast enough to make MIDI messages sound as if they are being

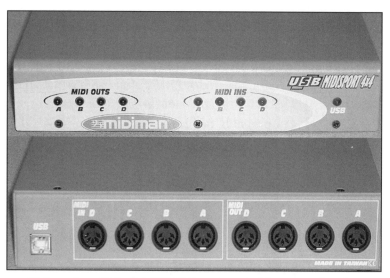

Midiman (now M-Audio) USB Midisport 4x4 multiport MIDI interface

transmitted or received simultaneously, even though each bit is processed sequentially (which is why we call them MIDI *sequences*). But keep in mind that the average MIDI message is at least two bytes (16 bits) long, and often three bytes (24 bits) long. It takes a small amount of time for a device to transmit or receive literally every bit of a complete MIDI message.

At short distances (or, more precisely, cable lengths), MIDI message transmission or reception time is negligible, so no appreciable delay is heard. However, it takes longer for any MIDI data sent to arrive at its destination if the distances (i.e., the overall lengths of the cable connections) between devices are longer. The last device in the MIDI chain could receive its information much later than the device at the start of the chain, resulting in audible MIDI delays between the first and last devices. That's why it's important to keep MIDI cable lengths to a minimum, and to use multiport interfaces or patch bays to avoid daisy-chaining devices.

MIDI Channels

One of the most common problems that beginners first have is that they can't hear their MIDI instruments after connecting everything. Usually, it's because they didn't connect their instruments' audio outputs as well. After all, no sound travels over the MIDI connections—only information about musical performance parameters. The reason that you can hear sound when you play your synthesizer is because the instrument's sound engine is able to translate the MIDI data that was generated when you played notes on the keyboard. This separation of performance information from the actual sound-producing qualities of an instrument is one of MIDI's most powerful features.

Before we get into some of the data that's generated in MIDI, let's first discuss how MIDI broadcasts this data. MIDI transmits and receives data on 16 separate channels (i.e., for each In/Out pair). You can think of these channels as you would television channels. If you want to watch the news on channel 2, you need to tune your TV to channel 2. Likewise, the TV station has to be broadcasting on channel 2 for you to see this program.

The same thing holds true with MIDI. If you want a MIDI device to receive MIDI information on MIDI Channel 1, you have to set that device to receive on MIDI Channel 1. Likewise, in order for that device to receive the information, the transmitting device (such as your computer's digital audio sequencer) also has to send the desired information on MIDI Channel 1. If both of these conditions are not met, you will probably hear nothing unless the receiving or transmitting MIDI device is set to Mode 1 (I'll explain this concept in a moment).

So, if MIDI can transmit and receive data on only 16 channels, how are the manufacturers of some devices and software packages able to advertise that they can transmit or receive on more than 16 MIDI channels? Well, these types of devices take into account the previously mentioned multiport interfaces, which have more than one set of MIDI Ins and Outs. Each set of ports transmits and receives information on just 16 channels. This means that you can broadcast MIDI information on 32 individual channels if your interface has two sets of MIDI ports. Similarly, you can broadcast MIDI information on 64 or 128 individual channels if you own a multiport MIDI interface with four or eight sets of MIDI I/O, respectively.

MIDI Modes

While most people can readily understand the concept of MIDI channels using the television channel analogy, this next bit of information concerning MIDI data flow is a little trickier to grasp.

MIDI devices can send or receive MIDI data over these 16 channels in one of four possible modes. Mode 1 is *Omni On/Poly*. A MIDI device that transmits information in this mode sends the same information out on all 16 MIDI channels at once. By the same token, a MIDI device that receives information in this mode will play all incoming MIDI data, regardless of the channel on which the information was originally transmitted. Most MIDI devices don't use this mode anymore, although this was a handy feature in the early days of MIDI when it literally took two or three separate synthesizers to create a layered sound. MIDI instruments set to this mode would always transmit or receive MIDI information from other devices, irrespective of the channel settings. Even so, as of this writing, a few current devices like the Alesis DM5 Drum Module can receive information in Mode 1. This can be a problem if an instrument in Mode 1 receives MIDI data meant specifically for other devices, as you'll hear the instrument attempt to play every note in a MIDI sequence. To correct this problem, you can do one of three things: change the instrument's setting to a specific MIDI channel, make sure that the instrument is connected to its own MIDI interface port, or make sure that the software is transmitting MIDI data meant only for that MIDI device. Either way, then, it won't receive MIDI data from channels it shouldn't be using.

Mode 2 is *Omni On/Mono*. This mode is similar to Mode 1, but with the following difference. Devices in Mode 1 are *polyphonic*—that is, they are able to send or receive a second *Note On message* (a MIDI message that tells a device to play one note) without having to send or receive a Note Off message for the first note (i.e., the device can play two different notes at once). Devices in Mode 2 are *monophonic*, meaning that a Note On message for a second note will automatically signal a Note Off message for the first note, even if no Note Off message was sent for that first note (i.e., the device can play only one note at a time). We'll delve further into Note On and Off messages a little later. At any rate, Mode 2 was never used that much even in the early days of MIDI, and I can't think of any MIDI devices that need to use this mode now.

Mode 3 is *Omni Off/Poly*. MIDI devices that operate in this mode receive or transmit information on a specifically assigned MIDI channel, or, more commonly, specifically assigned MIDI *channels*. They can also transmit or receive multiple notes simultaneously on each assigned MIDI channel. In other words, the device is also polyphonic for each MIDI channel. Mode 3 is the most commonly used MIDI mode, and many MIDI devices are automatically configured to transmit or recognize MIDI data in Mode 3. This is the mode that you'll almost always use yourself in your MIDI setup, and it is most often used with *multitimbral* instruments, which are able to play different sounds or instruments on multiple MIDI channels simultaneously.

The fourth and final option, Mode 4, is *Omni Off/Mono*. It's similar to Mode 3, except that devices that operate in this mode transmit or receive only single-note information over specifically assigned MIDI channels. This is useful for MIDI guitarists, because each guitar string can be assigned to a specific MIDI channel. Inasmuch as a guitar string can play only one note at a time, transmitting note data in Mode 4 helps to ensure that each guitar string will properly trigger its own note when played. However, MIDI guitarists can also use multitimbral instruments in Mode 3 to accomplish the same result.

Status Bytes and Data Bytes

As I mentioned earlier, no actual sound travels over MIDI cables. What is generated and used by MIDI are the *details* of a musical performance. For example, playing a key on a MIDI synthesizer generates information that includes data on which key was played, how hard the key was struck, and the MIDI channel on which this key was played. If you hold down the sustain pedal or use the pitch bend or mod wheel, that information is generated, too. But how do MIDI devices know what MIDI messages are being sent, and on what channel?

To recap, MIDI messages are at least two bytes long, and often three bytes long. The first byte of a MIDI message is called the *status byte*, which identifies the type of MIDI message being sent and its channel. Each type of MIDI message (Note On, Note Off, Control Change, Pitch Bend, etc.—more on these a little later) is assigned a certain value, and each MIDI channel has its own identifying number as well.

The bytes following a status byte are called *data bytes*—information or data associated with the *type* of message (i.e., status byte) that was just sent. For instance, a Note On message consists of three parts: one status byte and two data bytes. The status byte first identifies itself as a status byte, and then provides a value between 128 and 255 to identify the type of MIDI message it is (in this case, Note On), and on what channel that MIDI message is being sent. The second byte following a status byte is always a data byte, and its value is always between 0 and 127. In this particular case, this data byte identifies which MIDI note is being played. For example, if it were middle C, the data byte would send a value of 60. That's because each key is assigned a particular value or MIDI note number. For instance, the MIDI note number for the first or leftmost key on a 61-note keyboard is 36, whereas the MIDI note number for the last or rightmost key on that keyboard is 96 (coincidentally, both are Cs, but in different octaves.)

The third byte is also a data byte, and it also provides a value between 0 and 127. In this particular instance, though, this data byte sends information about the note's *velocity* (the speed or force at which this particular note's key was struck—think of it essentially as the "volume" of the attack). So, how does MIDI know how many data bytes are supposed to follow a status byte? By the type of status message that is sent. For example, Note On and Off messages contain two data bytes, while Pan and Volume messages contain only one data byte each.

Bits, Bytes, and Nibbles

MIDI devices don't see numbers like we do. To them, all data is in the form of *bits*, or ones and zeroes. More to the point, MIDI devices (and computers, too) also see information in the form of *bytes*. If you're familiar with these terms, you know that eight bits equals one byte (i.e., a chain of eight ones and zeroes). So, a digital device doesn't see a number in decimal format (familiar old base 10) like humans do—it sees it in a binary form as a group of ones and zeroes. For instance, while you may see the number 189 as just that—"189"—a digital device sees it as 1011 1101.

However, reading binary numbers the way a digital device does is a little unwieldy for humans, even if they're computer specialists. But if you'll look at how I wrote that binary number in the last paragraph, you'll notice that I grouped those eight digits into two groups of four, which is how binary numbers are commonly written. Each four-digit group is called a *nibble* (computer people have a weird sense of humor), each of which has 16 possible values.

You can express each of those four bits, or nibbles, with a single digit if you use a "base 16" or *hexa-decimal* numbering system. In our own base 10 numbering system, you count from 0 to 9 and express larger numbers by combinations of those first ten numbers. In hexadecimal numbering, you count from 0 to 9, but express the next six digits using the letters A through F. The number ten would be 0A in hexadecimal format.

Reading MIDI Messages

So why am I throwing another confusing numbering system at you? Well, as I mentioned before, MIDI sends two types of data: status bytes and data bytes. A status byte has a value between 128 and 255, and states what sort of message it is and on what channel the message is being sent. You might be thinking "But how can MIDI send two messages using just one number?" It's easy to see how when you express that number in hexadecimal form.

For example, you could express a Note-On message on MIDI Channel 1 as 144, but that's just a number, even if it's in the familiar base 10 format. However, when that message is expressed in hexadecimal format (90) it can be broken down into meaningful information. For instance, all Note-On messages start with a 9 as the first digit. The second digit designates the MIDI channel for that Note-On message, and that value will always be between 0 and F (MIDI channels 1 to 16). Other MIDI status byte messages include Note-Off (8n, where n is the MIDI channel number), Program Change (Cn), Control Change (Bn), and Pitch Bend (En).

Data bytes are also more easily expressed in hexadecimal format, too. To recap, their range is from 0 to 127 in base 10 format. That translates to 00 to 7F in hexadecimal format. So when you see a number between those two values in MIDI messages, you'll know immediately that they are data bytes. Likewise, a number between 80 and FF in hexadecimal form indicates that these are status bytes. So the next time you see a MIDI message that looks like this:

94 3C 60

You'll know that this is a MIDI Note-On message for MIDI Channel 5 (94), and that the note is a Middle C (3C) played at a velocity of 96 (60). Well, maybe you won't know that just by looking, but at least you'll know that these numbers do express meaningful information, and that they weren't concocted just to confuse you!

Do You Speak My Language?

Some of you might be cringing at the prospect of having to learn how to read status and data bytes so that you can understand what MIDI messages are being sent and what their data values are. Relax, because I have some good news for you. Digital audio sequencers can display MIDI information in a variety of ways. One type of display, the Event List, shows all MIDI data in a "human" format. In essence, it takes all of those MIDI messages and converts them from their binary or hexadecimal expressions into ordinary language that we humans can understand.

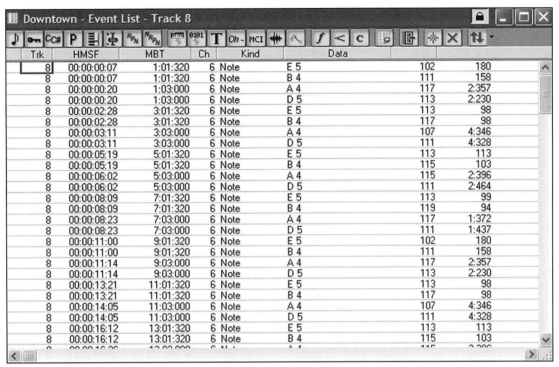

Caption: Sonar's Event List Window

For instance, the Event List view in Sonar shows, from left to right, what track the MIDI information is on; when the information occurred in both real-time and in measures, beats, and ticks (referred to here as "MBT"—more on this later); and what MIDI channel the information is on. The type of MIDI message is displayed in the next column. In this example, there are only Note messages. The next two columns show the data associated with that MIDI message—here, the particular note played and the velocity value, respectively.

The final column indicates the length of that MIDI note, which is usually expressed in terms of *ticks*. We'll talk more about ticks in the next chapter, but for now I want to point out that you don't see Note Off messages in the Event List. There are a couple reasons why. First, many sequencers receive and transmit Note Off messages, but hide them so that users don't have to search for them or match them up to their corresponding Note On messages whenever they want to edit a note's length. Second, many MIDI devices send a Note Off message simply as a Note On message with a velocity value of zero, which is just as good as shutting off a note. No matter how a Note Off message is generated or handled, it's information that you don't need to see in order to properly edit messages in a digital audio sequencer.

MIDI Implementation Charts

What if I were to tell you that everything you need to know about MIDI could be condensed onto one page? That would certainly make learning about MIDI much easier! Well, it obviously takes more than one page to explain everything there is to know about MIDI, but there is a single-page source of information that can tell you a lot about MIDI. It's called a *MIDI implementation chart*, and you'll find one in the back of every MIDI instrument and device manual. These charts are easy to read— I'll show you how. Just refer to this sample MIDI implementation chart for the legendary (but fictional!) ZP 5400 synthesizer, and I'll translate it for you.

Function		Transmitted	Recognized	Remarks
CHANNEL	Default	X	1-16	
	Changed	X	1-16	
MODE	Default	X	Mode 3	
	Messages	X	X	
	Altered	*****		
NOTE NUMBER		21-108	0-127	
	True Voice		21-108	
VELOCITY	Note On	1-127	1-127	
	Note Off	X	X	
AFTERTOUCH	Keys	X	X	
	Channels	O	O	
PITCH BEND		O	O	
CONTROL CHANGE	0, 32	O	O	Bank Select
	1	O	O	Modulation
	6, 38	O	O	Data Entry
	5	O	O	Portamento Time
	7	X	O	Volume
	10	X	O	Pan
	11	O	O	Expression
	16-19	O	O	GPC 1-4*
	64	O	O	Hold 1
	65	O	O	Portamento On/Off
	69	X	O	Hold 2
	70-79	O	O	Sound Controller 2-9
	80-83	O	O	GPC 5-8*
	84	X	O	Portamento Control
	98, 99	O	O	NRPN LSB, MSB
	100, 101	X	O	RPN LSB, MSB
PROGRAM CHANGE		0-127	0-127	
	True #	0-127	0-127	
SYSTEM EXCLUSIVE		O	O	
SYSTEM COMMON	Song Position	X	X	
	Song Selection	X	X	
	Tune	X	X	
SYSTEM REAL-TIME	Clock	O	O	
	Commands	X	X	
AUXILIARY MESSAGES	All Sounds Off	X	O	
	Reset All Controllers	X	O	
	Local Control	X	O	122
	All Notes Off	X	O	123-127
	Active Sensing	O	O	
	Reset	X	X	
Notes: *GPC: General Purpose Controllers		O=Yes X=No		

MIDI implementation chart for the ZP 5400

As you can see, the ZP 5400's MIDI implementation chart is divided into five columns. The first column, *Function*, lists the different MIDI functions of which this particular device is potentially capable. The second column indicates the different possible aspects of each of those functions. The *Transmitted* column indicates whether or not this device can transmit information regarding the items listed in the Function columns, and the *Recognized* column indicates whether or not this device can recognize information sent to it regarding those items as well.

Note that the *Recognized* column is not labeled *Received*, even though we've been talking all along about transmitting and receiving MIDI data. The fact of the matter is that every MIDI device receives *all* MIDI data sent to it. However, if there is present any MIDI information that is not meant for that device, the device will ignore it. Likewise, when a MIDI device receives data that it's not capable of acting on, it will ignore that as well. That's why there's a distinction between *received* and *recognized*.

The final column, *Remarks*, provides additional information on specific MIDI functions or features. The bottom row of the MIDI implementation chart also provides additional definitions or explanations on a device's special features or unique functions.

Channel

With the Channel function, there are two subheadings: *Default* and *Changed*. Default indicates the MIDI channel to which the ZP 5400 is automatically set when first turned on (or when it comes straight from the factory). Changed indicates the MIDI channels to which the ZP 5400 can be changed. In the past, some instruments automatically defaulted to MIDI Channel 1 when first turned on, and, in some cases, their MIDI channel settings could *not* be changed. In the case of the ZP 5400, it doesn't have a default channel. In other words, whatever channel you set the device to before you turn it off will be the same channel it "defaults" to when you turn it back on again. That's why there is an "X" (which means "No"—look at the last row of the chart) for both of these functions in the Transmitted column. Nonetheless, the ZP 5400 does have the capability of transmitting *and* receiving MIDI information over any of the 16 MIDI channels, even though it doesn't say so specifically in the Transmitted column.

Mode

There are three subheadings under the *Mode* function: *Default*, *Messages*, and *Altered*. Default indicates which MIDI mode the ZP 5400 is set to when first powered up—here, Mode 3. Messages indicates whether the ZP 5400 can send or receive mode change messages. As you can see in the MIDI implementation chart, the device neither sends nor receives mode change messages. This shouldn't come as a surprise, because most instruments these days operate only in Mode 3—they don't need to function in any other MIDI mode. Altered is another way of indicating whether a MIDI device can send or receive MIDI mode change messages. The asterisks in the Transmitted column indicate that this parameter is not used or does not apply.

Note Number

As I said before, each note or key is assigned its own MIDI note number. MIDI note values range from 0 for the lowest note to 127 for the highest note. If you stop to think about this, this is well beyond a grand piano's normal keyboard range of 88 notes. However, MIDI messages are composed of status bytes and data bytes. Status bytes always start with a 1 bit, which in binary terms ensures that the status byte will have a value between 128 and 255. Data bytes—like MIDI note numbers, for example—always start with a 0 bit, which means that their values will always be between 0 and 127. Although that's well out of the normal keyboard range, it's easier to keep the binary nature of MIDI consistent for processing purposes.

When you first look at the ZP 5400's *Note Number* section, you'll see that it transmits MIDI note numbers 21–108, and recognizes MIDI note numbers 0–127. If you look under the *True Voice* sub-heading, however, you'll see that the ZP 5400 only recognizes MIDI note numbers 21–108. Why is this important to know? Because the True Note range indicates what MIDI notes the ZP 5400 will actually play, even though it recognizes all MIDI note numbers.

So what will happen if you send a Note On message with a value of 20 or 109? Well, instruments like the ZP 5400 will usually wrap those notes back around to the nearest playable octave. A Note On message with a value of 20 will be transposed up one octave to MIDI note 32 (up 12 half steps), and a Note On message whose value is 109 will be transposed down one octave to MIDI note 97 (down 12 half steps). Likewise, if you transpose the MIDI notes on a sequencer track (a common editing task) out of the corresponding device's range, the same thing will happen. That's why knowing this information is important if you want to shift the octave range of a MIDI track and still have it play properly.

Velocity

Under the Velocity function, there are two headings: *Note On* and *Note Off*. Note On Velocity is simply how hard or fast you strike a key. The range goes from 1 to 127—1 is the softest and 127 is the hardest velocity. Note On messages with a velocity value of 0 are considered to be the same as Note Off messages. After all, you can't get any softer than a note with no velocity value at all!

What most people don't know (and this includes some experienced MIDI musicians) is that there is such a thing as a separate Note Off Velocity function in MIDI. This MIDI feature detects how quickly or slowly you release or lift off from a key. There aren't many MIDI devices that recognize this function, but there are some. One way in which this is used is to associate a MIDI instrument's onboard reverb settings with Note Off velocity. For instance, if you release a key quickly, its Note Off velocity value will cause that note to play with a short reverb time. Release the key slowly, and its Note Off velocity value will cause that note to play with a longer reverb time.

Aftertouch

One advantage of MIDI keyboards over conventional keyboards is that you can press down on a key after you've played that note to further modify its sound. This capability is called *Aftertouch* or

Afterpressure. As you can see from the ZP 5400's MIDI implementation chart, there are two types of aftertouch: *Keys* and *Channels*. *Key Aftertouch* will generate aftertouch information for each key being pressed. Not many keyboards transmit this information because aftertouch messages generate a lot of MIDI data, even when only one key is pressed. *Channel Aftertouch*, by contrast, generates aftertouch information for all keys in a MIDI channel, taking the key that was pressed the hardest as the value for all of the keys played. Because aftertouch generates a large amount of information, digital audio sequencers often filter out this data by default. However, if you use aftertouch frequently to modify your MIDI instruments' sounds while playing, you should change your digital audio sequencer's settings so that this information isn't filtered out.

Pitch Bend

Many MIDI keyboards have *pitch bend* wheels or levers that let a player alter the pitch of a note or a group of notes. Pitch bend wheels and levers differ from mod wheels (more details in just a moment) in that a pitch bender will always snap back to a position of "0" (i.e., no pitch bend) when released. Also, pitch benders generate a large amount of data as well. Even so, the number of semitones that a pitch bender will bend a note depends on the pitch bend range setting of the affected MIDI device. Most instruments have a pitch bend range of two semitones (a whole step) up or down by default, but this can always be changed.

Control Change

Control Change (CC) messages control a variety of a MIDI device's functions and sound output. Sometimes, control change messages are referred to as *Continuous Control* messages, which implies that the values for these messages always range in a continuum from 0 to 127. However, a few control change messages such as CC#64 (*Hold 1* or *Sustain Pedal*) have only two values: 0 or 127.

I'm not going to go into the details of every control change message listed in the ZP 5400 MIDI implementation chart. Instead, I'll discuss only those control change messages that you'll most frequently encounter and, more importantly, use. By the way, the names for these messages correspond to those in the Remarks column on the chart.

Modulation (CC#1)

As I mentioned earlier, keyboards usually have both pitch bend and modulation wheels. Pitch benders, logically enough, bend the pitch of a note or a group of notes. *Mod wheels*, on the other hand, generate modulation data that alters a MIDI instrument's sound. How the modulation data alters the sound depends on the synthesizer parameter associated with mod wheel data. For example, moving a mod wheel may add vibrato to a sound in one instrument program, whereas in another it may open a filter so that the tone can be altered from "dark" to "bright" in real-time.

Unlike pitch bend wheels, mod wheels don't snap back to a default position—the user must manually move the mod wheel position back to the "neutral" position. If that isn't done, the sound will continue to be altered in accordance with the position of the mod wheel and whatever parameter is associated with it. Friends of mine who work in customer support for music stores tell me that customers who complain that their instruments make weird "warbly" sounds often find that the problem goes away once they make sure that the mod wheel has been moved back to the neutral or closed position.

Volume (CC#7)

This control change message affects a program's volume level. While this seems pretty simple to understand, there are some special conditions that apply to this message. First, this control change message is channel-specific, as are all control change messages. For example, if your drum module is set to Channel 10, this message will alter the overall volume of *all* of the drum sounds on that channel—you can't use this message to individually control the volume of each drum sound in the kit. Second, this message can only make a program sound as loud as the *digitally controlled amplifier* (DCA) setting in the synth program will let it. If the instrument's sound is not as loud as it needs to be even after raising the volume setting to 127, then you have to increase the output level in the synth program's DCA parameter (check the manual for details). Third, overall output level is determined by the volume setting of the instrument's audio outputs—raising the MIDI volume level to 127 won't help that much if the instrument's audio output setting is only 25%. Similarly, raising the MIDI volume level to 127 won't help much if the channel or the master volume level of the mixer to which the synth is attached is set too low.

Pan (CC#10)

This control change message determines where a specific MIDI device sound's output is placed in the stereo field. In order to properly hear the effect of this parameter, the MIDI instrument's stereo outputs must be connected to one stereo or two mono input channels of an outboard mixer (or otherwise hooked up to something that allows for the panning—or at least the accurate monitoring—of left and right audio channels). Furthermore, the two mono mixer channels must be panned *hard left* (all the way to the left) and *hard right* (all the way to the right), respectively (a stereo input channel must be panned to the center). If this isn't done, the pan control message will be as good as nonexistent.

Hold 1 (CC#64)

The other term for this control change message is *Sustain* because this message is sent whenever a keyboard's sustain pedal is pressed down or released. While other control change messages generate values that range from 0–127, *Hold 1* generates only two numbers: 0 or 127. That's because a sustain pedal has only two positions: down and up. It's either on or off.

One of the most common MIDI sequence editing problems involves notes that won't shut off after a sequence stops. This usually occurs because a Sustain message with a value of 127 (Sustain On) was sent, but no corresponding message with a value of 0 (Sustain Off) was sent before the end of the sequence. Note that you can fix this by manually inserting a Sustain control change message with a value of 0 at the end of the sequence (check with your software manual on how to do this—but don't worry, it's always a very simple procedure). Don't forget to insert the message in the proper MIDI port and channel.

Other Control Change Messages

As you can tell from reading the implementation chart, there are numerous types of MIDI control change messages. Some types are useful to specific instruments, such as the *General Purpose Controllers* (referred to as "GPC" in the example; CC#16–19) which may be assigned to record and play back real-time changes of some of the synth's parameters. A digital audio sequencer might more easily handle other types of control change messages. For example, the *Bank Select* messages, which let you switch among different banks of a MIDI instrument's programs, are done transparently in most digital audio sequencers so that the user doesn't have to deal directly with the number assignments.

In other cases, it may take a combination of control change messages to work with a MIDI device's specific features. For instance, controlling the *Portamento* (note sliding) feature requires at least two control change messages: *Portamento On/Off* (CC#65) and *Portamento Time* (CC#5). Portamento On/Off turns the portamento feature on or off, while Portamento Time controls the speed of the slide from one note to another. In some instruments, *Portamento Control* (CC#84) is also used. This message specifies the source note from which to slide. If Portamento Control is not used, the portamento source note is always the previously played note.

Program Change

Most MIDI devices are able to store their individual parameter settings into their onboard memories as programs. Most people think of programs as sounds, which is true insofar as MIDI instruments and sound modules are concerned. But there are other MIDI devices such as effects processors that are able to store settings as individual programs, too. Programs are occasionally called *presets* because you can set up a program's parameters beforehand and later call them up with the touch of a button. Frequently, though, a program is referred to as a *patch*, which is a holdover from the days of modular synthesizers when synth programmers literally had to plug patch cables from one part of a synth into another to change sounds.

No matter if it's called a program, a preset, or a patch, most MIDI devices have them, and those devices can at least receive MIDI messages that cause presets to be selected or changed. Some MIDI devices, such as MIDI keyboards and sequencing software, can transmit that information as well. As you can tell from the implementation chart, it's possible to send or receive 128 patch changes over MIDI. Actually, you can send more when you combine this message with the Bank Select control change message mentioned earlier. That's because MIDI devices with more than 128 programs usually group the extra presets into separate banks, each of which can have up to 128 presets. But as I said earlier, usually you won't have to create a Bank Select message to go along with the *Program Change* message when you're working with your digital audio sequencer. That will usually be done without your even knowing it.

You'll notice that there is also a *True # (Number)* subheading in the Program Change function. Just like True Voice in the Note Number function, this distinguishes between the theoretical number of onboard patches the device can recognize and the actual number of available presets in that device.

It's mainly the older synthesizers that have this discrepancy, and MIDI handles this problem in a fashion similar to how it handles the True Note problem: It wraps the patch number back around. For instance, if you send a program change message of 96 and the device only recognizes 0–95, the final value will be 1.

One of the more confusing aspects of program change messages is the start number. Many people are used to having 1 indicate the first patch number. However, those who are used to working with computers (as MIDI programmers often are) often indicate the first program number as 0. If you find yourself consistently off by one whenever you send a program change message, you can do one of several things. First off, you can just remember that the first program is numbered 0, and send program changes with that fact in mind. If you don't want have to make a mental note of that fact, you can set up your digital audio sequencer to make that adjustment for you. However, you generally won't have to send number values for program change messages. Digital audio sequencing programs usually list each program's name for many MIDI devices, so you can just select the name of the patch you want. The program will do the grunt work of sending out the proper program change number to the corresponding device.

System Exclusive

So far we've covered *channel commands*—that is, MIDI messages that can be sent out over specific MIDI channels. Now let's look at *system commands*—that is, messages that can be received by all MIDI devices, regardless of the MIDI channel(s) on which the devices are set to receive.

One important system command is the *System Exclusive* message. This type of message enables devices to send specialized data only to other connected devices that can use it. In other words, this message allows one device to send data that is meant *exclusively* for another device. Although you probably don't think of a MIDI device as a system, it is, and each MIDI device or system has a unique identifying number. For example, the Korg Triton keyboard workstation has a unique identification number that is composed of the company's identification number plus a separate identification number for the Triton model. This can let a MIDI user address MIDI messages that are exclusive to just the Korg Triton.

System Exclusive messages are generally used with editor/librarian software that let you edit a MIDI device's parameters using a computer. You can then create your own custom banks of programs to send to a device.

System Common

The *System Common* heading has three functions: *Song Position, Song Select,* and *Tune*. The Song Select message asks a sequencer to load a specific song from its memory, while the Song Position message sets a sequencer to begin playing from any point within a song. The Tune message asks all of the receiving MIDI devices to tune themselves. None of these messages are used that much anymore, but if you acquire a vintage piece of MIDI gear that uses any of these messages, you'll at least know what they're for.

System Real-Time

System Real-Time messages synchronize the performance timing among MIDI devices. These types of messages are short (only one byte long), and because they synchronize the timing of MIDI devices, it's important that System Real-Time messages are sent at precisely the right time. In fact, these messages will be sent in the middle of other MIDI messages, if necessary. Put simply, System Real-Time messages have priority over other MIDI messages.

The System Real-Time parameters are composed of two functions: *Clock* and *Commands*. Under normal circumstances, a MIDI device such as a drum machine or keyboard with an arpeggiator or onboard sequencer will use its own internal clock as a timing reference. However, these devices can also control or be controlled by the internal clock of another device or computer software. If either or both situations are the case, they will almost always be noted as such in the Clock section of a MIDI implementation chart.

If a MIDI device can work with real-time clock messages, sometimes it can work with real-time command messages (i.e., via the Transport controls) as well. A Start command, for instance, will tell a receiving sequencer or drum machine to start playing at the beginning of whatever song it's ready to play. A Stop command, conversely, will tell a receiving sequencer or drum machine to stop playing. A Continue command will tell a receiving device to start playing from whatever point it last stopped. This differs from the Start command, which will always tell a receiving device to start from the beginning of a sequence.

Auxiliary Messages

The *Auxiliary Messages* are also system messages that perform a variety of tasks. For instance, *All Sounds Off* and *All Notes Off* perform similar but subtly different functions. All Notes Off sends a general Note Off command that ordinarily shuts off any notes that may still be playing when a sequence ends. However, any notes with Sustain On data will continue to sound even if a Note Off command is sent. All Sound Off messages ensure that all notes—even those with corresponding Sustain messages—are shut off. Similarly, the *Reset All Controllers* message ensures that control change messages such as sustain, mod wheel, and pitch bend are reset to their default states.

Most MIDI devices don't send the above listed MIDI messages, but they do receive them. A digital audio sequencer, on the other hand, uses these messages in a variety of ways. The All Sounds Off message is usually associated with the *MIDI Panic* button or feature in digital audio sequencing software (i.e., it will send an All Sounds Off message). The Reset All Controllers message is usually automatically sent whenever the sequencer is stopped. This avoids unnecessary complications, such as recording accidentally transposed notes because a pitch bend message wasn't reset to 0 when the sequencer was stopped in mid-session.

The *Reset* (or *System Reset*) message differs from these other messages even further. When this message is sent, the receiving MIDI device is requested to reset itself to its default settings. Depending on the device, the Mode and Channel settings may change, and Local Control will be turned back on (more details momentarily). All voices will be turned off, any onboard sequencer will be stopped, and play will start from the beginning of the sequence. Likewise, its arpeggiator may be turned off and reset as well. However, most devices don't recognize this message nowadays because their Mode and Channel settings are already at their default values. Moreover, the other Auxiliary Messages take care of these functions anyway, so this is a redundant command for most devices.

Many MIDI devices send and receive *Active Sensing* messages, which are automatically sent and received every 300 ms. But what does Active Sensing do? Basically, it's an automatic message that ensures that MIDI devices are properly connected. In the real world, MIDI cables can get unplugged, and sometimes at the worst moments. For example, if a Note On message is sent to a receiving device and its MIDI cable gets accidentally unplugged before it receives the corresponding Note Off message, that note will continue to play. You won't be able to turn off that note with any of the Auxiliary Messages mentioned earlier because there's no way for the unplugged device to receive them. However, if the receiving device doesn't get an Active Sensing message within 300 ms, it assumes that the connection between it and the transmitting device has been broken, and it turns off all of the notes it was playing.

Local Control or *Local On/Off* is another important Auxiliary Message that's useful for keyboards to receive. By default, we are able to directly play and hear an instrument because we have *local control* over the device's sound engine. However, there are times when you'll want to separate the MIDI data-generating portion of a keyboard from its sound engine (i.e., its internal sounds—what you hear when you press one of its keys), as you will see in the next chapter. In other words, you'll want to turn *off* the local control of that MIDI device. If you don't, what will happen is that the keyboard you are playing while trying to record MIDI data will sound everything *twice*—once because you're playing it (that's where the "local control" figures in) and a second time because it's receiving MIDI data from your software! Turning off local control means that everything will play *just once* as MIDI information feeds back into the keyboard. A Local On/Off message (CC#122) of 0 will turn off local control, while a value of 127 will turn it back on.

Even if an instrument doesn't receive Local On/Off messages, it may be possible to set up this option from its own general parameters. However, check with your keyboard's manual just to be on the safe side. In either event, make sure that your instrument can turn off local control of its sound-producing aspects.

CHAPTER 6
RECORDING *MIDI* TRACKS

We've now come to the part of the book that you've been waiting for—how to create and edit MIDI tracks! Before we go into details of this procedure, though, there are a couple of things you should keep in mind.

First, you're going to learn the *fundamentals* of recording and editing MIDI tracks here. Although it will seem as if I'm delving deep into the MIDI recording and editing process, the techniques I'm going to show you are only *basic techniques.* As you become more experienced in working with MIDI, you'll discover additional production techniques. In fact, if you're serious about creating music with MIDI, you'll be continually educating yourself about the production process. Consider this book as just a starting point.

Second, this chapter is not a substitute for your digital audio sequencer's manual. While I make every effort to discuss the features of MIDI production that are common to all digital audio sequencers, you should remember that each program has its own particular way of implementing these features. If you want to get the most out of your digital audio sequencer, *you must read the manual.*

All four of the major programs come with tutorials. Moreover, most programs include a separate manual for learning the basics, as well as a larger manual that covers all of the program functions in more detail. Use the basic manual and/or tutorial to start learning how to work with the program. However, at some point, you will have to read "the big book" in order to use the program more effectively. I recommend that you read your larger program manual using the following method (and remember that this comes *after* you've learned the basics via a tutorial or "basic manual"):

• *Read the manual completely through.* But don't even try to understand it—*just read it!* I know that this advice sounds strange, but the truth is that there really is too much information in these manuals to absorb all at once. The result is that most people get frustrated because they attempt to understand all of this complex material in one pass. I can tell you from experience that this can't be done, so don't try it. Just *read* the manual for now.

• *Read the manual again!* As you read the manual the second time, you'll find yourself beginning to understand some of the material, although not necessarily all of it. I believe that's because your mind subconsciously absorbed some of the information from the first read-through. Also, because (ideally) there was no overt attempt to retain information from the first reading, you were more relaxed and better able to absorb without effort.

• *Start working with the program.* Keep the manual close by so that you can refer to it as the need arises. You'll discover that even if you don't know how to do a specific task in the program, you'll be able to more easily find the relevant information in the manual. I believe this happens because your mind remembers, to a certain extent, the location of the information in the manual. You'll also find that you can more easily understand the program because you weren't forcing yourself to learn that information to begin with.

I know that this technique may sound a little weird to some of you, but students of mine who have followed this have confirmed to me on several occasions that it works. And I believe that if you use this technique and follow the overall concepts mentioned in this chapter, you'll find that learning how to create and edit MIDI tracks is pretty easy, not to mention fun!

Some of these programs have extensive help files that you can access for easy reference. Increasingly, software makers don't even print their manuals—instead, they create PDF files of them that you can install on your computer. Admittedly, this makes it a little more difficult to just read the manual in the comfort of your own chair (unless you have a laptop)! The upside is that online manuals not only save on printing costs—which (conceivably) lowers the price of the software—but you can randomly access the necessary information when you need to find it. But you can also just print out a manual yourself if you'd like to have a hard-copy.

Creating a New Song File

Obviously, the first step in creating MIDI tracks is to open your digital audio sequencing software. Usually, the program opens to a template or default file that contains a configuration for digital audio and MIDI tracks, but no actual MIDI or digital audio data. For example, some programs open up with a default environment of eight audio tracks and 16 MIDI tracks set to a *General MIDI* device (see "Appendix C: General MIDI and Standard MIDI Files"). Some programs such as Sonar and Cubase include template files of different audio and MIDI configurations. For instance, Sonar has templates for jazz trios, quartets, quintets, big bands, and other types of group arrangements. Cubase has templates for 16-track MIDI sequences, 24-track audio, and music for video.

However, these pre-existing templates won't always conform to the types of projects with which you work. That's no problem, because you can tailor these templates to your needs and then save them as new template or default files for later use. On the other hand, sometimes it's easier to build a song environment from scratch. For example, Sonar's "Normal" template has one MIDI and one audio track, and you can add more as needed. Cubase likewise has an "Empty" template with no tracks of any type—you add what you need as you go along.

Empty song template from Cubase SX

For the purposes of this book, you should create a new file by adding tracks as you build the song. As you do further work, you will probably see a pattern that develops regarding track configurations. For example, you may often use four or five MIDI tracks for recording your MIDI instruments and modules, and eight digital audio tracks for recording other instrumental and vocal parts. Once you see a pattern developing, you can create a template file for that particular configuration.

Setting Up Song Parameters

Before you start recording tracks, there are a few parameters you'll need to set up in your new song file. Some parameters will need to be set every time you create a new song file, and other parameters can be saved in a template file.

Data Path and Folder

When you first add a track or open a new file, many digital audio programs ask where you want the song file information to be stored. This is important, especially if you're going to record audio tracks with MIDI tracks, because each audio track consists of an audio file and a smaller *pointer file* that assists in rapid screen redraws of digital audio data. A pointer file "points to" information contained in a digital audio data file. When you manipulate audio data in digital audio programs, you do it through the pointer file so that the original audio file is unchanged. It's best to keep all song-related information in one location so that the program can find the data quickly and easily. Also, keeping all song data in one place makes it easier to archive the data later on.

In most cases, a digital audio program will have a default file path to which it stores data and, for most programs, this default path is set to a folder on the main hard drive. However, if you use a second hard drive just for digital audio data, you should change the default path in the program's options or preferences (check your manual) so that you can more easily store your digital audio—and, indeed, your overall song information—to the desired drive. It's much easier to properly set up drive path preferences just once than it is to do it each time you create and save a song.

The audio program will probably also ask if you want to use an existing folder or create a new folder in which to store all of the song data. Obviously, the only time you'll need to create a new folder is when you're creating a new song. Otherwise, just store any subsequent song data for an existing song into an existing folder.

Key and Time Signature

Experienced musicians who can read music know that two pieces of information are vital to performing a song—the key signature and the time signature. Knowing a song's key signature can be helpful when it comes to editing MIDI tracks or creating a score using information recorded in the MIDI tracks. For example, some programs may feature a *diatonic transpose* function, which transposes MIDI note data according to a song's key signature. This can sometimes mean the difference between a note being transposed a half step or a whole step during the editing process. Setting a song's proper key signature can also help to reduce the occurrence of notes from outside that key signature; minimizing the number of accidentals can make a score generated from MIDI tracks easier to read.

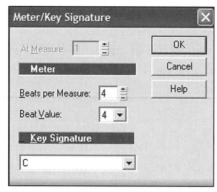
Key and time signature settings in Sonar

Likewise, knowing a song's time signature is important, especially if you are creating and editing music with MIDI. If you have no experience using key or time signatures, I have a few suggestions. First, set the key signature to C major for all of your songs until you understand how to use this information (this is often the default setting anyway)—this key signature has no sharps or flats. Likewise, set the time signature to 4/4 because it's the most commonly used time signature (it's also often the default setting). Finally, learn a little music theory because it will help you to create MIDI tracks much more easily. There are a number of fine books and programs available to help you in this department.

Tempo

It's not enough to know a song's time signature—you also need to know the speed at which the beats in a measure will occur. We indicate this by *tempo*, which is expressed as beats per minute (BPM). Obviously, songs can be played in a variety of tempos, and often tempo is determined by song style. For instance, the average tempo of a pop song is usually around 120 BPM, give or take a few beats per minute. As you create your own music, you'll also notice that your songs' tempos have a tendency to stay within a certain range. For instance, your upbeat tunes may have tempos of 130–160 BPM, while any ballads or slow songs you create may have tempos of 80–100 BPM.

Setting the tempo is also essential to using quantization properly, as you will see later. However, how do you go about setting the proper tempo? One way is to just enter a number value that you think is correct for the beats per minute. As I said earlier, you'll notice that your songs will tend to have a certain range of tempos. You can start off with an approximate tempo and adjust its speed after playing a part just for practice. Some programs also feature a *tap tempo* function, which helps you to set a tempo by tapping on a computer key, a keyboard key, or a sustain pedal for one or two measures. The program extrapolates based on this and then sets the number of beats per minute that most closely matches the tempo of your tapping.

An alternative approach is to set the tempo slow enough so that you can play parts in real-time without any mistakes. This is especially useful if your keyboard chops aren't the greatest, or if you're playing a part for the first time. You can always speed up the tempo to the desired BPM later without affecting the song's pitch. However, do this before you lay down any audio tracks in your digital audio sequencer.

Metronome

Although you'll have to set up the key signature, time signature, and tempo for every new song you create, you will be able to set up your digital audio sequencer's metronome function as part of a song template or default file. For those of you who are unfamiliar with a metronome, it's a device that generates a steady beat so that a performer can more easily keep in time with the song's tempo. Digital audio sequencing programs include this function as a standard feature. What's more, a digital audio sequencer's metronome has several options that the average user will find extremely helpful. Here's a quick rundown on the best way to set up your program's metronome function.

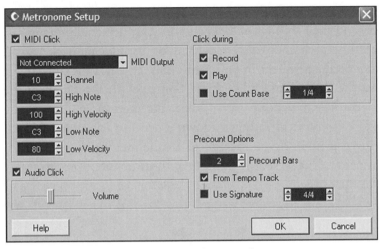

Metronome Setup window in Cubase SX

When you open the dialog box for setting up the program's metronome, you will see a variety of options. One option will let you choose between using your computer's internal speaker or a MIDI device (such as a synthesizer) as the source of the metronome's sound.

If you choose MIDI as your metronome sound source, you'll need to set up some additional parameters. First, you'll have to decide what MIDI note you'll use, and what MIDI device will generate that note—generally, you'll want to use a drum machine or a percussion patch on a synth module. Inasmuch as drum machines and modules trigger different drum sounds by playing particular notes, the MIDI note you select will determine which drum sound you hear. For instance, for the metronome setting in the screenshot, an Alesis DM5 drum module is the sound source for the MIDI note that will be played. The MIDI note itself (C3, or MIDI Note #36) indicates that the sound that will be triggered is a bass drum sound, according to the way the DM5 "maps" its sounds (when you're working with drums in MIDI, often different notes will trigger the sounds of different percussion instruments—e.g., bongos, hi-hats, cowbells, snares—so check with your manual for more information). I can just as easily select another MIDI note that generates a different sound, such as a closed hi-hat hit, a cowbell, or a sidestick.

While the actual MIDI channel for using the metronome is implied due to the program setup options used in this particular example, some programs will also request that you specify which MIDI channel and interface port should be used for the MIDI metronome note. Usually, that will be MIDI Channel 10, because percussion modules frequently use that particular MIDI channel. Obviously, you should also choose the port to which the drum machine or module is attached.

You don't have to worry that MIDI notes played by a metronome will be accidentally recorded into any MIDI tracks you create. Digital audio sequencing programs have been designed to independently generate MIDI metronome beats that don't get recorded into MIDI tracks, even if you're using the same device to record those tracks at the same time. Nevertheless, try to select a sound that you're unlikely to use when recording drum tracks. It can be confusing to try to record a cowbell part onto a track when the beat already playing in your headphones is *that same cowbell!*

You'll also notice in the metronome setup that there are two notes that can be played—one accented and one unaccented (here, high and low). The accented note represents the first beat in a measure and is played louder than the unaccented notes. You'll also see that both the accented and unaccented notes trigger the same sound in this illustration. Using the same sound makes it easier to listen to the metronome and to keep in time with the music. (As an experiment, try using two different sounds for this feature, and you'll know why I say that!)

There are other click options to consider, and their settings will depend on your personal preferences. If you want to hear the metronome at all times, whether you're recording or just playing back a song, select the Always On option (or the functional equivalent in your program). If you want to hear the metronome only during recording, select the Recording Only option. Some people want to hear the metronome count off the beats before recording, but don't want to hear the metronome during the actual recording. This is especially the case if you've already laid down a drum track and you don't need to hear the metronome anymore to keep time. If you can do so, set the metronome to Count-Off Only (or, again, the functional equivalent). Finally, set the number of measures you want to count off. Most people set the count-off to two measures.

Local Control and MIDI Echo

As I mentioned in the previous chapter, you are able to directly play and hear a MIDI instrument in real-time because you have local control over its sound engine. However, you'll ideally want to separate an instrument's MIDI data-generating portion—which is usually a keyboard—from its sound engine (synth or sampler) when you are working with digital audio sequencers. In other words, you want to turn off that MIDI device's local control. Most digital audio sequencers automatically send a Local Off message to all devices. Most synthesizers can recognize this message, but even if one doesn't, it may be possible to set up this option via its own general parameters. As always, check your manuals for specific information regarding this feature.

Why is it important to turn off a keyboard's local control? Well, digital audio sequencers "echo" whatever is received from any MIDI input ports and channels to any active output ports and channels. Although this may sound like a bad idea, it's actually the best way to operate your program with your MIDI setup.

Let's say you're using a multitimbral synth keyboard with your digital audio sequencer. Most multitimbral synths assign the keyboard itself a separate MIDI channel (usually 1). If you play your synth using local control, you'll only be able to play whatever sound is assigned to MIDI Channel 1 on your instrument. In that scheme, the only way you can play a part on a different MIDI channel is to change the keyboard's MIDI channel so that it corresponds to the new part.

However, if the digital audio sequencer is set up to automatically echo back MIDI information, you don't have to change the synth's keyboard channel every time you want to record a new MIDI track. All you have to do is set the MIDI channel of the track you want to record, which is usually automatic if you're working from a template file. The program will then re-channel the MIDI input from the keyboard to play the correct part, no matter what channel that part is set to. By extension, you can even play a part on a completely different MIDI port and channel using the multitimbral synth's original keyboard channel setting. The digital audio sequencer automatically routes the incoming MIDI data to the correct port and channel based on the track setting.

Another reason to turn off your keyboard's local control is to avoid what I call "MIDI feedback." When Local Control is on, a MIDI instrument sends out MIDI data of whatever you play to both its internal sound engine and the digital audio sequencer. But because the digital audio sequencer echoes that same data back to the instrument, the data triggers the sound engine a *second* time, almost immediately after the first time the data is generated. The instrument's outputted sound is altered, and the output you hear is almost like a phasing effect. If this continues, the MIDI output gets fed back into the MIDI input, which triggers yet another output to the sound engine and the sequencer. This loop continues until the program (or the instrument) freezes up from the continual feedback of MIDI data. Needless to say, you don't want that to happen.

To make sure that you can easily record MIDI tracks regardless of their channel settings, and to avoid MIDI feedback, set your digital audio sequencer's echo mode to "automatic," and its echo mapping to the Local Control port.

MIDI Filtering

You can also decide what sorts of MIDI data you want to record beforehand. For example, you may want to record MIDI note data, but not pitch bend information. Perhaps you have an instrument that can generate polyphonic aftertouch, and you want to ensure that its data is not filtered out. In any case, there are probably various types of MIDI information you'll want to record, and some you'll want your digital audio sequencer to ignore. Go to your program's MIDI Filtering section (or its equivalent) and select the kinds of MIDI data you either want to record or filter out. For instance, I usually want to record note data (obviously!), as well as Control Change data, patch changes, Aftertouch, and Pitch Bend information. I don't need to use System Exclusive data while sequencing, and I don't have a MIDI instrument that can generate or use polyphonic aftertouch, so I don't set the program to record these types of information. As you become more familiar with the types of MIDI information you generate, you will become more comfortable determining what kinds of information you can and want to filter out. By and large, though, you'll find that recording the same types of MIDI data that I do will be perfectly fine for you, too.

Setting Quantization Resolution

The next step is to set the song's quantization resolution. Before we get into the details of doing that, however, a little background information concerning quantization is required. MIDI note lengths are expressed in terms of *ticks*, or *pulses per quarter note* (ppqn). For instance, the original MIDI specification states that quantization resolution is 24 ppqn. In other words, a quarter note equals 24 ticks, an eighth note 12 ticks, a 16th note six ticks, and a 32nd note three ticks. If you notice the trend, you'll see that you can't accurately express a 64th note with this quantization resolution. After all, you can't have 1 1/2 ticks. Here's why.

Quantization is related to the word *quantum*, which roughly means "discrete amount." When used to refer to measurement, it's a way of stating that a measurement point exists or it doesn't. For example, a MIDI tick is either there or not there; there's no such thing as a half-tick. When you use quantization in MIDI, you're measuring where notes and other MIDI events start and stop at precise intervals (ticks). A note or event that doesn't fall on a precise point or tick will be moved to the nearest quantize point in the song's timeline. However, because a note like that isn't really being played exactly as it was recorded, its timing will be off.

It's rather like using a ruler that's accurate to the nearest quarter of an inch to measure various lines. As long as all of the lines have lengths that are measurable to the nearest quarter-inch, you can accurately measure those lines. However, lines that aren't measurable to the nearest quarter-inch can't be precisely measured. So what do you do? If you quantize your measurements, you can move the start or end of those line lengths to the nearest quarter-inch and use these new measurements to represent those lines. But they will be improperly represented, because these are not the exact measurements of the original lines.

A better solution to this problem is to use a more precise "ruler"—that is, to increase the number of measurable points to 1/8″ or 1/16″ intervals. This way, you can get more precise measurements of lines you couldn't accurately measure before. The same thing holds true in MIDI. If you likewise increase the number of quantize points—let's say, to 48 ticks—then you can accurately *timestamp* (record when an event occurred) down to 64th note intervals. Increase the quantization resolution to 96 ticks, and you can accurately timestamp events down to 128th note intervals.

Obviously, the greater the quantization resolution, the more precisely you can timestamp MIDI events. However, the question is, "How precise does a song's quantization resolution have to be?" Well, here's where things get a little weird.

Time Is Relative

Imagine that you're traveling down a highway, observing the telephone poles as you pass them by. Even though you know that they are spaced equally apart, they seem to be closer to each other the faster you drive. Likewise, they appear to be further apart from each other the slower you go. In short, how fast you drive determines the *apparent* interval between the telephone poles.

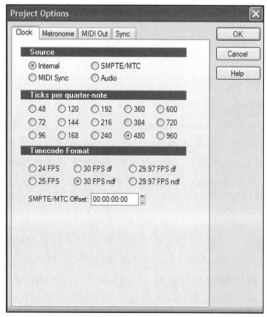

Quantization resolution setting in Sonar

The same thing holds true with MIDI quantization. While the number of pulses per quarter note is always constant, the speed at which those ticks pass by is determined by tempo expressed as beats per minute, which is a *relative* measure. However, unlike our previous telephone pole analogy, the distance (time intervals) between ticks really does depend on speed (tempo). The slower the tempo, the greater the time gap there is between each tick. The faster the tempo, the smaller the time gap there is between each tick. To make sure that you accurately record (timestamp) MIDI data at slower tempos, you need to make sure that the quantization resolution is set high enough to avoid large time gaps between each tick.

On the other hand, using the highest quantization resolution for songs with faster tempos doesn't necessarily ensure the greatest precision, either. After all, MIDI itself is affected by the limitations of its own transmission speed, so there are only so many ticks that can occur in a given second (you really don't need to worry about this—but you do need to be aware of it).

The best approach to setting quantization resolution is to strike a balance between precision and usability. The *minimum* resolution I would select is 96 ticks, especially when synchronizing to hardware devices with their own sequencers. These devices often have a maximum quantization resolution of 96 ppqn. And while there is a wide range of settings with various degrees of precision, I generally select a quantization resolution that also makes it easy to calculate ticks in my head (don't panic—you don't have to know how to calculate ticks in your head in order to use a digital audio sequencer!). Sometimes I prefer to assess MIDI events roughly in terms of ticks, and using a manageable quantization setting to do that mentally is helpful.

For example, out of all of the quantization settings shown in the previous screenshot, I would probably choose 240, 480, or 960 ticks. The first setting (240) is simply ten times the basic MIDI resolution, so all I'd have to do is add a zero in my head to work with the quantization values in this setting. The second setting (480) is just double that of the first, while the last setting (960) is ten times the minimum recommended resolution of 96 ticks, which, as I said earlier, is used by many MIDI hardware devices with their own sequencers. In each case, I just add a zero to the number of ticks I see based on smaller settings of 24, 48, and 96 ticks, respectively.

Note Value	Quarter note=96 ticks	Quarter note=240 ticks	Quarter note=480 ticks
Whole note	384	960	1920
Dotted half note	288	720	1440
Half note	192	480	960
Dotted quarter note	144	360	720
Quarter note	96	240	480
Quarter note triplet	64	160	320
Dotted eighth note	72	180	360
Eighth note	48	120	240
Eighth note triplet	32	80	160
Dotted 16th note	36	90	180
16th note	24	60	120
16th note triplet	16	40	80
Dotted 32nd note	18	45	90
32nd note	12	30	60
32nd note triplet	8	20	40
64th note	6	15	30
128th note	3	Not measurable at this quantization setting	15

Quantization values for notes

Also, remember that MIDI quantization has two separate but contradictory purposes. The first function is to make sure that MIDI events are recorded exactly as they occur, which we've already discussed at length. To do that, you need to use a high enough quantization resolution to precisely time-stamp them. However, you also can use quantization to correct performance errors that occur during recording so that they fall "on the beat" (we'll cover this in greater detail in the next chapter). In other words, you can purposely correct performances to lower quantization resolutions so that they sound better. If you're going to do that, it's best not to set the quantization resolution too high in the first place.

Ultimately, you'll learn to set quantization levels according to the overall tempo of your song (slower tempo = higher quantization resolution), its time signature, and the type of music you create. You'll also learn to set quantization levels in accordance with your overall perception of timing accuracy. Some people are more sensitive to timing than others. Some just *think* they are sensitive because they're aware of the quantization setting beforehand and their eyes fool their ears. Don't allow higher settings to trick you into hearing timing differences you can't really perceive.

The bottom line is that there is no absolute answer regarding setting quantization resolution. I've provided the tools to assist you in making that decision, but you'll have to develop the experience to determine that answer for each song on your own.

Laying Down MIDI Tracks

Now that you've started a new song file and have set all the parameters mentioned previously, it's time to start laying down MIDI tracks. Let's create a simple pop tune that consists of just a few parts: drums, bass, guitar chords, guitar arpeggios, and a synth solo. The first part you should record and edit is the drum track. After all, that is the anchor for the song, and you'll want to make sure that it's perfect before you record the other parts.

Step 1: Add or Insert a New MIDI Track.

Because this project was started with a blank template, you're going to have to create a MIDI track to record into. Obviously, you could also create a new sequence file using a template that's been set up to let you record MIDI tracks. However, you also need to learn how to add tracks as you need them, so you're going to do that for now. Besides, you get an additional benefit from adding tracks as you go: Your track display won't be cluttered with tracks that you don't use and will have to delete later.

The specific menu for adding a new track in a song or sequence file can differ from one application to another, but all digital audio sequencing programs have similar methods of invoking this feature. With that understanding, go to the menu in your specific program that allows you to add or insert a track, and elect to add a new MIDI track.

Step 2: Select the Desired MIDI Port and Channel.

Once the new MIDI track appears in the main sequencing window, select the MIDI port and channel into which you want to record MIDI information. Because the drum track is to be recorded first, set the MIDI port to where the drum module is attached, and set the MIDI channel for that port to 10. MIDI Channel 10 has become the *de facto* setting for recording MIDI drum tracks, so this is just following an easy-to-use convention.

Also, remember to select the MIDI port and channel from which you're generating the information that will be recorded. As I mentioned earlier, digital audio sequencers echo MIDI data out from MIDI input ports and channels. Even so, you want to make sure that the data that's being echoed is coming from a source of your own choosing. Otherwise, you could be in the odd position of triggering a previously recorded synth part into a new track. It may not cause MIDI feedback, *per se*, depending on the selected input and output ports or channels, but it's still something you don't want to do.

Some of you might think that you have to set MIDI Track 1 to MIDI Channel 1, but there's no law that says you have to do that. MIDI *tracks* in a digital audio sequencer are not the same as MIDI *channels*. In fact, you can record or combine multiple MIDI channels to one sequencer track, or split one channel of MIDI data over multiple sequencer tracks. There are times when you may want to take advantage of both of these options, but for now, remember that you can associate any MIDI channel with any MIDI track.

Step 3: Select the Desired Sound Patch to Trigger.

If you followed the suggestions that I provided in "Chapter 4: Hardware and Software Setup" for setting up your hardware and software, then you should see the appropriate instrument that corresponds to the MIDI port and channel you selected. Moreover, you should see the proper patch list associated with this. If so, select the name of the patch whose sound you want to trigger when recording the MIDI track (in this example, the sound patch should actually be a specific drum kit that you want to hear). If nothing else, select a patch number if you have no associated patch list to use for that device.

Step 4: Set the Record Start and Stop Times.

One of the great features of digital audio sequencers is that you can set the start and stop times for recording data at any point in a song's timeline. For example, you can set the start time at measure 1:00:000 and the stop time at measure 3:00:000 to record a two-bar drum pattern. By the way, the first number represents the measure number, the two zeroes after the colon indicate the beat in the measure, and the three zeroes after that represent the number of ticks in that beat. You can just as easily begin recording a part starting at 8:03:000 and ending at 17:02:237.

Similarly, you can set a start time without setting a stop time—for instance, when you're recording a track *linearly* (from the start of a song to its end) and you don't know for certain *where* it will end. However, you'll usually record sections or clips of songs, building up an arrangement as you go along. Under these circumstances, start and stop times for recording parts will vary according to the section of the song you're working on, as well as the specific tracks in that section.

Step 5: Set the Desired Record Option.

Digital audio sequencers let you record MIDI tracks using two main options. The first is *sound-on-sound*, which lets you add or blend MIDI data with information previously recorded on a track. The second record mode is *overwrite*, which erases the previously recorded information on a track and replaces it with the new MIDI data. There is also a third record option—*auto punch*—which is a particular alternative that deserves special discussion (and will receive it a little later in this book).

Sound-on-sound is a useful recording option for recording drum tracks since it can be difficult to play all of the desired drum sounds on a keyboard in just one pass. Often, it's easier to play the bass drum sound in the first pass, the snare sound in the second pass, and the closed and opened hi-hat sounds in the third pass. By using the sound-on-sound record option, you can input all of the MIDI drum information onto one track. However, in order to create drum tracks in this manner, you will need to make sure that your program is also set to *loop recording* so you can continue to record the drum track layer-by-layer without stopping (the section will just keep looping—you can keep on playing and recording until you tell it to stop). Of course, you don't *have* to set the track to loop recording, but you'll have to manually start recording any subsequent passes to add new drum sounds if you don't. Needless to say, that can be a pain in the posterior.

The loop recording feature may operate differently in overwrite mode, depending on the program. For instance, Sonar will write new MIDI information to a new track and mute (but not erase) the previous track when you combine loop recording with overwrite. The advantage to this recording method is that you can later splice together a perfect take from portions of each recorded track. The disadvantage is that you can quickly use up a large number of tracks while trying to get usable takes! You're better off making sure that you're able to play a part well before using this technique.

Step 6: Arm the Track and Hit Record.

To record a track, you first have to click on the track's Record button to *arm* it (activate it for recording). Then, click on the Record button in the program's Transport controls, and begin playing after the count-off beats. Unless you arm the track for recording, nothing will be recorded even if you hit the Record button on the program's Transport. So remember: Arm the track *before* you start recording!

Step 7: Stop When You're Done Playing, and Disarm the Track.

I know this sounds like an obvious instruction, however, it's important to stop the sequencer so that you can take the program out of Record mode. Doing this ensures that you won't accidentally record additional MIDI data into your possibly perfect track. Stopping the sequencer also provides another important benefit if you've been recording in loop mode—it forces you to listen to a loop from the beginning. Often, a loop sounds correct to the person creating it because they begin to make mental adjustments for added MIDI data as it cycles through the loop. One of the more common mistakes is that some people begin to hear 3rd and 4th beats as 1st and 2nd beats, and then input their MIDI information accordingly. The only way to notice this mistake is to stop the sequencer and listen to the loop from the beginning.

Furthermore, many beginners forget to do another important thing once they're done recording—disarm the track's Record button! One potential side effect of failing to disarm the track is that you may accidentally add MIDI data to that track later on, even if you've set up to record another track on a different MIDI channel. Also, remember that digital audio sequencers rechannel MIDI input to any active tracks. You could potentially trigger unwanted drum sounds in Track 1, even though you meant to play notes for a guitar patch on Track 2 and MIDI Channel 2. Needless to say, that could effectively ruin your drum track.

Step Recording

If you are trying to record an extremely difficult part and you just can't get it right even when you slow the tempo down, then it may be time to use your program's *step recording* feature. As its name suggests, this feature lets you record MIDI information into a track one step (note) at a time. However, the number of steps in a measure depends on the quantization setting. For instance, if the level is set to quarter notes, then there will be only four steps in a measure. If it's set to quarter note triplets, then there will be six steps in a measure.

When you step record notes, remember that you can change the quantize level on the fly to input a series of notes. For instance, if you need to input a quarter note, an eighth note, and a 16th note, you can set the quantize level to quarter notes and then input the quarter note. Afterwards, change the quantize level to eighth notes, and enter the desired eighth note. Next, change the quantize level to 16th notes, and input the proper 16th note. You can then change to a new quantize level, or simply advance to the next step, which would be a 16th note.

Also remember that the quantize level and the note duration are not the same thing. For example, you could set the quantize level to quarter notes, and the note duration to eighth notes so that you can play eighth notes only on the major beat divisions. You can also change note duration values on the fly here, just like you can do with quantize level—you can change the articulation of a note while step recording. For instance, you can step record a quarter note *legato*; that is, its full value. You can also step record a quarter note for what you *consider* its normal value, which may be two-thirds the length of its full value; i.e., a dotted eighth note. You can step record a *staccato* (short) quarter note, which may be a quarter of its actual value. In that case, you would change the duration setting to 16th notes.

Depending on how sophisticated the step time function works in your program, you may have a variety of other options that help you to enter notes quickly. For instance, some programs let you use your keyboard's sustain pedal to advance to the next step (all of the programs let you advance a step using computer keyboard commands). Digital Performer, for example, lets you enter note values that extend beyond one step by holding down the note on your MIDI keyboard while using the sustain pedal to advance to the next step. In any case, consult your software manual to learn how to use the step record features of your particular digital audio sequencer—sometimes it's just the right tool for the job.

Punch-In Recording

If you're recording a track linearly, you may want to use the auto-punch option to correct recording errors, provided there aren't too many mistakes in the track. For those of you who are unfamiliar with auto-punch, here's how it works.

Step 1: Go to the point in the recording where the mistake occurred.

Step 2: Search for a spot where nothing is being played on that track both before and after the point where the mistake is located. It doesn't have to be a full measure of silence; a rest note will do.

Step 3: Set the punch-in time for the location of silence before the mistake, and the punch-out time for the location of the silence after the mistake.

Step 4: Arm for recording the track you want to correct.

Step 5: Move the cursor to the point before the punch-in location, so that you can get a sense of the track's timing and feel in order to play along with it.

Step 6: Hit the Record button on the program's Transport controls.

The program will begin to play, but when it reaches the punch-in spot, the program will automatically record the MIDI information you play, while erasing the MIDI data that was there previously. When you reach the punch-out point, the program will automatically stop recording, although it will continue to play until you hit the Stop button on the Transport. If all went well, you should now have a perfect take.

I have to admit that I don't use the auto-punch option very much anymore. I prefer to get the right take or a take that's pretty close to perfect right off the bat, as opposed to using auto-punch to correct a take. A take in need of a couple of corrections is easy to edit, and I would rather edit a track than play part of it again. Besides, it's been my experience that working with auto-punch can cause a loss of "feel" because the correction was recorded "out of context."

I also prefer to create multiple takes and compile a perfect take from those. When recording multiple takes, the feel is usually maintained from take to take, and it tends to remain present even in compiled tracks. Sometimes, too, the feel of a track changes or develops over time during the recording process, and recording multiple takes lets you capture the best feel for the track and use it.

Besides, digital audio sequencers provide you with a large number of tracks to record to, so why not take advantage of all of those tracks? After all, punch-in recording was originally developed because older recording systems had a limited number of tracks to work with. Now that this limitation has been practically removed, why continue to use the old method if there are better alternatives?

Recording Additional Tracks

If you're recording a popular song arrangement, the two elements that lay the foundation for the tune are the rhythm and bass tracks. Those two parts have to sound right together before you can create the rest of the song. That's why I make sure that the drum track is properly quantized, and all of the notes are correct before moving on to recording additional parts (I'll discuss more MIDI editing features in the next chapter). After the drum part is recorded and edited, I generally record the bass part on its own track and MIDI channel next. The procedure for doing this is the same as it was for recording the drum part. I also immediately edit the bass part after recording and listen to how it sounds in context with the drum track.

When I'm satisfied that the drums and bass sound good together, I add the other parts as desired, following the same recording procedure. One of the things I've discovered over the years is that the more time I spend making sure that the drum and bass tracks sound good together, the less time I have to spend making sure that the other parts sound good. After all, I took the time to lay the proper foundation on which to build my song, so recording the other parts is usually easier and doesn't require as much editing.

Once I've finished the basic editing on the various parts I've created, I often use the sound clips I've recorded to build up an arrangement—I'll show you how to do this in the next chapter. Afterwards, I prepare the finished tracks for mixdown, using the MIDI parameters that make this possible. From there, I can either play these MIDI tracks in sync with the digital audio tracks as I record them, or convert the MIDI tracks into audio tracks. There are advantages and disadvantages to both methods, as you'll see a bit later

CHAPTER 7
EDITING MIDI TRACKS

Digital audio sequencers make it easy to edit MIDI tracks almost automatically. Even so, no automatic editing process is completely foolproof, and sometimes the results you want may not be the results you get. Furthermore, you have to decide what *really* has to be done to make a track sound better, and avoid letting the technical capabilities of your digital audio sequencer make your decisions for you. For example, in the early days of MIDI, some people thought that if tracks weren't exactly quantized, then they weren't *perfect*. Obviously, that's not so, but it does demonstrate how one can easily get caught up in the technical features of a program's functions to the detriment of the music itself.

In fact, the most important thing you'll learn from working with your digital audio sequencer is knowing when a track sounds fine just the way that it is. Because the technology exists to make "perfect" tracks, it's easy to spend too much time tweaking tracks to make them "just right." While I admit that paying attention to details is important to making great music, it's also just as important to not get lost in the details of your music. I know people who have spent a year attempting to perfect recordings that were already excellent 11 months earlier. Unfortunately, their unwarranted concern that the tracks were not perfect led them to "over-tweak" their songs to the point where they no longer sounded good. Their apprehensions regarding the quality of their tracks became a self-fulfilling prophecy. Don't let this happen to you: Know when to stop editing!

With that in mind, I'd like to show you some examples of basic MIDI editing techniques as applied to a short tune I created. I'll explain to you some of the problems and pitfalls I encountered, as well as discuss the editing techniques I used to perfect the tracks that I recorded.

Common MIDI Recording Problems and Their Solutions

The most common MIDI recording problems concern notes that weren't properly played for whatever reason. For instance, a note might not have been played right on the beat when it should have. In fact, a whole track may suffer from bad timing—it may be inconsistently ahead of or behind the beat. Equally likely, a note may have been flubbed somehow. Maybe the wrong note was played, or you accidentally hit an extra key at a time when you intended to play only one note. In any event, the take is not perfect. Fortunately, correcting these mistakes requires only a few basic MIDI editing techniques that you can easily employ.

In the following editing examples, we will be working primarily in the program's "Piano Roll" view to fix these mistakes. It's the easiest way to work with MIDI note information, although the Event List view can be helpful sometimes, too. The Piano Roll view is also more accurate than the Score Edit view when it comes to portraying all of the details of MIDI note information. Granted, the Score Edit window is useful for editing MIDI information that is meant to be seen, such as a multistave score or leadsheet. By contrast, the Piano Roll view is better for editing MIDI information that is meant to be heard.

I would also like to mention that the illustrations of the following MIDI editing examples were generated in Cakewalk's Sonar. Note that this was done only for consistency's sake: I want you to be able to see the editing changes clearly from one stage to the next. Each of the four digital audio sequencing programs offers outstanding Piano Roll views and Drum Edit variations on it as well. The editing techniques described here are applicable to all four programs, so you shouldn't have any problems applying these techniques to your specific software.

Problem #1: Duplicated Notes

One common problem that occurs from loop recording MIDI tracks is duplicated notes. It isn't hard to see how this can happen: you don't stop playing at the end of a loop, and a few extra notes are accidentally recorded in the next pass of the pattern. As you can see in the screenshot, there are duplicated notes of the first two closed hi-hat eighth notes in the drum track I recorded. It's usually pretty easy to spot duplicated notes in Piano Roll view because the notes closely overlap each other. That's because it's almost impossible to play new notes at *precisely* the same spot in a measure as notes that were recorded in a previous pass.

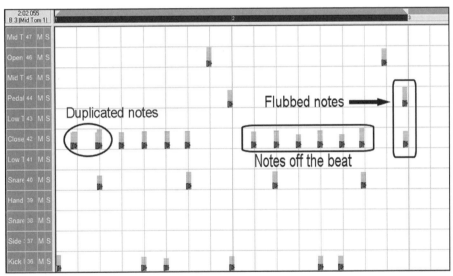

Non-quantized drum track in Piano Roll view, indicating some of the more common MIDI recording mistakes

The easiest way to correct this problem is to select the Erase tool while in Piano Roll view, and simply click on each duplicated note that you want to erase. If you have several duplicated notes, you may have another editing option, duplicated on which program you use. For instance, some programs can automatically delete overlapping or duplicated notes that occur after the first note in a quantize point. Some programs also include a separate "deglitch" function that removes notes with extremely short durations, which usually occur because a key was accidentally played for a brief moment. In any event, use these processes with caution, and always check the results of your edited material. No automatic editing process is completely foolproof.

If you can hear but not see the duplicated notes, switch over to Event List view. If you see the same note played twice on the same bar, beat, and tick (or just a few ticks off), then delete the second occurrence of that note. That one is probably the duplicated note. Even if it isn't, the remaining note can easily be corrected through quantizing, as I will demonstrate in a moment.

Problem #2: Flubbed Notes

Flubbed notes are another problem common to newly recorded MIDI tracks. Nobody is perfect, and even the best musician will occasionally hit a wrong note or accidentally hit two notes when one was meant. Well, to err may be human, but we don't want anyone to hear our mistakes, either. Fortunately, flubbed notes are pretty easy to fix. Just go into the Piano Roll view and go to the measure where the wrong note occurred. As you can see in the screenshot, I accidentally hit the notes that triggered both the closed hi-hat and the pedal hi-hat sounds simultaneously. Real drummers don't do that, so one of those notes will have to go. Because this occurred after an open hi-hat sound, I'm going to keep the pedal hi-hat sound and delete the closed hi-hat sound. As before, I just select the Erase tool and click on the offending note to remove it.

If I had simply played a wrong note at close to the right time, I would have the option of just moving the note to the proper pitch and time. Digital audio sequencers allow you to drag selected notes vertically to alter pitch and horizontally to alter their locations. However, if you play several wrong notes in one take, it's better to correct your mistakes using other methods rather than to individually move or delete several wrong notes. Sometimes, for instance, it's much faster just to record a part again than to spend an inordinate amount of time trying to edit a poor take.

If you can't seem to get a good take playing at your set tempo, try recording with the tempo slowed down. You can always speed up the playback tempo afterwards. Yet another alternative is to create multiple takes and then assemble a perfect take from the good parts of each. Digital audio sequencers make it easy to cut and paste together a perfect take (check your manual for details). However, this particular technique works best when you're recording a linear track, not a short clip of just a few measures.

Problem #3: Notes Not on the Proper Beats

Another common problem that occurs from recording MIDI tracks is that the MIDI events don't always fall on the proper beats, as you can see in the screenshot. The easiest way to fix this particular problem is to quantize the MIDI information to the best resolution appropriate for this track, clip, or pattern. Quantization is such an important and complex editing tool—even when it is used in the most basic manner—that it's worth taking some time to examine how it works in greater detail.

Quantization Options

As great a tool as quantization is, it is not a magic wand that automatically fixes all poorly recorded MIDI parts. Even if it were, this is a wand that you have to know how to wield, or else the results can be completely unintended. The screenshot here contains the Quantize dialog box for Sonar. You can see that there are a variety of options and settings related to this feature.

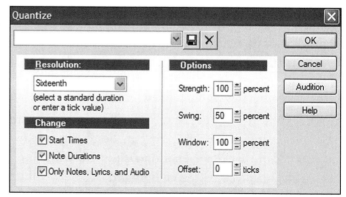

Quantize Dialog Box in Sonar

Resolution

When you quantize MIDI data, you process it to make sure that it falls on the proper beat or subdivision of a beat. How precisely you quantize MIDI data depends on how coarsely or finely you set the resolution of the quantize points. Quantization resolution can be set to a variety of levels, from whole notes to 32nd note triplets (or even smaller) for all MIDI events (the quantization resolution shown in the screenshot is set to 16th notes). Naturally, this is a feature common to all digital audio sequencers. You can also choose what MIDI event data you want to move to the nearest quantize point as well. Obviously, the most common type of MIDI event you'll want to quantize is note data, although you also may want to move other types of data associated with MIDI note events, such as sustain pedal or pitch bend information.

Start Times and Durations

Sonar's Quantize dialog box gives users the option of moving the start times of any MIDI event data to the nearest quantize point, as well as setting note durations to quantize to (the other digital audio sequencers offer this function as well). For example, if you were to select Note Duration settings only, the length of each note in this example would be adjusted to 16th notes, but the start times wouldn't change. (Actually, Sonar adjusts note durations so that they end one clock tick *before* the start of the next quantize point—this ensures that the notes don't overlap. However, the adjustment may lengthen the durations of some notes and shorten the durations of others.) If you were to combine that setting with Start Times, the result would be MIDI notes moved to the nearest 16th note of a beat, with each note's length changed to a 16th note. As you can see, independently adjusting these three parameters—Resolution, Start Time, and Duration—can yield dramatically different results, depending on the combination of settings.

Quantize Strength

All digital audio sequencers allow users to determine just how complete the quantization effect will be. For instance, changing the Strength parameter will influence how close to the quantize points any selected MIDI data will be moved. A setting of 100% means that MIDI data will be moved exactly to the nearest quantize point. However, that may sound too mechanical for some people's tastes. Fortunately, it's possible to set the Strength to a desired percentage so that MIDI event data will be moved closer to but not exactly on the beat. This lets users tighten up the timing while retaining a more human feel to the track. Understand, however, that those notes already on the beat will not be moved away from the quantize point, because they're already at the quantize point. Likewise, if a note is closer than the set percentage of the quantize point, it will be perfectly quantized as well. As always, though, consult your program's manual to see how this function is handled in your sequencer.

Swing

Many new MIDI users assume that they have to quantize notes to evenly spaced points in a measure. On one hand, that's true, but on the other, it isn't. I'll explain. Some song styles don't contain notes that are positioned on a perfectly even time grid, even though they may be written as if they were. For example, a series of eighth notes in a jazz tune is *written* as if all notes were played evenly. In reality, though, they may be *played* with a "swing" style, with the first note's time value extended and the second note's time value shortened. This series has a pattern that sounds like the first and last notes of an eighth note triplet—which, as you will see in a bit, is an important piece of information.

This swing style is so common that digital audio sequencers include a Swing function in the Quantize feature. Basically, the Swing option "distorts" the timing grid so that each pair of notes is spaced unevenly, giving the quantized material a swing feel. For instance, a swing value of 50%—the default setting—means that the grid points are spaced evenly apart. A value of 66% indicates that the time between the first and second grid points is twice as long as the time between the second and third points (the screenshot shows the difference between a "straight" pattern and quantized with a Swing setting of 66%). A setting of 33% does the inverse by setting the time between the first and second grid points to half as long as the time between the second and third

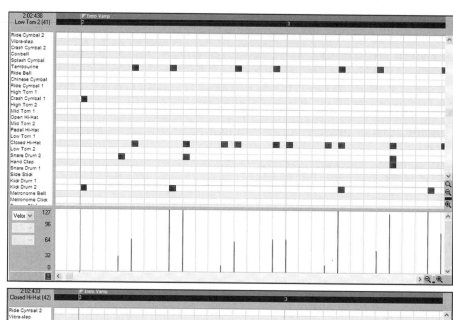

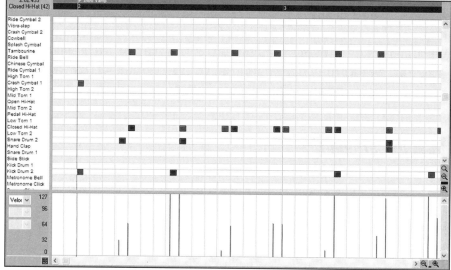

Before Swing Quantize and after Swing Quantize

points. Of course, you can set the percentage to other values, too. For example, a setting of 55% will add a slight bounce to a track, while more extreme settings (like 25% or 75%) will result in highly syncopated MIDI tracks.

However, if you know that you're going to be using the standard Swing setting of 66% for quantizing a track, you may be better off setting the quantization resolution to a triplet value. Swing quantizing a straight pattern results in a swing pattern where the notes fall on evenly spaced triplet-note boundaries. Knowing this gives you the option of writing or playing it that way in the first place, and saves you the extra step of swing quantizing the part afterwards.

Quantize Window

Another way to keep the feel of MIDI tracks while tightening up their timing is to adjust the Quantize Window, which is another common quantization feature of digital audio sequencers. Under normal circumstances, the Quantize Window is set to 100%, which means that all notes will be shifted to exact points on the quantization grid. That's because the Quantize Window extends to half the resolution distance on each side of the quantization point. For instance, a quantization resolution setting of 16th notes will have a Quantize Window of a 32nd note on either side.

However, if you adjust the Quantize Window to 50%, it extends to only a quarter of the resolution distance on each side of the quantization point. For example, a quantization resolution setting of 16th notes will have a Quantize Window of a 64th note on either side. Those MIDI notes or events that fall outside of that window will not be moved to the nearest quantize point.

By adjusting the width of the Quantize Window, you can determine how exact the quantization process will be. Higher settings mean more precision, so there may not be much of a practical difference between settings of 90% and 100%. Conversely, lower settings of 10% or 25% mean less precision. However, there may not be much of a practical difference between quantizing a part with a small Quantize Window, and not quantizing a part at all. As you become more experienced in using the Quantize Window, you'll become more aware of which settings are usable and which ones are not.

Quantize Offset

Some programs provide additional options for "normal" quantization. For instance, Sonar lets you shift the quantization grid earlier or later by a given number of clock ticks. Normally, the resolution grid is aligned evenly with the starts of measures and beats, but if you offset the grid by three ticks, then a note that was originally near 1:01:000 would be moved to 1:01:003—three ticks beyond the usual quantization point.

Oddly enough, this seemingly special option can be used quite frequently. For example, let's say that you recorded a MIDI track using a particular sound or patch. Later, you decide to change the original patch to a different sound. However, this sound has a faster *attack time* (the time it takes for the note to sound fully after it is triggered), so the actual sound seems to occur consistently ahead of the beat. You could slide the track backwards a few clock ticks to adjust for the difference between the MIDI note start and the actual start of the sound. However, you may want to tighten up the sound of the track but alter some of its feel as well. By offsetting the quantize point, in combination with some of the other quantization options, you might get a better-sounding track than if you had simply slid the track backwards a few ticks.

Applied Basic MIDI Editing

Now that I have outlined some of the MIDI recording problems that can occur and some of the tools that can be used to fix those problems, I would like to show you how I used these tools in a song I sequenced. I hope you will see not only *how* these tools were applied, but also *why* they were applied. So let's go, track by track, to examine how I used some basic MIDI editing tools to improve a song to my satisfaction.

The Drum Track

As you saw back a couple of screenshots, there were a number of things wrong with the drum track as it was first recorded. There were a few duplicated notes, some mistakenly played notes, and the track's timing wasn't very tight. I opened the Piano Roll view of my digital audio sequencer and, with the Erase tool, deleted the two duplicated notes. At first, I didn't notice the simultaneous closed hi-hat and pedal hi-hat notes at the end of the pattern, although I could hear that something was wrong. However, the problem didn't become apparent until after I quantized the track.

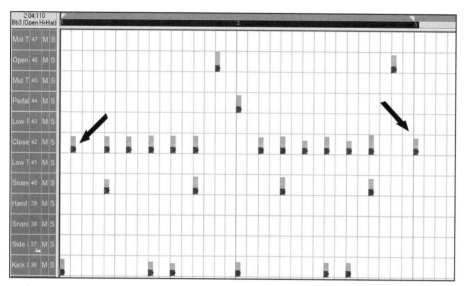

The initial results of quantizing the drum track to 16th notes. As you can see, some notes have been moved to the wrong quantize points.

I quantized to 16th notes, but the results were not what I expected. What should have been the first closed hi-hat note was moved to the wrong quantize point—a 16th note too late. The last closed hi-hat note was moved to the first beat of the third measure, which was an obvious mistake because the pattern was only two bars long in the first place. Actually, that beat probably should have been on the first beat in the first bar, but was played at the wrong time during loop recording. That's also when I first noticed the simultaneous notes mentioned previously.

I undid the quantization process and reset the resolution for eighth notes. This corrected the timing of the track, but I still had to fix the hi-hat problem at the end of the pattern. The answer was actually pretty easy—just delete the pedal hi-hat. After all, the open hi-hat would be closed on the first beat of the next measure. This also meant that I would have to create a second pattern with a pedal hi-hat on the first beat of the first measure. This second pattern would actually be the main pattern that I'd use throughout the song—the original pattern with the stick closed hi-hat in the first measure would be used just for the first two measures.

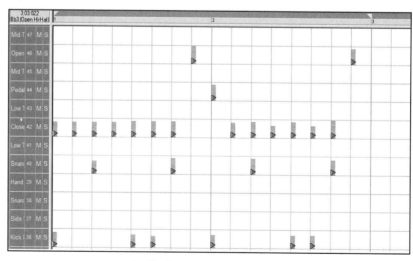

The final, corrected drum pattern

The Bass Track

The only real problem with the bass track was that there was a pair of overlapping notes at the end of each measure. Although overlapping notes aren't necessarily a bad thing, these particular overlapping notes sounded sloppy, especially when compared to the staccato eighth notes in the preceding measures. Inasmuch as the first note overlapped the second note, all I needed to do was to shorten that first note. I simply used the Drawing tool in the Piano Roll view to grab the end of the note and move it left to shorten it (click and drag).

Some of the staccato notes don't fall precisely on the beat. Some people would have been tempted to quantize these notes to "correct" them. However, in this instance, I left them as they were recorded to impart a more human feel to the tune, especially since the drum track is already locked into the beat. Besides, you can see that these staccato notes are off the beat by only a very small amount—they're not really worth changing.

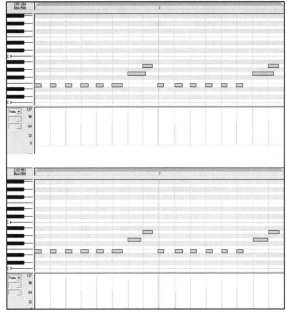

Bass track before and after editing

The Chord Track

As I mentioned earlier, the more time I spend making sure that the drum and bass tracks sound good together, the less time I have to spend making sure that the other parts sound good. This little chord

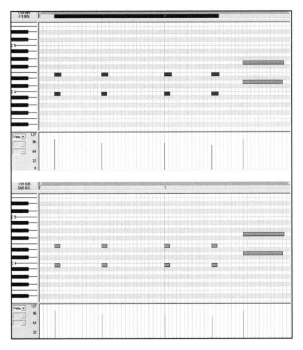

track I recorded next is a perfect example of this. The timing on the track was perfect—no quantization was required. However, the note lengths for the staccato chords were a little too long for my taste. To correct that, I selected just the staccato chords, and quantized only the note durations to 16th note triplets. This made the chords just the right length for that quick, biting sound—they now stand out in sharp contrast to the longer dotted quarter note chord at the end of the second bar.

Furthermore, the upper note of the chord was a little longer than the lower note. I wanted both notes to end at precisely the same time. Overall, the note length of the chord was just right, so I just set the lower (and shorter) note to the same length as the higher note.

Chord track before and after editing

The Guitar Track

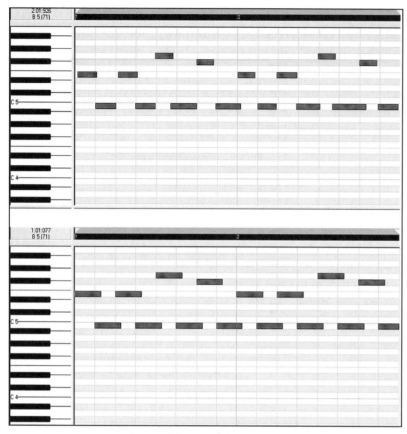

Guitar track before and after editing

I wanted this track to sound like a guitar whose notes are allowed to ring out on their strings. To achieve that sound, the ends of the notes had to overlap. I did a pretty good job of getting that effect just by playing the part live; however, I wanted the effect to be more pronounced. I could have simply quantized the note durations to a particular value, such as a quarter note triplet. I could have also used the Change Length function to stretch the note lengths to a new value. Both methods would have worked, but in the end, I just quantized the note durations to make them overlap.

You'll notice that the last note in the pattern isn't as long as the other notes. I had to decide whether I would create a new part that would extend the length of that note into the next measure. After all, it looked as if that was the right thing to do, based on what I saw in the Piano Roll view. Of course, that meant that I would have to alternately paste in offsetting patterns to maintain the effect throughout the song. I soon realized that this shortened note actually gave the loop a bit of breathing space—this two-bar pattern has a natural phrasing already. It just goes to show that the tools in your digital audio sequencing program are just that—tools! As always, your ear should be the final judge.

Velocity Editing Tools

Sometimes a note is played at the proper pitch, time, and length, but it's either too loud or too soft compared with the rest of the notes that were recorded. Other times, the entire track or pattern sounds stiff or mechanical because each note sounds equally loud. These are problems with *velocity*, the part of a MIDI note message that indicates how hard or soft a key was struck when played. This velocity value in turn determines how loud or soft the note sounds when it's played back.

Digital audio sequencers provide a variety of tools for handling problems with velocity. Which tool you use for fixing a note velocity problem depends on the type of problem you want to correct, and sometimes there is more than one way to fix a particular problem. For now, though, here are the most common types of velocity problems, and the best ways in which to fix them.

"Standout" Notes

Let's say you've recorded a MIDI track that's almost perfect, except that one note was played too loudly or too softly—so much so that it stands out compared to the other notes in the track. How do you go about fixing this? Well, the first thing you need to do is identify the standout note, and what its velocity value is *in relation to the velocities of the other notes in the track!* I emphasize this point for a good reason: You want the standout note to blend in properly with the other notes in the track. To do that, you have to know what velocity value will ensure that the affected note does just that when corrected.

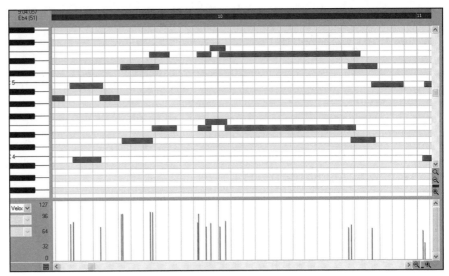

The Velocity graph below the notes in the Piano Roll view indicates the relative velocities of the notes being played. This graph is useful in determining which notes are too loud or too soft.

One way to see the velocity values of all notes in a track is to view the velocity levels in the Piano Roll view. The upper portion of the window shows the notes, while the lower pane in the Piano Roll view can be set to graphically illustrate the velocity levels of those notes (check your manual for more information). Working with this view is the best way to examine the velocity levels of monophonic tracks. Tracks with chords don't display velocity values as well because the vertical line for one note can mask the velocity levels for other notes occurring on the same beat or quantize point. To see the individual velocity values of each note in a chord, switch over to the Event List view. Each note in a chord will be grouped together at approximately the same point in time in the Event List, depending on how precisely you played these notes, which makes it much easier to find the velocity values for each note in a chord.

Once you're able to determine the velocity values of the other notes in the track, change the standout note's velocity value to a number that corresponds to the other notes. For example, if the note is supposed to be accented, look at the velocity values for similarly accented notes in the track and change it to match. Likewise, if the note is unaccented, examine the velocity values for notes that are unaccented, and change the standout note's velocity to match.

Keep in mind that there will be a variety of ways in which you can alter a standout note's velocity. One way is to just type in a new velocity value in the Event List view. Another way is to redraw the vertical line that represents its velocity level in the Piano Roll view. However, that may not be the best route, especially if you're trying to change the velocity value of a note in a chord.

A third way to change a velocity level is to right-click (Windows) or option-click (Mac) on the standout note in the Piano Roll view. Depending on the program, this will either highlight the note or cause a note edit dialog box to appear. If the note is highlighted, its parameters will probably appear in a task bar above the Piano Roll view. Simply change the velocity value from there. If a dialog box appears, the note parameters will be there. Just change the velocity parameter in the dialog box.

Fluctuations in Velocity

Sometimes the velocity levels of the notes in a MIDI track fluctuate wildly—that is, notes are either too loud or soft, but are rarely at the right level. Fortunately, this problem is not as severe as might seem at first glance. If you stop to think about it, chances are that the *basic* feel of the track is there. The wild fluctuations in velocity are often an exaggeration of that basic feel. All that needs to be done is to reduce the fluctuating velocities to a smaller range of variations so that the MIDI track in question plays with a more realistic feel.

To do that, digital audio sequencers allow you to reduce velocity ranges by setting minimum and maximum values. Let's say, for instance, that the velocity levels for a track fluctuate between 48 and 127. You can reset the minimum and maximum velocity levels to 84 and 110, respectively, and then process the track so that the differences between velocities aren't so exaggerated. The track will play back more smoothly, but its basic feel will remain essentially the same as before. This is called *velocity compression*.

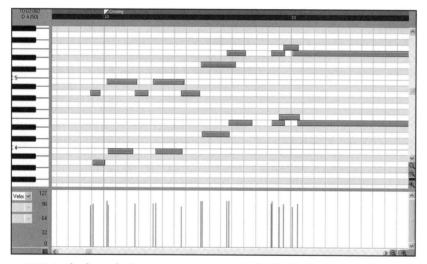

MIDI track after velocity compression. The velocity levels are more consistent compared to the original levels in the previous screenshot.

This process is similar to what an audio compressor/limiter does, except that it operates on MIDI velocity data. In fact, some digital audio sequencers use the compressor/limiter paradigm to set MIDI velocity editing levels. We'll discusses compressor/limiters later in this book, but for now you should know that *peak level* corresponds to the desired maximum velocity level, *threshold* corresponds to the minimum desired velocity level, and *gain* corresponds to how much the velocity levels of the notes that already fall within the minimum and maximum settings will change in relation to that range.

On the other hand, sometimes there is too little variation in velocity. The feel may be *almost* there, but because of the small amount of fluctuation in the overall velocity levels, the track sounds a little wooden. Fortunately, this can be easily fixed by a process that is the mirror image of velocity compression—*velocity expansion*. Velocity expansion alters the variations in velocity so that high velocity levels are made higher, and lower velocity levels are reduced even further.

Basically, you set a velocity threshold that determines the center point for velocity expansion. For instance, a setting of 72 means that any velocities above that will be increased, and any velocities below that will be further decreased. How much velocity gain or reduction occurs is determined by an offset amount. For example, an offset amount of five will increase or decrease a note's velocity level by a value of five. In keeping with our example, if the original velocity level was 76, its new level will be 81. If its original velocity level was 70, its new level will be 65. As you can see, the difference between velocity levels has been expanded to a wider range, which should result in a more human feel to the track.

Depending on the program, you can also set a minimum and maximum threshold of change for expanded velocities. After all, you don't want to create the opposite problem of wildly fluctuating velocity values. Of course, you can always perform velocity compression afterwards to compensate for any unexpected fluctuations that may occur as a result of velocity expansion, but let's not forget that you can also always undo any MIDI editing process and reset the parameters. This is preferable to using a second processing tool to correct the mistakes made as the result of using the first.

Groove Quantizing

I've alluded to the concept of "feel" several times in this chapter. As you may have guessed, "feel" can be described in terms of quantization—that is, how precisely (or imprecisely) notes are played in relation to a particular quantization resolution. Perfectly quantized tracks may sound mechanical if not played properly. By the same token, tracks that are played with too much imprecision sound terrible, too.

However, another important element of feel is the velocity levels of the notes as they are played. Notes played at constant velocities often sound stiff or mechanical. In short, they lack a sense of variation that makes them sound as if a human played them. Of course, too much variation makes them sound as if an *incompetent* human played them, which you don't want, either. As the old joke goes, you don't want perfection, just a darn sight less imperfection.

So far, I've treated the quantizing process and the velocity editing process as two separate functions. I did that purposely so that you would understand and be able to use the two processes by themselves. However, there is a process that combines both—*groove quantizing*. All digital audio sequencing programs have this feature, and it can be a powerful tool when applied properly. Although it's often used to create realistic-sounding MIDI drum tracks, it can be used for any type of MIDI part.

Groove Quantizing Drum Tracks

Most of you reading this book are probably not drummers, so you probably don't think of rhythm the way drummers do. You may be able to create perfectly quantized drum patterns, but creating a drum track that has the right feel is a more arcane process to you. That's why the Groove Quantize feature, which allows you to introduce a more humanized rhythmic feel into MIDI tracks, was developed in the first place.

Let's take a rhythm pattern whose notes are perfectly quantized and whose velocities are constant.

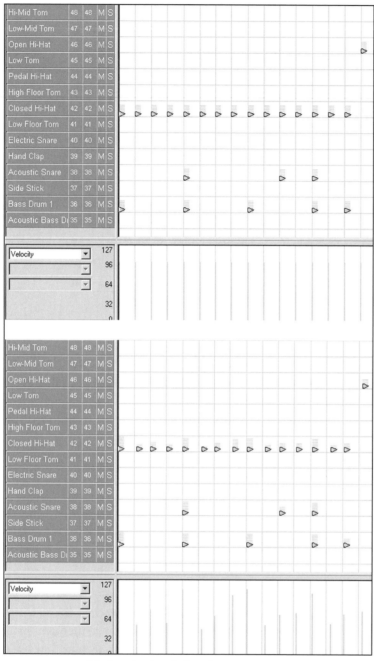

Drum track before (top) and after (bottom) groove quantizing

This is not an uncommon occurrence, inasmuch as drum patterns written in step time or drawn in a note at a time often have no variations in velocity. But you can groove quantize a drum track so that it sounds as though a drummer played the part.

The first step is to select the drum pattern, clip, or track you want to groove quantize. Next, select the Groove Quantize function according to the procedure outlined in your program manual. You can select a preset pattern to work with—in this case, I chose a Light Shuffle preset. Once the pattern has been processed using the specific preset pattern, you should see a change in velocity values for specific notes on the quantize grid (see the bottom half of the screenshot). You should also see a shift in note placement for various beats on the grid. For instance, you can see that the velocities of the hi-hat notes vary from note to note, but in a regular pattern. You'll also notice that not all of the hi-hat notes fall perfectly on the 16th note points of the grid—there is some variation in the timing that makes the hi-hat swing ever so slightly. In short, it sounds more realistic, as if an actual drummer played the part.

Groove Quantizing Other Tracks

You can use Groove Quantize to create parts with a particular "feel" on other MIDI tracks, too. You can use the preset patterns mentioned earlier, which can be helpful if you're trying to lock down a bass part with a drum track. More often, though, you will probably want to apply the feel of an existing MIDI pattern or track to the track you want to groove quantize. Fortunately, you can copy the desired MIDI pattern information from another track in the song, or from a track in a different song. Either way, you can groove quantize a track based on MIDI timing and velocity information from any other MIDI pattern or track. Check with your manual for more information.

Some programs even let you extract MIDI timing information from audio clips so that you can apply that information to MIDI tracks you want to groove quantize. You will probably have to insert points for each beat division and subdivision in the audio clip so that the program can convert its timing into MIDI information. However, it doesn't require that much of an effort, and the end results of groove quantizing tracks from audio clips can be extremely satisfying. For instance, you can apply the feel of your favorite song to the song you're creating. Perhaps you've found an intriguing phrase whose timing you want to apply to your MIDI track. By using an audio clip as the basis for a pattern, you can groove quantize a MIDI track to give it the exact feel you want.

The Final Word

As you can see from reading this chapter, there are a variety of ways in which you can edit MIDI note data in order to correct mistakes and create particular feels. Keep in mind, however, that what you've just read only scratches the surface of what is possible with these editing tools. There are many ways to process MIDI data, and this can be done simply for creative purposes and not just for correcting recording mistakes. I advise you to read your program's manual to learn more about its MIDI editing capabilities.

Now, let's move on to basics of digital audio.

CHAPTER 8
DIGITAL AUDIO BASICS

Learning the fundamentals of digital audio is necessary in order to make good recordings with your computer. Fortunately, though, it's easier than learning the basics of MIDI. After all, MIDI is a specialized music production method that requires you to manipulate data based on performance messages in order to create finished "recordings." To do that, you have to learn how to speak its particular "language." On the other hand, audio recording is a more intuitive process. At its most basic level, even a child can do it. Even so, there is more to recording digital audio than just hitting the Record button.

Unfortunately, there's also a fair amount of conflicting information concerning the digital audio production process—but then, that shouldn't be too surprising. After all, the analog recording process has existed for several decades, while the digital audio recording process has been in the mainstream for only about 15 years. Moreover, it doesn't help that some people attempt to apply the tried and true techniques of analog recording to digital audio production. What's more, they often try to provide a rationale for doing so based on what they perceive as digital audio principles, even when the explanations don't always coincide with the facts. The reason why this misinformation is still perpetuated is that often the explanations sound reasonable on the surface—based on most people's experiences with *analog* recording.

Rather than detail all of the myths and misunderstandings regarding digital audio—which could easily fill a whole other book—I'm just going to explain the basics of digital audio production. This should give you enough background to understand how to properly record, play back, and process digital audio. I will point out the differences between analog and digital audio production techniques, and, where necessary, clear up any misconceptions concerning those processes.

Recording Fundamentals

The first step in the recording process is to convert the energy contained in sound waves—which are actually changes in air pressure—into electrical energy. A device that can convert one form of energy into another form is called a *transducer*. A microphone, for example, is a transducer that takes sound waves and converts their changing air pressure levels into changes in electrical voltage (see "Appendix B: Microphone Basics" for more details). Electric guitar and bass pickups are transducers that detect changes in air displacement caused by string vibrations and convert them into electrical energy. Speakers, which are driven by electrical voltage, are also transducers that transform the variable electrical voltage back into changes in air pressure that we can hear.

Overall, the process of transforming sound wave energy into electrical energy is identical for both analog and digital recording. However, analog and digital recorders process and store those changes in electrical energy in fundamentally different ways, and it's those differences that will determine how you work with analog and digital audio recording systems.

Analog Audio Recording

In simple terms, an analog recorder takes the electrical energy of converted sound waves and passes it to the record head of the deck. As it's doing this, a reel (or cartridge) of magnetic tape passes over the record head. The magnetic tape is coated with electrically charged particles whose polarities are arranged in random order on the tape itself. As the tape passes over the record head, the particles' polarities change in response to the changes in voltage passing through the head. The pattern of this response mirrors—or is *analogous* to—the changes in voltage as they occur over time. That's why we call this process *analog* recording.

You might think that analog recording is the preferred recording format because it has a one-to-one correspondence with the sound source. That's not true at all, even though many audio professionals do prefer the sound of analog recordings, as they often seem "warmer." Many of us have been raised on analog, so we're more used to its sound. Moreover, some of us older recording artists first learned audio production techniques on analog recorders, so we're more comfortable with this format. However, due to nostalgia for the "good old days" of analog audio, one can forget that there are several good reasons why digital audio was developed in the first place.

Tape Noise

One problem with analog is that in the recording process the tape makes physical contact with the record head, generating a particular type of noise called *tape hiss*. While professional multitrack analog decks are designed to substantially reduce the amount of hiss, and there exist tapes with smoother coatings to glide over the heads with less friction, tape hiss can never be entirely eliminated. One way to combat tape hiss is to record tracks *hot*—as loud as possible—in order to mask the noise. People still try to record digital audio tracks as hot as possible to this day, although they have seemingly different reasons for doing so. For instance, even experienced engineers and producers believe that if you don't digitally record tracks hot enough, your effective sample rate will be substantially reduced—this is simply not true.

Tape Width

In order to record analog tracks as hot as possible, the tape has to be wide enough to accurately record the dynamic range of the signal. If the *amplitude* (i.e., "width" of the signal) is too high—that is, too loud—the signal will not fit onto the tape. The loudest parts of an analog signal will be *clipped*—the highest waveform peaks will be cut off short of their maximum heights, distorting the audio signal. This is also known as *analog distortion*.

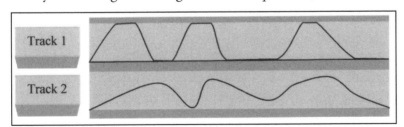

Illustration of analog distortion on tape. The signal on Track 1 has been clipped and is flattened out along the edges, unlike the signal on Track 2.

Interestingly, a little analog distortion can be pleasant to the ears, which is another reason why engineers and producers like to record a signal on analog as hot as possible. However, if the signal is recorded at too high a level, the distortion causes the audio signal to sound muddy, indistinct, or "fuzzy." Recording a signal just right is a real art. Of course, distortion isn't always a bad thing, either. One of the most common guitar effects is distortion, which is created by taking the sound of the electric guitar and *overdriving* (over-amplifying) its signal. In fact, this effect was first called "fuzz tone" back in the 1960s.

Bleedthrough is another analog recording problem that can occur if a signal is recorded at too high a level. Each track in a multitrack recorder occupies a specific section of tape. These tracks run parallel to each other, with a little bit of space between them on the tape. If an overly hot signal is recorded onto a track, two things can happen. There might be some distortion on that track because the analog signal won't "fit" into the area on the tape allotted for its signal (clipping), or the signal might "spill over" into the area between the tracks or—if it's *really* hot—onto an adjacent track (*bleed through*), creating a "ghost" effect of low-level audio on that second track.

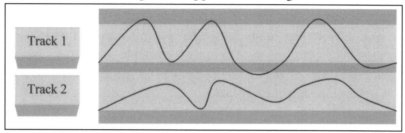

Illustration of tape bleedthrough of a signal from Track 1 onto Track 2. Not only will Track 1 sound distorted, but faint traces of Track 1 will be heard on Track 2 as well.

One way of minimizing bleedthrough is to not use adjacent tracks for recording—for instance, you can isolate vocals by recording them between two empty tracks. Another way to minimize bleedthrough is to group similar instruments on adjacent tracks. For example, drum tracks can be grouped together because they really don't affect each other the way dissimilar instruments on neighboring tracks can.

Yet another way of handling signal distortion and bleedthrough is to make sure that the track areas on the tape are wide enough to accommodate the recorded signal. Of course, this also means that the tape itself has to be wide enough to accommodate the number of tracks the tape deck can record. For instance, many 8-track decks use half-inch tape, while 24-track decks use two-inch tape.

Tape Speed

While wider analog tape sizes make it easier to record audio tracks without distortion, tape width alone doesn't solve the problem. Only so much of an audio signal can fit onto a tape at any given moment. So, how can the process of recording to analog tape be improved? Increase the amount of tape that represents a given moment! To do that, you don't need a *wider* tape—you need a *longer* tape. How do you do that? It's easy—you just increase the tape speed! Those of you who are familiar with analog tape decks know that they record at different speeds. The faster the tape speed, the better the fidelity of the recording. For example, the average cassette deck records at a speed of 1 7/8 ips (inches per second). Some multitrack cassette decks record at 3 3/4 ips and some reel-to-reel decks record at either 7 1/2 or 15 ips. Professional two-inch 24-track decks record at 30 ips!

Each of those tape speeds also represents a given length of tape. Depending on the tape deck, one second of time can be 7 1/2, 15, or 30 inches long. That's more space on which to store a signal, which results in a better signal with less chance of distortion. An analog tape recording of a second of material might look something like the image on the right.

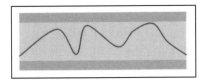

An analog signal recorded on a short (slow) length of tape

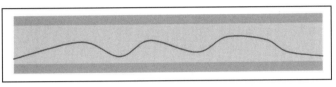

The same analog signal recorded on a longer (faster) tape

A slower tape can be densely packed with signal information, and bleedthrough can occur if the levels get too high. However, if that same signal is recorded at twice that speed, it will look like the image on the left.

The signal now "fits" into the track because it has been elongated. Note that this doesn't mean that the signal is distorted or that the tape somehow doesn't match the sound source any longer. It's still the same waveform—the increased tape speed (length) simply allows the waveform more "storage space." Another benefit of the increased tape length, besides less distortion, is that you can record the signal even hotter, giving you a better signal-to-noise ratio. Of course, you still run the risk of causing distortion if you record the signal *too* hot, but that can happen no matter how wide the tape is or how fast it runs.

Other Analog Problems

Analog tape has to run at a speed that's fast enough to record each second of a signal onto a relatively long length of tape. This introduces yet another problem: In order to accurately record a signal to analog tape, the tape speed has to be constant because any change in speed can cause *wow* (unwanted variations in pitch) and *flutter* (unwanted variations in volume level). Unfortunately, recording to analog tape at a constant speed is difficult because the deck's motors must operate at a very high degree of precision. For instance, the weight of a tape on a reel changes as the tape traverses from one reel to the next, and this affects speed constancy. Also, the faster a tape moves, the harder it is for a deck to maintain a constant speed. Making a tape deck's motors run at a constant speed is obviously difficult, and the precision motors that can do this are very costly.

Also, tape is not an ideal storage medium. As I had mentioned earlier, tape has a magnetic coating of particles whose polarities are arranged in a random order. Unfortunately, these particles fall off the tape surface whenever the tape is used. If enough of them fall off in a particular section of tape, you will lose what was recorded. When played back, you will hear a momentary silence or a signal extremely reduced in strength, which is a phenomenon called *tape dropout*. Once you lose those particles, the audio they represented is gone. Additionally, the tape particles are shed onto the analog deck's tape heads and capstans, which then must be cleaned regularly.

Further, tape stretches a little bit each time it is played or used for recording. In fact, each time you fast-forward or rewind a tape, you're stretching it. Stretching will eventually distort the analog "image" on the tape, and the abuse that occurs from even this general use will contribute to the previously mentioned problem of tape dropout.

Why do I mention all of this? As beginners, you'll often hear that analog recording is superior to or better than digital recordings. I don't believe that's necessarily so, and you shouldn't either. They're different, that's all. I've heard outstanding digital recordings, and lousy analog recordings. I've also heard dreadful digital recordings and wonderful analog recordings.

The difference between a good recording and a bad recording depends partially on the quality of the equipment used and (infinitely more important!) the expertise of the person making it. A skilled producer or engineer can rise above the limitations of the recording equipment and make excellent recordings. An unskilled producer or engineer will make bad recordings, regardless of the quality of the recording gear.

Finally, remember that digital audio was developed for some very good reasons. For one thing, it eliminates the previously mentioned problems that have plagued analog recording for years. For another, recording audio in a digital format allows recording artists, producers, and engineers to work with recorded material in ways undreamed of just a couple of decades ago.

Digital Audio Recording

The first step in digital audio recording is the same as for analog recording—convert the energy contained in sound waves into electrical energy. But whereas an analog recorder continuously passes that electrical energy to the record head of a deck which in turn writes the voltage changes onto magnetic tape, a digital recorder *samples* (takes a reading of) those changing voltages at regular intervals. It converts those readings into digital data (expressed in binary form), using an A/D, or *analog-to-digital converter*. This digital information is stored to a storage medium such a hard disk or CD. To hear this digital information as audio again, it is retrieved from the storage medium and passed through a D/A, or *digital-to-analog converter*. The advantage of this process is that the recording media doesn't introduce noise into the audio signal. The only thing recorded on the media is *data*, not the audio signal itself.

And because the only thing recorded is data, there is no need to worry about bleedthrough on adjacent tracks, nor should there be any concerns over analog distortion. Likewise, there's no need to fuss about tape speed constancy, wow, or flutter because the data goes through a buffer that ensures a constant flow of information to and from the converters. Heck, you don't even need tape! All you need is a storage medium (like a hard disk) to store this information. And although all hard disks have a magnetic coating that is similar to analog tape, dropout or data loss is less of a problem because there is error checking and redundancy built into the digital audio recording process.

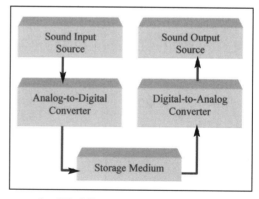

A simplified illustration of the digital audio recording and playback process

Sample Rates and Resolutions

All things being equal, the quality of a digital audio recording depends on two factors: its *sampling frequency* (expressed in kHz) and its *resolution*, or bit depth. For instance, you may have seen this magic number prominently displayed in advertisements for various audio interfaces: 24-bit/96kHz. As of this writing, we're also beginning to see a new magic number: 24-bit/192kHz. If you're unfamiliar with these expressions, this is what these numbers mean.

As I stated earlier, audio is recorded digitally by taking samples of a waveform at regular intervals. Samples are basically snapshots of an audio waveform's voltage levels (which represent changes in a sound wave's amplitude) at any given moment. A good analogy is movie film, which is a series of snapshots taken at regular intervals. When the film is played back properly, you see motion. When you play back samples, you hear audio.

The *sample frequency*—the number of samples taken per second—partially determines how accurate the representation of the waveform will be. For instance, a sample rate of 88.2 kHz (or 88,200 samples per second) will produce a more detailed waveform than one recorded at 44.1 kHz, or 44,100 samples per second. After all, it would contain twice as many snapshots of the changes in the waveform over the same amount of time. It should be able to more quickly detect changes in voltage levels as a result.

However, sample rate alone doesn't determine the degree of digital audio accuracy. *Sample resolution* is important as well. Sample resolution is expressed in terms of *bit depth*, which refers to how well a digital audio converter can discriminate between changes in audio levels over time (that is, amplitude). For example, 8-bit resolution means that a digital audio converter is capable of detecting 256 discrete levels of change (or *quantization intervals*) in an audio waveform's amplitude. That may seem like a lot at first, but it really isn't.

Still, where do we get this 256 number? Well, if you know something about computers, you know that a bit, which is the smallest unit of digital information, has only two values: 0 or 1. You may also know that there are eight bits in a byte. To calculate all of the possible combinations of values that these eight bits can express, multiply 2 (the only two values a bit can express) by itself 8 times (the number of bits in a byte). The result will be 256.

So, if 8-bit resolution has 256 quantization intervals, 16-bit resolution means that it has double that amount, right? No! Remember that you have to calculate all of the possible combinations of values, so 16-bit resolution means that you multiply 2 by itself 16 times. That will give you a value of 65,536 discrete levels of change that can be detected in an audio waveform. By extension, 24-bit resolution provides 16,777,216 discrete quantization intervals!

Bit depth also correlates to *dynamic range,* which is the difference between the softest and loudest sound levels that can be distinguished by our ears. In digital audio recording, each bit increases the dynamic range by about 6 dB ("dB" stands for "decibels," by the way). The dynamic range for 16-bit recordings is theoretically 96 dB. Likewise, the theoretical dynamic range for 24-bit recordings is 144 dB. However, you may have noticed that I said *theoretical* dynamic range. Because of various design factors that are too numerous to mention here, many 16-bit recording systems have a dynamic range of 93 dB at best, while many 24-bit systems have dynamic ranges of 108 dB to 112 dB. To put it into perspective, though, a digital audio system with 93 dB of dynamic range is still better than many professional analog recorders, while a digital audio system with 108 dB of dynamic range is outstanding.

As you can see, digital audio has solved many analog recording problems while offering superior performance to analog audio systems in many areas. Digital audio also provides exciting possibilities for manipulating audio in ways undreamed of not so many years ago. However, this new recording paradigm has also introduced new problems of its own into the recording process.

Digital Distortion

As I mentioned earlier, analog distortion is as much a blessing as it is a curse during the recording process. When mishandled, recordings can sound muddy and indistinct. When properly used, it can add warmth to a track. The reason why this is possible has to do with the nature of the analog tape medium: You can oversaturate a tape with just enough signal to make the output sound good. But how can we tell the difference between properly oversaturated material and too much signal?

Obviously, your ears can help with that. Also, by reading the meters the tape deck, the mixer, or both, you can learn to associate its readings with the necessary amount of tape saturation. Unfortunately, the problem is that the meters on these mixers and tape decks are calibrated to a decibel reference that lets users drive a signal over 0 dBu (all you need to know about dBu for now is that it is referenced to a voltage level). While driving a signal beyond 0 dBu is appropriate for recording "hot" analog signals, doing this in a digital audio recording system can lead to disastrous results.

For one thing, the decibel reference for digital audio is based, logically enough, on the loudest possible signal that can be digitally recorded, based on the sample rate and resolution. This number is written as 0 dBFS (the "FS" stands for *full-scale*), and it's not the same as 0 dBu. As you can guess by the term "full-scale," you can't get any louder than 0 dBFS in digital audio systems. Signals lower than 0 dBFS are designated with a minus sign in front of them; –6 dB, for example. The lowest possible signal in a 16-bit system is –96 dB (so 0 dBFS would equal 96 dB), while the lowest possible signal in a 24-bit system is –144 dB. In practice, meters in many digital audio programs and devices may go down to only –72 dB, which is considered a good working noise floor.

Therefore, if you try to oversaturate digital audio the way you do with analog recording, you'll experience *digital distortion*. Depending on the severity and length of the overdriven signal, digital distortion may sound like either a small pop or crackling sound at best, or noise caused by someone jiggling a bad cable attached to a loud amplifier at worst. In short, there's nothing pleasant or musical about this sort of distortion.

Also, to avoid clipping and digital distortion, one has to record at a level lower than 0 dBFS. For example, Alesis recommends in their ADAT digital audio multitrack reference manuals that users shouldn't exceed –15 dBFS to –10 dBFS on average when recording audio tracks. I usually set levels between –6 dBFS and –12 dBFS using my computer-based digital audio recording system, depending on the number and type of tracks I'm recording. For those raised on analog recording, this goes against everything they've been taught: *Record audio tracks as hot as possible.* However, digital audio has such a wide dynamic range that it isn't necessary to record digital audio tracks as loud as possible. Besides, trying to record tracks as hot as possible in the digital audio realm can lead to other production difficulties, as you will discover later.

Quantization Error

Each time a waveform is sampled, two things occur. First, each sample measures the amplitude (which corresponds to resolution) of a waveform at that precise moment. Second, each new sample detects those changes in amplitude over time (which corresponds to frequency). However, due to the inherent nature of digital audio, you'll never have a digitally perfect representation of an audio waveform. For one thing, there will always be a brief time gap between each sample, regardless of the number of samples you take in a second. In short, you just can't digitally represent a continuous waveform, no matter how fast you sample it.

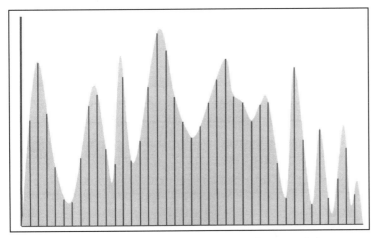

A continuous waveform (shaded background) and its sampled representation as indicated by vertical lines

Also, no matter how finely you can measure the changes in waveform amplitude, they will not always be perfectly exact. Just as sampling a continuous audio waveform creates a time gap between each sample, it can also create a "level gap" or difference between the waveform's actual amplitude and a sample's measurement of that amplitude. That's because bit resolution is like marks on a ruler—its readings are only accurate to its nearest measurable point or discrete interval. If the audio level at a particular sample point is not exactly at a measurable interval, a digital audio system has to round up the sample level's value to the nearest measurable point. Naturally, those rounded up measurements won't be correct because of this. This discrepancy between the measured interval and the actual interval is the definition of *quantization error.*

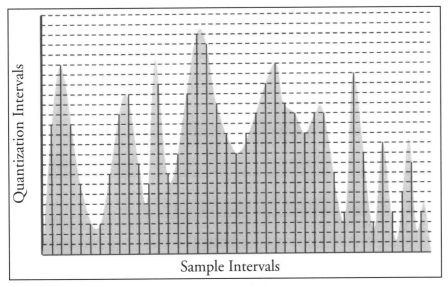

The difference between a waveform's actual and measured amplitudes determines the amount of quantization error.

The amount of quantization error determines the degree of *quantization distortion*. As you can see in the previous graph, some of the distorted samples are fairly close to the actual waveform level, but a few distorted samples are far away in comparison to the actual level. So how do you reduce quantization error and distortion? By making the ruler more precise! The way to do that in a digital audio system is to increase the bit resolution so that smaller changes in sample levels can be detected. For instance, if you increase the bit resolution from 16 to 20 bits, the digital audio system will now be able to detect 1,048,576 discrete levels of change. Even so, that may result in the same number of distorted samples—however, the *degree* of quantization distortion will probably be much lower overall. Increase the bit resolution to 24, and the digital audio system will be able to detect 16,777,216 levels of change in amplitude for the sampled audio waveform. That will further reduce the level of quantization distortion, and probably diminish the occurrence of distorted samples, too.

However, no matter how much you increase the sample resolution, there will always be a sample whose level falls outside of the measurement interval, no matter how small that interval is. The bottom line is that you can never completely eliminate quantization error—and, by extension, quantization distortion—from digital audio systems. On the other hand, the mere presence of quantization error doesn't necessarily mean that quantization distortion is noticeable to the human ear. If the sample rate is fast enough and the bit resolution is deep enough, the amount of quantization distortion is of no practical concern. So this begs the question "What's the correct sample rate and resolution for making digital audio recordings?"

Choosing Your Sample Rate and Resolution

Some of you might think that using the highest possible sampling rate and resolution is the proper answer to the previous question. In a perfect world, this would be true. However, this isn't a perfect world, and there are several things besides audio quality to consider when selecting a sample rate and resolution for recording digital audio. For instance, it's obvious that at best you can only sample at the highest rate your audio interface allows. Leaving that limitation aside, the simple answer, for now, is that 16-bit/44.1 kHz resolution is the *minimum* for producing quality digital audio recordings. Even so, you'll find that there are several relevant factors to consider when working with digital audio in general, and some of them have surprisingly little to do with the quality of your recordings.

However, first let's sidetrack into how we arrived at choosing the sample rates we currently use. A lot of people have some serious misconceptions as to why we use the sample rates that we do. It's important that we go back to the beginning so that we can get a little historical perspective, and correct some of the false assumptions that have been allowed to develop over the years.

The Nyquist Theorem

A physicist named Harry Nyquist developed a theorem for recording digital audio. Part of this theorem states that the sample rate must be at least twice the highest desired frequency in order to create an accurate digital recording. We know that the human ear can detect a range of frequencies from 20 Hz to 20 kHz. Therefore, to capture accurately and faithfully frequencies up to 20 kHz, a digital audio system's sample rate must be at least 40 kHz. But because of inherent limitations in equipment design, digital audio systems need to record at a slightly higher rate in order to ensure digital audio accuracy. That's why the minimum professional sample rate is 44.1 kHz.

As I mentioned earlier, sample rate alone doesn't determine digital audio accuracy. Sample resolution, or bit depth, is just as important, too. So why was 16-bit resolution chosen as the proper bit depth? Well, bit depth is related to dynamic range—each bit in a digital audio system represents roughly 6 dB of dynamic range. For instance, a 16-bit system has a theoretical dynamic range of 96 dB. Even so, most 16-bit systems have dynamic ranges of about 93 dB, once again due to limitations in equipment design. However, at the time digital audio recording systems became widely available, 93 dB of dynamic range was considered outstanding, even for analog recording systems. That's why a sample resolution of 16 bits was initially used for professional digital audio recording systems.

So, if sampling audio at 16-bit/44.1 kHz was considered the professional quality setting, why do we now sample at higher rates and resolutions? Well, that's a good question, and some audio professionals wonder why, too. Some think that a sample rate of 44.1kHz is sufficient because the *anti-aliasing* filters in digital audio systems effectively eliminate any artifacts above 20 kHz. Aliasing occurs when digital audio systems attempt to sample frequencies above the selected sample rate. Aliasing generates unwanted samples that are related to both the input frequencies and the sample frequency, but sound harsh and unpleasant. To avoid this, digital audio systems use anti-aliasing filters to prevent frequencies above the sample rate from being recorded.

Also, digital audio systems *oversample*—that is, they sample several times over the stated sample rate to ensure that a digital recording is as accurate as possible. For instance, some systems use 64x oversampling (i.e., 64 times the stated sample rate) to record audio digitally. These systems then select those samples that most closely match the actual voltage values of the analog signal, thereby reducing quantization error and distortion.

Additionally, some digital audio systems record at a higher resolution than the final playback resolution. For example, some systems record digital audio at 20-bit resolution but play back at 16-bit resolution. Recording at a greater bit depth does two things. First, it gives the system a little more headroom. After all, bit depth is related to dynamic range, and an increased dynamic range means a better signal-to-noise ratio. Second, raising the bit depth lowers the noise floor. When the recorded audio is played back at 16-bit resolution, its least significant bits (the lower bits where the noise is likely to be) are eliminated, making the transition from signal to silence much smoother.

Besides, even though 20 kHz is the upper limit of human hearing, most people really hear up to only 12 kHz to 15 kHz. Why increase the sample rate if most people can't hear the difference anyway? Furthermore, some feel that 16 bits provide more than adequate resolution for accurate digital audio. As mentioned earlier, digital audio systems oversample anyway, and many systems record at a higher resolution than the playback resolution, too. In one sense, increased sample resolution is already built into 16-bit systems because of these two factors. So why increase the bit resolution further?

The opposing argument is that all frequencies—even those beyond the range of human hearing—interact acoustically to create a waveform. Capturing a broader frequency range with more accurate resolution is necessary to reproduce sound waves with the required fidelity. Furthermore, we don't yet fully appreciate the impact of high-frequency content above 20 kHz on our listening experience, either. For example, we might not hear certain frequencies so much as "feel" them. Also, some ultrasonic frequencies may add to our listening experience by carrying spatial and location cues that would be lost if not recorded. You should record audio material at the highest sample rate and resolution that's technologically possible, just for those reasons alone.

However, bear in mind that recording devices (such as microphones) and playback systems (such as CD players) can't capture or reproduce these higher frequencies anyway, so why record at these rates? Well, the answer is that higher sample rates and resolutions *do* improve the quality of digital audio recordings, but in a way that most people don't usually think about.

When discussing sampling at higher rates and resolutions, some people have a tendency to think in terms of capturing sounds with higher frequencies that are out of our range of hearing. After all, the Nyquist Theorem states that the sample rate must be *at least* twice the highest desired frequency in order to record digital audio accurately. However, there's no law that says that you have to sample at twice the sample rate—you can sample at four or eight times the sample rate, too. If you think of sampling this way, frequency can simply be thought of as *the regularity of an occurrence*, i.e., how often something happens. When you sample audio, you basically take a snapshot of a continuous audio waveform's amplitude at that precise moment. How often you do that—whether it's 44,100 times a second or 192,000 times a second—is the frequency (or regularity) at which the audio is sampled.

Keep in mind that when you sample audio digitally you're attempting to represent a continuous phenomenon (i.e., an audio waveform) in a discontinuous manner (i.e., as a collection of individual samples). As I illustrated earlier, the representation of a waveform improves when the changes in a waveform are detected more rapidly (i.e., sampled more *frequently*). So as you can see, sampling digital audio at higher rates has less to do with capturing ultrasonic frequencies—rather, it has more to do with determining how accurate the digital representation of the waveform will be.

Similarly, increasing the bit resolution will improve the signal-to-noise ratio of the digital audio recording. More to the point, increasing bit resolution will diminish the level and occurrence of quantization error and, by extension, quantization distortion. This will also improve the quality and accuracy of a digital audio recording.

Storage Capacity and System Speed

However, increased audio quality and digital accuracy come with a price. Recording audio digitally generates a lot of data. Moreover, the amount of data increases according to the sample rate and/or bit resolution. To determine how much data a recording generates at a particular rate and resolution, here is a simple formula:

$$(b \times r) / 1024 / 8 = n\text{KB/sec}$$

In this equation, b = bit depth, r = sample rate, and n = the number of kilobytes (KB) of data produced in a second.

For example, if you want to know how much data will be generated by recording a single audio track at 16-bit/44.1 kHz, you simply multiply the bit depth (16) by the sample rate per second (44,100). The answer will be 705,600 bits. That's a pretty large number to work with, so let's make it more manageable by turning it into kilobits. To do that, you just divide by 1024, which gives us 689.0625 kilobits, which is still a large number. Besides, as computer-literate people, we're used to talking about *kilobytes*, so let's divide this number by 8 (the number of bits in a byte) to make it even more manageable. That will leave you with 86.1328125 kilobytes of digital audio per second, which you can just round off to 86 KB/sec.

If you want to simplify this calculation, you can also use this formula:

$$(b \times r) / 8192 = n\textbf{KB/sec}$$

since dividing $b \times r$ once by 8192 is the same as dividing it by 1024 and then again by 8.

What if you were to record audio at 24-bit/44.1 kHz? Well, that would generate about 130 KB/second of data. That doesn't seem like so much until you start calculating how much data is generated for a song. A minute's worth of 16-bit/44.1 kHz audio generates a little over 5 MB of data per minute (just multiply the 86 KB by 60, which are the number of seconds in a minute, and then divide by 1024 to convert kilobytes to megabytes). By contrast, a minute's worth of 24-bit/44.1 kHz audio generates about 7.6 MB of data per minute. A four-minute, 16-track song could generate either 320 MB or over 486 MB of data, depending on whether you select 16-bit or 24-bit resolution for the 44.1 kHz sample rate.

Bit Depth	Sample Rate (in kHz)	Kilobytes per second (KB/sec)*	Megabytes per minute (MB/min)*	Data per song (16 tracks @ 4 minutes)
16	44.1	86	5	320 MB
16	48	93.75	5.5	352 MB
24	44.1	129	7.6	486.4 MB
24	48	141	8.2	524.8 MB
24	88.2	258.4	15	960 MB
24	96	281.25	16.5	1056 MB *(1.03 GB)*
24	176.4	517	30.3	1939.2 MB *(1.89 GB)*
24	192	562.5	33	2112 MB *(2 GB)*

*Per monaural track

Approximate data amounts for various sample rates and resolutions

Why is this information important to know? First, you need to make sure that the hard drive you use for storing digital audio information is large enough to accommodate the amount of data you generate. As you can see, recording a typical song can generate 320 MB to 2 GB of data, depending on the sample rate and resolution. Fortunately, most hard disks have extremely large storage capacities, so this isn't as big an issue as it once was. Even so, I would recommend that the hard disk on which you store your digital audio data have a storage capacity of at least 40 GB.

However, hard drive capacity isn't the only concern. How *fast* a hard drive can stream data to and from the disk is more important. To stream 16 tracks of data recorded at 24-bit/44.1 kHz, a hard drive has to transfer data at a rate of just over 2 MB per second, which most hard drives can easily handle. However, streaming 16 tracks of digital audio recorded at 24-bit/192 kHz requires a hard drive to move that data at a rate of almost 9 MB per second. More likely, though, it would have to stream data at a rate of nearly 12 MB per second, and some drives would have difficulties maintaining that transfer rate. That's because many digital audio sequencers and multitrack recording programs process 24-bit audio data files in 32-bit chunks because it's easier for the computer to process the data that way. The result is that your audio program generates larger 32-bit audio files (it just pads those last eight bits with zero values). Therefore, the amount of data in a typical song recorded at 24-bit/44.1 kHz would not be 486 MB, but rather 646 MB!

As you can see, selecting a sample rate that your computer can process is just as important as selecting a sample rate for the sake of fidelity and accuracy in audio reproduction. 24-bit/44.1 kHz sample rates can be handled by most computers and hard drives. In fact, most current computers and hard disks can now successfully process multiple tracks of 24-bit/96 kHz audio. On the other hand, it takes a fast computer with fast hard drives that can sustain high transfer rates to process multiple tracks of 24-bit/192 kHz digital audio. Only high-end digital audio workstations (or DAWs) can record large numbers of tracks at this sample rate right now. If your system is more modest, you may need to limit the number of tracks you record or otherwise intend to work with.

Sample Rates and Software Synthesis

If you plan on using software synthesizers and/or samplers to create music, you should set your audio device's sample rate to 16-bit/44.1 kHz or 24-bit/44.1 kHz at most. That's because software synths and samplers can require a significant amount of computer processing power. The need for processing power increases as the sample rate increases in either bit depth or sampling rate. This can make a difference in how many soft synth or sampler tracks you can play at once. Besides, you usually won't hear any significant improvement in the quality of a soft synth's output if you set your audio devices to higher sample rates. All you will do is make your computer work harder than it really has to.

Some software synthesizers and samplers let you work in real-time at a lower sample rate and resolution, but *render* their output at a higher sample rate. All digital audio sequencers allow users to convert a soft synth's output to digital audio data by processing how the corresponding MIDI data affects the soft synth's behavior. This conversion process is called *rendering*, and it is done *off-line*, i.e., not in real-time (and in a sort of "behind-the-scenes" way). Because the computer doesn't have to be concerned with playing these soft synths and samplers in real-time, there is no concern about such issues as virtual instrument latency, or how hard the processor has to work to create real-time synth audio output.

If your soft synths have the capability to work at lower sample rates in real-time while allowing rendering to occur at higher sample rates, you can first create virtual synth MIDI tracks at the lower rate. Then, when you're ready to record audio tracks, you can render the virtual synth tracks into audio tracks at a higher rate so that they match the sample rate and resolution of the subsequent digital audio tracks.

Sample Rates and Effects Processing

Nearly every digital audio sequencer and multitrack recording program uses software-based digital signal processors, either within the software itself (i.e., *native*) or as effects plug-ins. Nearly all of these native effects and plug-ins process digital audio at 24-bit or 32-bit resolution. However, this can pose a problem if the audio material was first recorded with 16-bit resolution. That's because these effects process 16-bit audio internally at the higher 24-bit or 32-bit resolution and then resample the output back down to 16-bit resolution. This introduces quantization error into the data, which can become more pronounced as the original material gets repeatedly processed with a variety of virtual effects.

One way to minimize the potential problem of quantization error due to virtual signal processing is to set the sample rate at 24-bit resolution to begin with. Another way is to use virtual effects processors sparingly. Many people have a tendency to over-process audio tracks with EQ, compression, and other types of effects. It's better to record an audio track properly than to try and fix the track later with EQ, compression, and other signal enhancers.

On the other hand, don't feel as though you have to avoid recording at 16-bit resolution or not use plug-ins with 16-bit audio tracks. To keep things in perspective, remember that it takes repeated processing of the same material many times over before noticeable quantization error occurs. However, overprocessing 16-bit audio with plug-ins is a common beginner's mistake, and I admonish you to be aware of both the potential problem and the various ways you can avoid it.

Sample Rates and Mastering

The best way to select a sample rate is to determine the final format of the finished product *before* you begin recording. Most of the time, your finished product will be in CD format, although you may want to create DVD audio tracks. If you are creating tracks for audio CDs, you should select sample rates that are exact multiples of 44.1 kHz (44.1 kHz, 88.2 kHz, or 176.4 kHz) because you're going to have to *downsample* (convert to a lower sample rate and/or bit depth) those higher sample rates to the CD audio rate of 16-bit/44.1 kHz. It's easier to divide those values evenly by two or four rather than by 2.1768707482993197278911564625854 or 4.3537414965986394557823129251701—you would have to divide digital audio data recorded at 96 kHz and 192 kHz by these numbers, respectively, to downsample them to 44.1 kHz! There's also a lower chance of quantization distortion occurring when you downsample rates that are even multiples of the final sample rate.

Likewise, audio that is going to DVD audio format should be sampled at 24-bit/96 kHz (which is the DVD sample rate) or 24-bit/192 kHz, which is exactly double the DVD audio rate. As in downsampling to CD audio, it's preferable to downsample to DVD audio by an even multiple, too.

On the other hand, selecting the bit depth is less of an issue. Downsampling 24-bit audio to 16-bit audio is not as much of a problem as downsampling from differing sample rates. Most programs have a variety of *dithering* schemes that smoothly scale down 24-bit audio to 16-bit audio. However, you don't want to resample 16-bit audio up to 24-bit audio, so make sure that you start off with the highest bit rate possible.

Final Considerations

As you can see, selecting the proper sample rate and resolution is more than a matter of capturing the highest quality audio signal possible. Sample rate and resolution selection also depends on a variety of other factors, such as the speed and power of your computer and its hard drives, whether you are using software synths and samplers, and the final format of your digital audio tracks. Your choice of sample rate and resolution will by necessity be a compromise of these various factors.

More importantly, you'll probably change sample rates and resolutions based on which stage you're at in the song production process. If you're a typical user, you'll probably start off at 16-bit/44.1 kHz resolution to create virtual instrument tracks. Then, when you're ready to record audio tracks, you'll change to a higher sample rate or resolution, based on what is most suitable for your system and the number of tracks it's capable of handling. Before you start recording, though, you should render your virtual instrument outputs to audio tracks at this new sample rate or resolution. Afterwards, record the digital audio tracks and later process them with virtual effects processors. As you mix down the tracks of your song, you may downsample and dither them to 16-bit/44.1 kHz to make a master file suitable for an audio CD.

No matter what sample rate and resolution you ultimately select, don't worry that your audio could have been better if only you had used better equipment or selected a higher sample rate. After all, the technical elements of digital audio production will improve as the years go by, if past history is any indication. In a few years, 32-bit/384 kHz sampling rates will probably become possible and practical. Are you going to wait until then to start creating your audio masterpieces? If you adopt that mentality, you'll still be waiting to record your hits until 64-bit/768 kHz digital audio becomes available ten years from now, or when some new form of audio recording is introduced in 20 years.

My advice to you is to just make sure that the audio you create *now* is the best work you can do with what you have at your disposal. If that means recording at 16-bit/44.1 kHz, so be it. If that means being able to record at 24-bit/192 kHz, that's fine, too. Ultimately, the average listener won't care whether you recorded your material with the latest technology or not—all that will matter is that your music sounds good. And, if you take the time to do the best work possible, regardless of the technical limitations imposed on you, your music will indeed sound good.

CHAPTER 9
CREATING DIGITAL AUDIO TRACKS

Creating audio tracks in digital audio sequencers is in many ways similar to creating MIDI tracks. In both cases, there is a basic routine you should follow in order to record tracks in a consistent manner. But before we go into the details of recording digital audio tracks, you need to make sure that your system is ready to start working with digital audio. For instance, you should have already followed the directions for setting up and testing your audio interface according to the guidelines detailed in "Chapter 4: Hardware and Software Setup". If you haven't, do so now.

Make sure that you have properly connected the sound source you're recording to the correct input channel(s) of your mixer or audio interface. Also, be certain that you're using the right kinds of cables with the input and output channels of your audio devices. For instance, using an unbalanced cable in an audio jack that requires a balanced cable will lead to an *impedance mismatch*. This is a sure-fire way of introducing noise (and often a weak audio signal) into your recording setup. Needless to say, you don't want that.

Finally, make sure that you have selected the desired audio sample rate and resolution for recording and playing back digital audio in the audio setup options of your digital audio sequencer. As I had mentioned in "Chapter 8: Digital Audio Basics," the sample rate and resolution you choose will be determined partly by the sampling capabilities of your audio interface. Beyond that, your choice of sample rate and resolution will depend on the various factors detailed there. For the purpose of this example, the sample resolution and rate are assumed to be 24-bit/44.1 kHz since the audio will be mixed down to a CD. Setting the sample rate at 44.1 kHz will allow you to avoid potential quantization errors that can occur as a result of downsampling audio from 48 kHz to 44.1 kHz. If it is also your intention to create audio for a CD (and it probably is), then set your numbers likewise if your hardware and software setup are capable of it.

Recording in the Computer Room

As a home recordist, you will probably be recording in the same room as your computer. As you know, computers can be noisy, so take as many steps as you can to minimize this noise before recording. For example, you can place your computer under a desk and hang a thick drape in front of it. However, make sure that you don't cover the computer's air vents or it may overheat!

Naturally, computer noise isn't a problem if you're recording *line sources* (i.e., ones that don't require any form of microphone) only. However, that doesn't mean that computer-generated sources of noise can't cause problems with line-level recordings. For example, sitting or standing too close to a computer's CRT monitor while playing an instrument that has pick-ups (like a guitar or bass) will also cause the instrument to pick up the RF noise generated by the computer monitor (note that this is not a problem with LCD monitors). Poorly shielded hard drives also generate operating noise that can be picked up by poorly shielded audio interfaces. In the former case, the solution is simple: Don't play too close to a monitor, or use an LCD monitor instead. In the latter case, making sure that you have quality components in your system is the best safeguard.

Another way to minimize computer noise when recording with microphones in the same room is to use a cardioid mic positioned away from the computer (refer to "Appendix B: Microphone Basics" for more details). It rejects sounds from the back of the mic capsule, and that will usually reduce any recorded computer noise to a manageable level. Even so, you may have to use some noise reduction software or a plug-in afterwards to treat tracks recorded with microphones (there will be more details on this later in the book).

Of course, you'll want to hear what you're recording while you're recording it. If you're going to use external monitors to do that, make sure that you use them only when it is safe to do so. If you're recording a line source, you can safely monitor the recording through external monitors. On the other hand, you should never use external monitors in the same room where you're recording a sound source with a microphone. If the mic is too close to the monitors, it will induce feedback. At the very least, the monitored signal can leak into the microphone, and you probably don't want to hear or record the combination of both the original signal and the slightly delayed signal from the monitors!

You should also monitor through headphones when recording vocals. However, make sure that the output level of the vocalist's headphones is not too high when recording, especially if the vocalist tends to stand extremely close to the mic. The output from the headphones could be picked up by the mic, and the combination of both the original and monitored signal could ruin your recording. Of course, you can further minimize headphone leakage by using headphones that have a circumaural design.

Basic Audio Track Recording

Let's add audio tracks to the MIDI tracks you recorded earlier. After all, digital audio sequencers are designed to record and play back both MIDI and audio tracks in a single program environment.

Step 1: Add or Insert a New Audio Track.

As in the case of MIDI tracks, the specific menu for adding a new audio track in a song or sequence file may differ from one application to another. Keeping that in mind, go to the menu in your specific program that allows you to add or insert a track, and elect to add a new audio track.

Note that you can add in more than one audio track. However, the number of new audio tracks you can record at once depends on how many input channels your audio interface has. If it has two inputs you can record only two channels at once, if it has four inputs you can record only four channels, and so on.

Step 2: Select the Desired Input and Output Bus.

Once the new audio track appears in the program window, select the audio interface input *bus* you want to record into, and the audio output bus through which you'll monitor your recording. Buses usually refer to left/right pairs of input or output channels. For instance, an audio interface with just two channels of I/O has one input bus and one output bus.

Note that this doesn't mean that you can record and play back only two audio tracks in your digital audio sequencer. You can record and play back as many audio tracks as you want within the scope of the performance limitations of your computer. However, you will only be able to *record* two channels of audio at any given time, and all audio tracks—including the tracks being recorded—will be routed through the two-channel (i.e., stereo) output bus.

Input buses in Cubase. Even though all of the audio interface's channels are available for use, users are required to highlight (activate) the channels that will actually be used.

If your audio interface has more audio inputs and outputs, naturally you will have more audio routing choices. For instance, if you have a four-in/eight-out audio interface, you can choose one of four (or all four) input channels for recording, and likewise you'll have a choice of eight channels from which to monitor digital audio playback. Although you will probably monitor the audio inputs using their matching audio outputs, you don't have to do that.

One final note concerning buses—make sure that you've *activated* the buses that your program will use. Some digital audio sequencers automatically select all of an audio interface's input/output channels during program setup. However, some programs such as Cubase also require you to activate the input buses you want to use in a song, even if all of the buses were selected for use in its audio interface control panel.

Step 3: Select Between Mono and Stereo Audio Tracks.

Computer-based digital audio sequencers can record an audio track in either mono (one audio channel) or stereo (two audio channels, one panned hard left and the other hard right). This differs from hardware-based multitrack decks—they have only mono tracks. To record stereo tracks on a hardware-based multitrack, you need to use two mono tracks simultaneously.

If you want to record a mono track with your digital audio sequencer, you will need to specify which channel on the input bus you want to use. The usual convention is that odd-numbered tracks use the left channel inputs, while even-numbered tracks use the right channel inputs. It's a convention that grew out of using hardware multitrack decks, and it's been followed in digital audio programs, too. However, some programs use the left input channel *exclusively* for recording all monaural tracks, but let you route its output to a left or right channel. As always, check with your program's manual to determine how it records mono tracks.

If you want to record in stereo, select the stereo input parameter. Depending on your program, you may have to ensure that the stereo track is on an odd-numbered track as, again, some programs still follow the odd-left/even-right convention for working with digital audio tracks, and will automatically link two adjacent digital audio tracks (starting with an odd-numbered track) to record in stereo.

Some digital audio programs offer yet another recording alternative: They allow users to use *both* channels of an input bus to record *mono* tracks. The software does this by summing together the output of both bus channels into a mono signal. The chief advantage of this option is that you can record mono tracks from a two-channel source without having to repatch any cables in your audio setup. For example, I may want to record a synthesizer part into a mono track in my digital audio program. The synth has two physical audio output jacks, and they're already wired to my mixer in stereo. Rather than repatch the cables on my synth or mixer channels, or pan the synth output hard left or right through MIDI, I can just leave my cables and synth settings alone. The program will sum both channels of the input bus and record it as a mono track.

Step 4: Set the Record Start and Stop Times.

As I had mentioned earlier, you can set the start and stop times for recording at any point in a song's timeline. This makes it easy to record individual patterns or song sections without having to record a track linearly. As in the case of MIDI tracks, you'll often want to record sections or clips of songs to build up an arrangement as you go along. Of course, you can also record linear tracks as well. In fact, your song arrangements will usually consist of a combination of clips and linear tracks.

Step 5: Set the Desired Record Option.

Digital audio sequencers will often let you record audio tracks in the same way as you would MIDI tracks. For instance, you can record audio using the sound-on-sound option, which blends digital audio data with previously recorded audio on the same track. You also have the choice of recording in overwrite mode, which erases the previously recorded material on an audio track and replaces it with newly recorded audio. Finally, you can use auto punch mode to record and replace digital audio on a track. It works the same way that auto punch recording for MIDI tracks does, except that the data you're working with is digital audio, not MIDI.

Step 6: Arm the Track.

To record an audio track, you first have to click on the track's Record button to arm it for recording. In some digital audio programs, clicking on a Record button will also cause a dialog box to open up, requesting a name for this new audio file. Note that this won't change the file name of your project file. Digital audio sequencers just save audio recorded through them as separate files, so don't worry—these audio files will still appear as tracks in your project. The sequencer knows where to find them.

Note that some programs will name an audio file by its track name if the track has been labeled (by you, that is—e.g., "bass," "vocals," etc.). If the track has no label, the file name will often simply be listed as "Track X," where "X" is the track number.

Step 7: Monitor Input Levels.

Before you begin to actually record on that track, check the input level of the signal you'll be recording. In other words, sing or play a portion of whatever part you plan to record to ensure that the levels are properly set. You don't want the overall signal level to be too low, but you don't want the signal level to be too high, either. An average signal level of –6 dBFS should be sufficient.

As I've said before, setting signal levels at –6 dBFS goes against the traditional analog recording technique of recording a signal as hot as possible. However, there is a real danger that digital distortion can occur if you apply this technique to recording digital audio. For one, you'll hear digital distortion if you use the same bus to monitor more than one track that has been recorded at 0 dBFS.

Finally, you have to remember that you will probably perform some type of processing on most audio tracks. This can increase their output levels past 0 dBFS, which, again, can cause digital distortion. To prevent that from happening, you need to provide a little headroom for working with *plug-ins*. Recording at a maximum level of –6 dBFS should give the plug-ins enough headroom to process a digital audio track while still avoiding digital distortion (we'll talk more about using plug-ins later).

Step 8: Hit the Record Button.

Once you've armed the audio track, given the track a file name, and have checked its input signal level, click on the Record button in the program's Transport window and begin playing after the count-off beats. Again, as in the case of MIDI, you have to make sure that you have also armed the track for recording as well. Otherwise, nothing will be recorded.

Step 9: When You're Done Playing, Stop Recording and Disarm the Track.

I know that I'm stating the obvious, but it's important to click Stop in the Transport window so that you can take the program out of Record mode. Also, remember to disarm the track's Record button once you're done recording. After all, you don't want to ruin a take by accidentally recording over it.

Overdubbing Audio Tracks

Recording new tracks alongside previously recorded tracks is a technique known as *overdubbing*. No matter how many tracks you're able to record in one pass, chances are that you will have to overdub additional tracks afterwards. This is especially true if you are recording all of the audio tracks for a song yourself. Naturally, you have to be able to hear what you're recording while simultaneously monitoring previously recorded tracks so that the new tracks are in sync with the earlier ones. If you're planning to use your audio interface exclusively for recording and monitoring digital audio tracks, you'll need to make sure that it has the zero-latency monitoring feature discussed in "Chapter 3: Choosing the Right Audio and/or MIDI Interface." You'll also need to make sure that your software supports this feature.

However, your audio interface or program doesn't necessarily need to support zero-latency monitoring if you plan to use an outboard mixer for directly monitoring recording sources and audio interface output sources. In fact, it may be preferable to use an outboard mixer even if your audio interface supports zero-latency monitoring. For one thing, you'll be able to record and monitor all parts in sync, just like you would if your audio interface had that zero-latency monitoring capability in the first place. For another, using an external mixer with an audio interface that has multiple outputs lets you assign groups of tracks within the program to different audio interface outputs. These various track assignments become, in effect, submixes that you can route to an external mixer. This in turn allows you to more easily work with digital audio tracks in a variety of ways. For instance, by assigning previously recorded tracks to different outputs than the current record output bus, you may be able to record tracks at slightly higher levels (up to –3 dBFS) without worrying as much about digital distortion. That's because you're not summing together several recorded tracks through a single pair of outputs.

You can also use your mixer to raise and lower volume levels as well as mute and solo various groups of tracks on the fly without affecting the settings in the program itself. In addition, you can monitor the tracks in conjunction with outboard signal effects processing, and this won't affect the outputted tracks as they exist in the computer. However, you have to make sure that you record the input sources dry to begin with.

Wet vs. Dry Recording

One choice that you'll have to make before recording is whether you'll want to record tracks *wet* (with signal processing) or dry. The common wisdom, and one that I follow myself, is to record them dry and then add signal processing later. There are several good reasons for that, especially in the case of digital audio recordings. For instance, if you apply audio effects plug-ins or the program's native signal processors to the signals you're recording, you'll introduce a delay into the monitored signal. After all, the inputted signal has to go through different software-based signal processing devices—each of which requires a little processing time—before coming back out again as a processed signal. Besides, audio interfaces with zero latency monitoring usually monitor the input signal from the input source, not the eventual output source. Under these circumstances, you won't hear the processed result of what you're recording anyway.

You could also use an outboard mixer connected to external signal processing devices to record and simultaneously monitor wet tracks. This would eliminate the previously mentioned delay problem, but it could also lead to some unanticipated editing difficulties later. Let's say, for example, that you've just recorded several takes on separate tracks of a vocal part with reverb on every track. You're going to use those separate takes to create a *comp track*—an edited track compiled from a number of takes existing on different tracks (a common audio production technique, and one you're probably going to use frequently). You create a comp track by splicing together the best portions of audio from different takes and pasting them to one "perfect" track. As you might guess, it's important that the comp track plays seamlessly so that no one can hear any differences among the spliced sections.

However, whenever you add reverb beforehand—or other processes like digital delay or flanging effects—you make it more difficult, if not impossible, to create splices that sound like one smooth track when played together. The reverb tail (decay) from one splice may not quite match the reverb level at the start of the following splice. You could experience a sudden jump or drop in the reverb sound, depending on which splices and takes are used. Likewise, mismatched delay effects (more on these in "Chapter 13: Advanced Mixing Techniques—EQ and Effects") from one splice to the next can cause a comp track to sound uneven—so much so that it would be obvious even to a casual listener that this was an edited track. This goes against the whole purpose of a comp track, which is to create a perfect take from several imperfect takes so that it sounds as if it was recorded right the first time.

You can use external signal processing devices to apply signal processing to monitored sources in a way that doesn't add the effects to any of the signals. For instance, I've found that most people want to hear reverb on all tracks, and they especially want to hear reverb added to their voices when they're recording vocal tracks. I've set up my system so that they can monitor tracks with reverb added, and yet not have the reverb effect recorded into the track itself. This way, they get to hear reverb with their recordings, I get dry recordings that I can more easily edit, and everybody is happy.

However, for every rule, there is an exception. Although I generally do record tracks dry, there are certain types of sound sources that I record with effects when I feel it's appropriate. For instance, I record electric guitar tracks with various effects because they're integral to the overall sound of the guitar. Likewise, I usually record outboard synth sounds using the synth's own onboard effects because these effects are often crucial to the sound patch being played. In both cases, I might remove the reverb from the signal path of these instruments' effects processors, but I usually do that whenever I want to use a single reverb for all tracks in a song. Otherwise, I leave their own reverb effects in.

Converting MIDI to Digital Audio

Digital audio sequencers, by definition, are able to record, edit, process, play back, and mix down both MIDI and digital audio tracks together in one program environment. However, the problem is that MIDI data and digital audio data are two completely different types of information. To recap, MIDI doesn't record sound—it records details of performance information that are used by MIDI instruments to generate sound. While recording MIDI tracks doesn't generate huge amounts of data, it does require that MIDI instruments always be present in order to hear that data as sound. Digital audio data, on the other hand, is a digital representation of actual sound recordings. While the amount of data these recordings generate can be huge, all you need is an audio interface to play back this data once you're done recording the tracks.

Each type of data, in its natural state, is incompatible with the other. You can't hear MIDI data solely via the audio capabilities of audio interfaces, per se, nor can you trigger MIDI devices with digital audio data. This isn't really a problem, though, if you're willing to mix the combined output of digital audio tracks and MIDI instrument tracks to a separate mixdown device such as a DAT deck or even a second computer dedicated to mastering tracks—that is, recording the mixed output of multiple audio tracks to a final stereo track. However, for our purposes right now, we want to be able to work with one type of track just to make things easier for us, and to do all the work from within one computer.

The easiest way to do this is to turn MIDI tracks into digital audio tracks. How do you do this? It's easy—you just record the output of the MIDI instruments into digital audio tracks. In fact, before you start recording digital audio tracks of other instruments, you'll first want to convert the MIDI tracks into digital audio tracks. However, before you do that, you'll need to prepare the MIDI tracks for digital audio conversion. How much preparation you need to do will depend on how you want to record your MIDI parts.

Mixing MIDI to Stereo Audio Tracks

By the time you're ready to record the output of your MIDI tracks as digital audio tracks, you should have already set all of the song parameters, especially the tempo, and key and time signatures. Furthermore, you should have already edited the MIDI tracks as detailed in "Chapter 7: Editing MIDI Tracks." However, if you're going to record all of your MIDI tracks to one stereo audio track, there is one last thing you'll need to do: Mix the individual MIDI tracks to a perfect stereo mix using MIDI control change messages Pan and Volume.

First, set the Pan message for each MIDI track to the desired point in the stereo field. The range for Pan messages is from 0 to 127. Each value represents a specific pan position in the stereo field: For instance, 0 is the equivalent of hard left, 63 is center, and 127 is hard right. Other values represent relative positions in the stereo continuum. For example, a Pan message value of 31 indicates that the instrument is panned to the left, halfway between the center and hard left positions.

It's likely that you had already "preset" the pan position for each part when recording and editing each MIDI track. However, make sure that you are satisfied with these settings. Once you've got everything as you want it for each track, insert the proper Pan message in the Event List at the beginning of the track and before any MIDI note data. That way you'll be sure that the proper message has been stored when you back up or archive the MIDI tracks of this song.

If you plan to move around the pan position of a MIDI instrument track in real-time, you'll need to insert change messages in the appropriate MIDI tracks. One way to do this is to go into the Piano Roll view and draw in the Pan message changes as you want them to occur over time. You can also create these changes using the program's automation features.

Next, set the Volume level message for each MIDI track to the proper level. The range for Volume messages is also from 0 to 127, with 0 representing no volume and 127 as the highest volume level. As with Pan messages, you will have probably preset the volume levels for each track during the initial recording and editing process. Unlike pan position, which is usually static, the volume levels of your tracks will probably change over the course of the recording. For instance, you may fade in or fade out the starts and ends of clips or tracks. Some tracks may be reduced in level at certain points in the song, while other track levels may be increased at certain times to emphasize a particular part. In short, mixing with Volume messages requires some track automation.

Automating MIDI Tracks

If you have a surface controller, you can record MIDI volume level changes in real-time. However, even the most experienced users won't always move faders to the right levels all of the time. Neither will they always move the faders at the right speed to create the desired fade curve. Fortunately, digital audio sequencers include editing tools that allow you to automate the volume and pan process to a high degree of precision. You can even use these tools to edit and correct Volume and Pan changes that were first recorded from a surface controller's output.

If you'll look at the figure below (a graphic representation of automated tracks), you'll notice that the MIDI tracks have lines running through them. If you look *closely*, you'll also notice that these lines change shape between the small rectangles that also appear on the tracks. Each small rectangle represents a *node*, or a point that anchors a line segment. The line segments between the nodes not only indicate the volume levels or pan positions, but also how they will change over time.

MIDI Pan and Volume automation

For instance, Track 2 has a slow fade-in curve, which you can see by the shape of the line from the first node to the second. Other tracks have abrupt volume changes that jump from one level to another.

But how do you create track automation if you don't have a surface controller? Easy: First, add a new volume envelope to the track (check with your software's instruction manual on how to do this). A straight line will appear, with a node at each end of the track. To create a fade-in, add a new node at the spot where you want the final volume level of the fade to end. Don't worry if the node doesn't initially appear at the exact point you want: You can drag the node to the right spot afterwards. Next, grab the first node and pull it straight down to the bottom of the track. You should now see an angled line between the first node and the new node you added. Next, select the type of curve you want the angled line segment to be. The default shape in most programs is linear, which is what that angled line represents. You can change it to a slow curve or a fast curve, or even a sudden jump from the first node's volume level to the next node's new volume level. Depending on your specific program, you may have other curve shapes available, too.

Anytime you want to adjust the volume level and the way that it changes, just add a node at the point where you want the change to begin, and another node where you want the change to end. Then set the desired fade curve for that line segment as described in the previous paragraph. You can always adjust the volume up or down by moving the proper line segment or node vertically. You can also alter the start and end points of the volume changes by moving the appropriate nodes horizontally.

Recording the Automated Mix

Now that you've automated all of your MIDI tracks, you're ready to record them as a stereo mix. First, make sure that you've routed the stereo outputs of your synthesizer to the desired inputs of your audio interface. If you're recording the outputs of multiple synthesizers to stereo, route the stereo outputs of their audio mixer to the correct audio interface inputs. If you're using the same mixer to monitor both your MIDI instruments and digital audio tracks, you won't be able to use the stereo output of that mixer. Instead, you'll have to assign all of the MIDI instruments to a separate mixer bus, and route the outputs of that bus to the proper inputs of the digital audio interface.

Next, set up the audio track into which you're going to record the MIDI tracks, following the procedure described earlier in this chapter. Depending on how you've routed your monitoring system, you may hear both the MIDI instrument outputs as they are triggered by the MIDI tracks and the digital audio recording of those MIDI tracks. You may hear a slight echo or delay between the MIDI tracks and the audio tracks as well, but don't worry—it's perfectly normal for this to occur, and it won't be recorded into the digital audio track.

Once you're done recording, stop the Transport and disarm the record button on the digital audio track. In addition, mute the MIDI tracks so that they no longer trigger your MIDI instruments. However, don't delete those MIDI tracks, because you never know when you may need to use their data to record a different or additional part to digital audio. You may also want to archive the MIDI tracks, if your program supports this feature. Archiving a track not only prevents it from being played, it also makes sure that the program won't try to process its data in any way. Simply muting a track may not necessarily prevent the program from processing the data, even if you don't hear it. However, don't worry about data being unintentionally recorded if you don't archive—this function is used to free up computer resources, nothing more.

Finally, play back the newly recorded stereo audio track to make sure that the MIDI instruments were recorded properly. If all went well, you should hear a fine stereo mix.

The Advantages of Individual MIDI-Generated Audio Tracks

One of the disadvantages of converting all of your MIDI tracks into one stereo audio track is that you have limited control over the individual instruments afterwards. For instance, let's say that you want to boost the bass drum to give it a little more punch. You can't increase its volume without increasing the volume of everything else in the stereo mix. You could add a little EQ in the bass frequency range to give the bass drum some extra "oomph" (and you'll learn more about EQ a little later in this book), but you'll also boost the bass frequencies of other instruments in the audio mix, such as the bass guitar sound. That might be acceptable if the bass guitar needs an extra boost, too, but it will be a problem if the bass guitar was fine before the change in EQ.

That's why it's usually better to convert the audio output of each MIDI instrument to its own track. In fact, you'll want to record the audio output of specific groups of MIDI sounds within an instrument to separate audio tracks. The drum kit with its individual sounds, for example, is often a good candidate for this.

In some ways, transferring MIDI instruments to individual audio tracks requires less preparatory work on the MIDI tracks themselves. For one thing, you don't have to spend time automating volume level changes in a MIDI track because you can do that later when it's an audio track. All you need to do is set the initial MIDI volume level so that you get a good signal level for the recording. Also, you may not have to set the Pan messages for the MIDI instruments, depending on how you actually record the sound. Instead, you can record the tracks from the stereo sources as mono tracks, provided your audio program supports that feature. As an alternative, you can record the tracks in stereo and later convert them into mono tracks, either within your digital audio sequencer or by exporting them to a separate editing program.

On the other hand, how quickly and easily you can record MIDI instrument output into digital audio tracks will depend on the length of the song and the number of audio tracks you can record at once. If you have an audio interface with only two inputs, the best you can do is record two individual tracks at a time. If you have an audio interface with eight channels of I/O, you can record up to eight tracks in one pass. The other influencing factor is the number of audio outputs each of your MIDI instruments has, and the number of parts each instrument plays. With that in mind, let me give you an illustration of how to go about recording MIDI instrument output into individual audio tracks.

Transferring MIDI Drum and Percussion Tracks

I prefer to record the drum tracks first. Before I do that, however, I first put each individual drum sound on a separate MIDI track. Most digital audio sequencers have an editing command or tool for splitting individual notes in a track and placing them on separate MIDI tracks. Inasmuch as drum sounds are assigned to specific notes, splitting the notes in a MIDI drum track is the equivalent of isolating each drum sound on its own track.

Be aware that each note should still be assigned to the same channel and port as the original drum track. Also, don't try to pan each individual drum sound with its own Pan message. Remember that this is a channel-wide message: changing the pan position for one note on one MIDI port and channel will change the pan position for all notes on the same MIDI port and channel. Besides, if there happen to be two Pan change messages on the same MIDI port and channel at the same time, only the Pan message with the higher value will be used.

The next step is to mute all of the MIDI tracks that you don't want to record in this pass. Which tracks you mute will partly depend on how many tracks you can record simultaneously with your digital audio interface.

The number of audio outputs of the source MIDI instrument will also determine how many parts you can record at once from that specific device. For example, my drum module has only four audio outputs, so I can record only four audio tracks at once from that MIDI device. This means that if I have eight tracks of MIDI drums to record, it will take two passes to do them all, even if I have an eight-channel audio interface.

Because each drum sound is triggered by a specific MIDI note, each sound should be on a separate MIDI track. Some sounds—such as the bass drum, snare drum, and ride cymbal—should always be recorded on separate audio tracks. Some sounds—such as closed, open, and pedal hi-hats—are really aspects of a single hi-hat sound and can therefore be recorded together to the same audio track.

Some groups of sounds belong together, such as tom-toms, crash cymbals, or congas—their individual MIDI tracks can be recorded together, and preferably in stereo so that their pan positions in the stereo field are maintained in the digital audio file.

Transferring Other MIDI Instruments

Other MIDI instruments generally reside on separate MIDI tracks to begin with, so there's no need to split them up further. However, there are other issues to consider when converting their output to audio tracks. How many parts can be played through a particular MIDI instrument? Will you have to record its output in multiple passes or can you do it in only one pass?

Another factor to consider is the number of audio outputs these instruments have. Many workstations and multitimbal modules have at least four outputs, so you can potentially record up to four parts in one pass. Of course, that depends on whether you want to record a part in stereo or mono. For example, if a particular sound patch uses reverb and stereo delay as part of its overall sound, you'll probably want to record that sound as a stereo audio track. On the other hand, a sound that relies less on the instrument's internal effects processor can probably be recorded in mono. If the instrument generates at least two such sounds simultaneously, you can simply set their MIDI tracks' pan messages to 0 and 127 respectively, and record both parts at the same time as separate mono tracks.

As you have no doubt realized by now, the number of MIDI tracks you can simultaneously record is ultimately determined by the number of inputs your audio interface has—and the more inputs it has, the less time you'll spend converting MIDI instrument output to audio tracks. I grant you that this can be a tedious process, but it pays off in the end by giving you increased control over the sounds these instruments generate. Also, converting MIDI tracks to audio puts everything into a common digital audio format so that you can easily perform all of the recording, editing, audio processing, mixing, and mastering tasks from within one production environment.

CHAPTER 10
ALTERNATIVE PRODUCTION TOOLS

So far, I've discussed working with MIDI and audio tracks as if they were two completely different entities with no common ground. However, technological advances have significantly blurred the line between audio and MIDI. Granted, that line hasn't been totally erased (yet), but the computer-based recording artist now has at his disposal a variety of virtual tools that combine some of the best aspects of MIDI and digital audio—tools that were almost unheard of just ten years ago. These production tools eliminate the need for hardware-based synthesizers and samplers and, in some cases, the need for performing with instruments (in the traditional sense) altogether.

While these new production tools provide alternative methods of creating music with your computer, it's important to understand how they work and why they were developed. Furthermore, it's important to understand their limitations so that you can more effectively use them in your music production environment. With that in mind, let's discuss the first technological advance—virtual MIDI instruments.

Virtual MIDI Instruments: An Overview

Unlike hardware synths and samplers, virtual MIDI instruments exist only in software. Because these instruments are computer-based, they offer several advantages over traditional hardware synths and samplers. First, virtual MIDI instruments don't take up any floor space because they only exist inside the computer! Compare that to a group of hardware instruments that can take up a significant portion of your recording room's space.

Second, the price of software-based instruments is much lower in comparison to their hardware-based counterparts. The average price range for a software synth is between $150 to $400. Compare that to the average price range for hardware synths, which can range from $700 to $2000 and up.

The cost of ownership for virtual MIDI instruments, compared to hardware MIDI instruments, is also lower. With hardware instruments, you have to spend extra money on ancillary equipment, such as multiple-tier keyboard stands, rackmount cases for modules, multiport MIDI interfaces, MIDI and audio cables for each instrument, and probably a separate mixer to monitor the outputs of all the instruments. If you use these same instruments to play out on gigs, you also need cases for each keyboard, mixer, etc.

By contrast, you need only one controller keyboard to play your virtual instruments. If you have a USB keyboard, you don't even need a separate MIDI interface. Also, you don't need to buy separate audio and MIDI cables for these virtual instruments. Neither do you need a separate mixer for these instruments, because their outputs can be controlled via the program's virtual mixer. And if you want to play out on gigs with these instruments, you can pack up your laptop and take them all with you, because all of your instruments reside on your computer's hard drive.

On the other hand, using virtual MIDI instruments has its disadvantages, too. You need a sufficiently fast computer to play more than three or four software instruments at any given time, and the number of software synths you can play simultaneously depends on the type of virtual instrument you use and the nature of the sound that the particular instrument plays. For example, a virtual instrument that creates sounds using a complex synth structure requires a certain amount of computer resources to begin with. If a particular sound this instrument produces consists of a complicated structure that makes a variety of changes over time, this will require more computer processing than a sound that changes little over time or doesn't play for very long. This isn't a problem for hardware-based instruments, because their processors have been designed to work optimally with the kinds of sounds they produce and, therefore, their performance will be uniformly consistent.

It's also important that the audio interface through which the virtual instrument plays has only a small amount of virtual instrument latency. After all, you want the virtual instrument to respond just like a hardware-based synth. However, don't get caught up in the belief that reducing virtual instrument latency to zero is necessary. Even hardware-based synths and samplers have a small amount of MIDI latency—it just depends on the instrument's design. However, the processing power of the computer is important as well and, in my opinion, the latest generation of computers finally has the capability to make playing multiple virtual instruments just as practical as playing a similar group of hardware-based MIDI instruments.

Virtual Instrument Plug-Ins

All of the four digital audio sequencers discussed in this book incorporate virtual MIDI instruments

into their programs via virtual instrument plug-ins. To recap, a plug-in is a small program that performs the function of a hardware effects processor or instrument in a digital audio sequencing program. We'll talk more about effects processing plug-ins in a later chapter. Right now I want to discuss virtual instrument plug-ins in more detail.

Although all four digital audio sequencers employ virtual MIDI instruments in their programs, each of them uses different plug-in formats. Check to make sure before you acquire a new plug-in that it will work with your software and audio interface!

The VB-1, LM-7, and A1 are all VST instruments that are included in Cubase SX. There are hundreds of additional VST instruments and VST-compatible host programs available, too.

Even though each plug-in format is incompatible with the others, there are utility programs called *wrappers* that provide a "shell" so that one type of plug-in format can work within the framework of a different plug-in format. The most common wrappers let VST instruments and effects plug-ins operate as DXi or MAS plug-ins. This shouldn't be surprising, because the VST format was the first successful *host-based* (relies exclusively on the computer's processing power to perform a task) processor and instrument plug-in format. Based on the sheer number of plug-ins available, VST is still the most widely used format.

But there are other types of plug-in formats for more specialized hardware/software computer-based digital audio systems, too. For example, Digidesign uses the RTAS (Real-Time Audio System) and DirectConnect plug-in formats with their Pro Tools systems. Creamware uses its own plug-in architecture for its SCOPE audio systems cards and software. These two systems use *DSP-based* plug-ins, which are used with proprietary digital signal processing (i.e., DSP) hardware. The hardware itself is a PCI card populated with a number of digital signal processing chips. The chief advantage of DSP-based plug-ins is that they don't task the processing capabilities of the computer itself. On the other hand, their biggest disadvantages are that they are usually used only with proprietary software systems and their prices can be a little steep.

Standalone Virtual Instruments

Software synthesizers and samplers don't necessarily need to be integrated into digital audio sequencers: They can exist as standalone instruments, too. The main advantage of using standalone virtual instruments is that you can play these instruments without having to open a digital audio sequencing program to access them, which is what you ordinarily have to do with plug-in instruments. This ability makes it easier to play these instruments in a live setting, too. Imagine going to a gig with nothing but a laptop and a keyboard controller and having access to any type of instrument you want to play, from classic electric pianos to virtual modular synths. You can do that with a good collection of standalone synths or samplers.

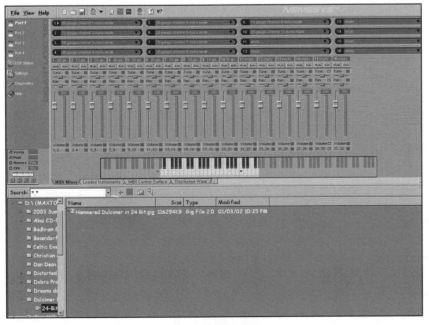

Often, standalone virtual instruments include plug-in versions of the instrument, too. These can allow you to integrate the instruments into your digital audio sequencer, just like any other virtual instrument plug-ins. Of course, some standalone instruments exist *only* as standalone virtual instruments. For instance, one of the most popular virtual samplers, Tascam's GigaStudio, exists exclusively as a Windows standalone instrument. This program also requires that your audio interface use a special GSIF (GigaStudio Interface) driver. However, it's such a popular program that a high percentage of audio interface manufacturers include a GSIF driver with their products.

A standalone virtual instrument can work in conjunction with a digital audio sequencer, even if it doesn't exist as a plug-in as well. For example, GigaStudio uses its own virtual MIDI router, which acts as a software version of a MIDI interface, to receive MIDI data from a digital audio sequencer running simultaneously on the same computer. There are also a number of free virtual MIDI routers available online, such as Hubi's Loopback Device, which can route MIDI data from digital audio sequencers to any standalone virtual instrument.

Of course, you can always run these standalone instruments on a separate computer. In this circumstance, they become like any other hardware synth or sampler, but that's not necessarily a bad thing. A rack of hardware synths can be replaced by virtual instruments installed on just one computer. And you can change virtual instruments as the situation dictates

However, some standalone virtual instruments require a lot of computer resources to work properly. Streaming samplers—such as GigaStudio, Native Instruments' Kontakt, and Bitheadz' Unity Session—are similar to digital audio programs in that they play huge sample files from a hard drive rather than from memory only. Like digital audio programs, streaming samplers need to stream audio from a hard drive at a fairly fast rate. Just as when working with digital audio programs, it's best if one uses a separate hard drive just for large audio sample files. Also, because streaming samplers require so many computer resources, it's usually more productive to use a separate computer for these programs.

In fact, using a second computer for virtual instruments and effects is rapidly becoming a common practice, even for beginners. For instance, IK Multimedia's AmpliTube is a computer-based virtual guitar effects processor that also models certain types of guitar/amplifier combinations. Another virtual guitar effects processing program, Dsound's RT Player Pro, offers a variety of virtual effects that appear onscreen as guitar foot pedal effects, or *stompboxes*. In addition, RT Player Pro lets you load VST instruments into its "effects rack" so that you can play them live without the need for a VST digital audio program.

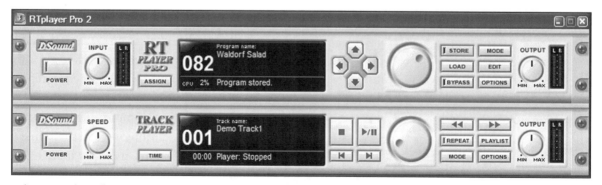

The DSound RT Player Pro 2 consists of two virtual modules: Player Pro and Track Player. The Player Pro can be used as a real-time effects processor and VST instrument player, whereas the Track Player can simultaneously play back audio files for live performance.

Steinberg has also realized that using a second computer for VST instruments is often more effective than attempting to play several virtual instruments and digital audio tracks simultaneously on one platform. Starting with Cubase VST 5.0, Steinberg has included VST System Link in its Cubase line of digital audio sequencers. VST System Link allows users to connect two computers together and synchronize their timing using a single bit of data running through any type of digital audio connection such as AES/EBU, S/PDIF, or ADAT. Moreover, you can connect between different platforms without any trouble, so if you have a PC and a Mac, you can use them both together.

Users can run Cubase SX with V-Stack (shown here), which acts as a shell for running VST instruments and effects in desktop production and live settings.

Initially, one had to make sure that each computer was running a compatible version of Cubase in order to take advantage of VST System Link. However, users can now use VST System Link with V-Stack, an easily affordable standalone program that's basically a version of Cubase with just the VST rack and mixer—it doesn't include MIDI sequencing and audio track recording or playback.

Soft Synth Studios

Yet another alternative to plug-in and standalone virtual MIDI instruments is a soft synth studio program. Soft synth studio programs combine several important elements of MIDI music production.

First, each soft synth studio has a collection of several different types of synthesizers and samplers that can be played simultaneously. Each soft synth studio also includes a number of virtual effects processors and a mixer as well. For example, Propellerhead Software's Reason has six software instruments and eight effects processors from which to choose. You can use these effects processors in-line with the virtual instruments or connect the effects plug-ins into the auxiliary sends and returns of the virtual mixer. (We'll discuss how to use virtual effects in more detail a little later on in this book.)

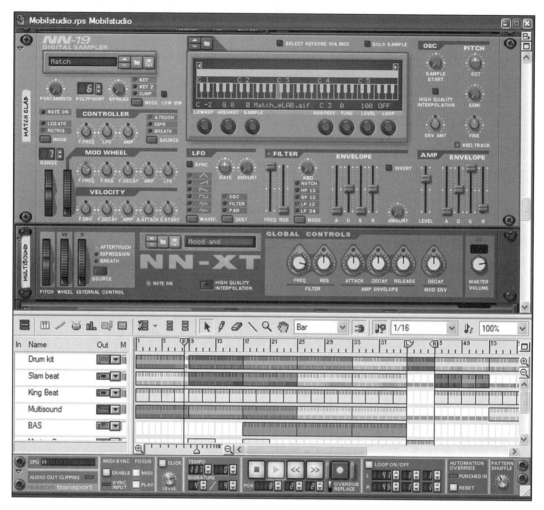

Propellerhead Software's Reason

Each instrument in a soft synth studio is played with a *pattern-based* MIDI sequencer (i.e., used for sequencing beats and loop-based music). Each instrument has a set number of different patterns that you can use, plus you can enter notes in the pattern with your mouse in real-time or use an external MIDI keyboard. These programs also include the basic MIDI editing functions required to polish the patterns for proper performance.

Songs in soft synth studios are created by chaining different patterns together. Each instrument has its own song track, so you can mix and match the patterns of the different instruments to produce a song. Some soft synth studios also let you use MIDI to control track playback in a variety of ways. For example, you can control volume and pan levels in real-time, and mute (or unmute) tracks.

The number of virtual instruments and effects you can simultaneously use depends partly upon the amount of computer processing resources each instrument and effect requires. Some don't need much power to produce sounds, while others can put a huge drain on your computer's resources. While most soft synth studios include a meter that indicates how much power the program is consuming, very few will tell you in advance how much processing power each instrument or effect will use. A notable exception is Arturia's Storm Music Studio.

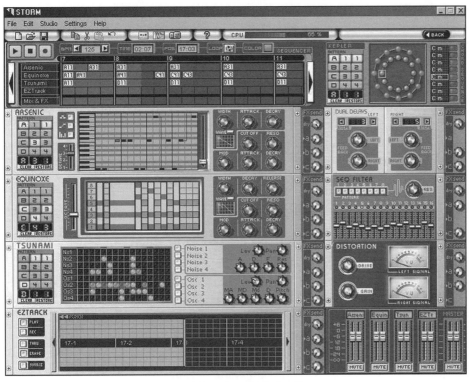

Arturia's Storm Music Studio

Storm has also been designed so that the user is limited to using four instruments and three virtual effects simultaneously. Although other soft synth studios can employ more instruments and effects, or multiple instances of the same instrument, that number will be limited by the speed and processing power of your system. There's a big difference between how a soft synth studio performs on a computer with minimal resources as opposed to a faster system. I like the fact that Storm will work just as well, by and large, on systems with minimal resources as it will on even faster machines.

The type of driver your audio interface uses will also influence soft synth studio performance. Many programs use ASIO drivers for fast performance, although the OS X versions of Reason and Storm use the new Core Audio and MIDI drivers. Some PC soft synth studios use drivers in the DirectX format, which is an older version of the WDM driver format. However, these programs, as a rule, prefer the ASIO drivers.

Converting Virtual Instrument Output to Audio

Even though virtual MIDI instruments exist only in software and rely on a computer's audio interface to be heard, the data that triggers these instruments is still in MIDI format. Just as you did for hardware synths in the previous chapter, you must convert the virtual instrument output into digital audio tracks. Fortunately, though, there are a variety of ways to accomplish this task and, in most cases, it's much easier than recording audio from hardware synths being triggered by MIDI data in real-time.

Virtual Instrument Plug-Ins

To convert virtual instrument plug-in output to digital audio, just export its output as a digital audio file in whatever audio format you're using (WAV or AIFF—Wave or Audio Interchange File Format, respectively). The general procedure is as follows.

First off, mute all of the tracks that you *don't* want to export to audio—otherwise they will all be exported into the same digital audio file. If you want to export specific drum sounds to separate audio tracks, make sure to perform note-splitting on the MIDI track that contains the drum data so that each part of the kit will be on its own track. The only tracks that you shouldn't mute are the specific tracks that contain the MIDI data you need to trigger the virtual instrument plug-in and the audio track through which the virtual instrument is routed. This is because most digital audio programs use a MIDI track for the MIDI data and a separate audio track to hear the virtual instrument's output. The exception is Cubase, which requires that a MIDI track only be routed to the virtual instrument's MIDI output in order to be heard.

Next, set the locator points (check with your software manual for instructions) for the start and end times of the MIDI tracks or clips you wish to export as digital audio.

Then, activate the Export Audio command from your specific program's menu. In some programs, it's a specific command, while in other programs it's a submenu item in the Export menu or command. A dialog box will then appear which will prompt you to enter the new audio file's name, as well as its location, data format, and other relevant information. Once this information has been entered, click on the OK or Save button. The program will process this information off-line.

Afterwards, mute the MIDI track you just converted, but don't erase or delete it. You may need to use this data again at a later time. If your program offers an Archive function, take advantage of it.

Next, access the Import Audio command. When the dialog box opens, select the new audio file you just created. The program will then import that file into a new audio track. Now you can treat that track the same way you would any audio track—because now it *is* an audio track.

Standalone Virtual Instruments

The process of converting the audio output of standalone virtual instruments can vary, depending on the nature of the virtual instrument software and the manner in which you are using it. For instance, if the standalone virtual instrument exists on another computer, you may have to treat it as you would an external hardware synth. So, first, you would have to cable the two computers, MIDI-wise, just as you would do with other hardware MIDI instrument/computer setups. You would also have to connect the outputs of its computer's audio interface to an external mixer, whose outputs should then be connected to the audio interface of the computer that would record the digital audio. Afterwards, you'd just have to follow the procedure for converting virtual instrument output to digital audio as it was described earlier.

If your audio interfaces allow it, you can streamline the connections between the two systems by using matching digital audio connections instead. Just directly connect the digital audio output of the standalone virtual instrument's audio interface to the digital audio input of the digital audio recording computer's interface. If your audio interfaces use S/PDIF or AES/EBU digital audio ports, you can transfer two channels of audio at once. Similarly, if your audio interfaces use ADAT digital audio ports, you can transfer eight channels of audio at once.

Keep in mind that you will still need to connect the two systems via MIDI so that the MIDI output of the digital audio computer can trigger the sounds created by the standalone synth on the other computer. Also, you'll have to make sure that you route the output of the standalone virtual instrument to the digital audio ports. Likewise, you'll need to ensure that the digital audio computer is recording incoming data from its own digital audio ports.

Converting the output of a standalone virtual instrument that resides on the same computer as a digital audio sequencer is a stickier problem. In most cases, the standalone instrument won't render its output into digital audio off-line as virtual instrument plug-ins do. Of course, if the standalone virtual instrument can also function as a virtual instrument plug-in, your best bet is to use it as such—then you can just convert its output to digital audio the same way as you would with any virtual instrument plug-in.

Failing that, there is another alternative, provided you have a multichannel, *multiclient* audio interface (i.e., one that can be accessed by more than one audio program at the same time).

First, set up your digital audio sequencer to use a limited number of audio interface channels. For example, you can set it up so that it records and plays back only on the first two channels of the interface. Then, set up your standalone virtual instrument to send its audio output to two different channels—for instance, Channels 3 and 4—of the same audio interface. Next, physically connect the outputs of, to follow the example already set, Channels 3 and 4 of your audio interface to Channels 1 and 2 (you may have to use an external mixer to do this properly). Finally, record the output of Channels 3 and 4 (the virtual instrument) into Channels 1 and 2 in the digital audio sequencer in real-time.

This method works if you have two audio interfaces in your computer. For example, you can assign the first audio interface to the digital audio program, and the second audio interface to the standalone virtual instrument. Then, you can just set up the audio routing as previously described, making exceptions for the fact that you are using two separate audio interfaces as opposed to one multichannel, multiclient audio interface.

Soft Synth Studios

Fortunately, converting the output of soft synth studios into digital audio data is easy. This is because soft synth studios let you export output to digital audio files, just like digital audio sequencers with virtual instrument plug-ins. Moreover, you can mute the different sequencer tracks in soft synth studios so that you can record the output of each virtual instrument as a separate digital audio file.

In some cases, you can incorporate soft synth studios into digital audio sequencing programs. The most widely used tool to do this is ReWire, which was also developed by Propellerhead Software. ReWire acts as a virtual audio/MIDI router between applications that support this feature. For example, Reason and Storm both support ReWire, as do Cubase and Sonar. Whenever Reason or Storm is connected to Cubase or Sonar, their outputs can be routed through these programs' virtual mixers, just as with other virtual instrument plug-ins. Furthermore, their audio output within the digital audio sequencers can be exported as audio files in the same manner as virtual instrument plug-ins.

Because this is an off-line process, converting the output of soft synth studios to audio occurs faster than real-time. It's a quick and easy procedure, even if you convert the output of individual instruments to separate audio tracks.

Real-Time Audio Pitch and Tempo Alteration

A couple of reasons why MIDI has been successful are because it allows musicians to speed up or slow down the tempo of a recording without affecting pitch and, likewise, alter pitch without affecting tempo. Neither of these capabilities is possible with audio recorded to tape, because changing the pitch of the recording changes the tape speed (i.e., tempo) as well. And, for a while, most early digital audio editing programs wouldn't let you change the tempo of digital audio tracks without altering pitch, either. To be sure, you could stretch or shrink the length of digital audio recordings, but always at the cost of altering the pitch of the material. Likewise, you could raise or lower the pitch of digital audio recordings, but doing so also altered their lengths. Eventually, digital audio editing programs made it possible to alter pitch and tempo independently of each other. Still, one had to go off-line in order to process these tracks. In short, you couldn't alter digital audio's pitch or tempo in real-time.

Clearly, the demand for a way to independently alter the pitch and tempo of digital audio in real-time was there. The desire for a solution to this problem was further fueled by the fact that real-time independent pitch and tempo alteration could be done in MIDI. Never mind that it was possible in MIDI only because it was a different type of technology—musicians wanted to be able to treat digital audio just like MIDI.

A Beat-Slicing Primer

ReCycled Audio Files

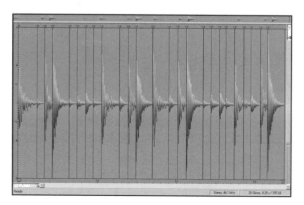

A beat-sliced ReCycle file

One of the first companies to tackle the problem of independent pitch and tempo alteration for digital audio was Propellerhead Software, and their solution was a program called ReCycle. This application is an example of what is called a *beat-slicing program*. As you may be able to deduce from this description, this type of software analyzes an audio file and divides it into individual beats. Although these types of programs work best with audio percussion tracks, they also work well with any type of audio with an identifiable rhythm or pattern.

Each beat can be identified by its attack. In some cases, the attack for a particular beat is high, while in other cases the attack is much smaller. If you stop to think about it, that's the difference between the major beats—which are usually accented—and the unaccented subdivisions between the major beats. Another reason for the differences between the attacks of some beat slices is due to the Sensitivity setting in ReCycle. If I were to reduce the Sensitivity setting, ReCycle would only identify the beats with higher attack levels and ignore the smaller attacks. Conversely, if I were to increase the Sensitivity setting, ReCycle would insert additional slice points where the attack levels are even lower.

Before beat slicing can occur, you have to tell ReCycle how many measures and beats there are in the audio file, and what its time signature is. For example, the loop in the screenshot is exactly two measures long, and it is in 4/4 time. ReCycle uses that information to calculate the tempo of the loop and to set up a 16th note quantize grid within the loop-editing window. As you can see, the lines on the quantize grid (the regularly spaced dotted vertical lines) don't always match the beat slice points (the solid vertical lines). But that's a good thing, because the beat slice information is what's important.

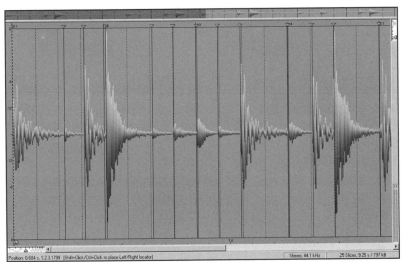

ReCycle beat slices vs. beat division. Notice that the correct beat slices don't always correspond to the fixed quantize point.

You can alter the base tempo in real-time from within ReCycle, as well as the base pitch (there are many other processing features available, but for our purposes, we'll limit ourselves to the discussion of its real-time pitch and tempo alteration tools). You can then save the processed audio file in a variety of formats, but the two we're most interested in here are the native ReCycle file (REX2) and Standard MIDI File (MID) formats.

The ReCycle file format contains all of the information concerning the base tempo, pitch, and beat slices of the audio file as it was saved. This information can be loaded into Cubase, Logic, Digital Performer, and Reason, which all support the ReCycle file format. The first three programs can only use the parameters contained in a ReCycle file to alter tempo in real-time without affecting pitch, whereas Reason also lets users alter pitch in real-time without affecting tempo.

When an audio file is saved as a ReCycle file, users also have the option of saving the timing of the beat slices as notes in a standard MIDI file. The initial reason for doing this was to trigger ReCycle slices that were transferred to an external sampler. While this function is still available in ReCycle, the major reason for saving beat slice information from MIDI files now is to preserve the timing information for Groove Quantizing a MIDI sequence. Unfortunately, only the note timing information is saved; the velocity value for all notes is set at 127. That's too bad, because this means that it's impossible to use both timing and velocity information simultaneously to groove quantize a MIDI part using data extracted from a ReCycle file.

Cubase now includes its own beat slicing capabilities, even though it imports ReCycle files, too. Although the terminology is different ("hitpoints" as opposed to "beat slices"), the functionality (altering tempo without altering pitch) is pretty much the same. In fact, Cubase owners can use the hitpoints to extract timing information and convert it to MIDI note data, just as with ReCycle files. That data can then be used to groove quantize other MIDI tracks, too.

Although ReCycle represents a great advance in the real-time manipulation of audio files, there are a few limitations to using its files. First, whereas Reason users can alter the pitch as well as the tempo of ReCycle files in real-time, Cubase, Logic, and Digital Performer users can alter only the file's tempo in real-time. Also, whereas Reason users can create ReCycle files without using the ReCycle program, Cubase, Logic, and Digital Performer users must use ReCycle in order to convert audio files into the ReCycle format. Cubase SX and SL users can now manipulate audio files in a manner similar to ReCycle, but the information is not saved as a ReCycle format file.

One final note—and the most important one, I think—there is no way to preview ReCycle files on the fly and in context with existing audio in programs that support this type of file, Reason is the sole program that lets users preview ReCycle loops. Moreover, you must copy and paste a ReCycle loop every time you want to extend the length of a track composed of ReCycle files. These limitations can often make it difficult to construct songs quickly using only ReCycle loops.

Acidized Audio Files

A few years ago, Sonic Foundry introduced Acid, a program that overcame many of the limitations of ReCycle files. Like ReCycle, Acid is a beat slicing program. Unlike ReCycle, though, Acid lets users manipulate both pitch and tempo in real-time. Furthermore, users can audition Acid loops in real-time and in context with existing audio tracks; it's also easy to "paint" loops to make tracks or song sections. These capabilities make Acid a complete music production environment for creating songs entirely with audio clips. By contrast, ReCycle is a beat-slicing loop *editor*—you must use a second program to construct a song using its file clips. However, whereas ReCycle is a cross-platform application, Acid is available only to Windows users.

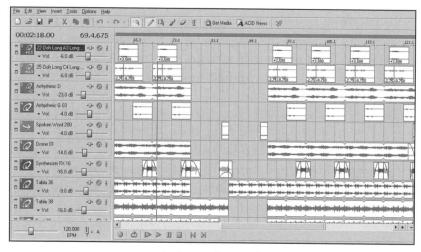

Sonic Foundry's Acid.

Earlier versions of Acid came bundled with a scaled-down version of Sound Forge, Sonic Foundry's well-known stereo audio editing program. This was done so that Acid users could make their own Acidized audio loops from ordinary sound files.

Acid files contain some of the same types of information required for ReCycle files. The Acid software needs the base tempo and number of beats in an audio file in order to manipulate its tempo properly in real-time, and it needs to know the base or root note of the audio file so that it can properly manipulate its pitch in real-time. It also needs to know whether the file should be manipulated by pitch. For instance, you usually won't need to alter the pitches in a percussion track, although you may want to alter the tempo, but you'll probably want to alter both the pitch and tempo of a non-percussion track as needed. The software needs to know whether the audio file in question should be played as a loop or as a one-shot file—this makes a difference in how the file is used by the software.

The most recent release of Acid does not include a version of Sound Forge. However, users no longer need it to Acidize an audio file—Acid itself now includes the editing tools necessary. In fact, you no longer even need Acid to create or use Acidized audio files! A number of programs for both Mac and Windows—Cakewalk's Sonar, Guitar Tracks Pro, Home Studio, and Digital Performer (Mac), to name a few—can work with Acid-format files.

Additionally, looping programs such as Phrazer (Mac) and Ableton Live (cross-platform) not only import Acid files, but they also improve on Acid's functionality. They can both trigger and mute audio loops in real-time using the computer's keyboard or via MIDI note messages. In effect, these programs let you perform a real-time mix of different audio tracks that can change every time you "play." By contrast, Acid users are not able to manipulate track playback in the same manner.

Cubase, Logic, and Sonar are also able to perform beat slicing and include the relevant data in order to manipulate an audio file's tempo and pitch in real-time (Digital Performer can't quite do this, but it does store tempo maps with its audio files so that they can be used in other projects with differing tempos). In short, you no longer need Acid to work with Acidized audio clips, or to create similarly beat-sliced audio files. Even so, it helps to know the advantages and drawbacks of using the various programs and file formats that make it possible to alter tempo and pitch in real-time.

The Pros and Cons of Using Beat-Sliced Files

One of the biggest advantages of using beat-sliced files is that you can quickly create realistic percussion tracks with them. After all, most musicians aren't drummers, nor are they always good at creating rhythm tracks with drum machines or drum editing software. Beat-sliced files give computer-based musicians a way to produce a natural-sounding drum track, or at least extract the timing from one so that the groove can be applied to a MIDI percussion track. Using *loop construction kits*—that is, drum loop file collections consisting of isolated drum sounds—one can create percussion tracks that include basic patterns, variations on those patterns, and drum fills.

Of course, you don't need to limit yourself to using looped percussion tracks to make music with beat-sliced files. Bass lines, synth parts, guitar rhythms, and various instrumental riffs can all be used to create multiple audio tracks. You can manipulate these files in a variety of ways to create unique tracks that bear little relation to their original source material. In fact, you'd be surprised at how creative you can be just by using pre-recorded pieces of audio exclusively. On the other hand, you are ultimately limited to using existing audio loops, so if you need to generate a truly original track, you'll have to create the audio material yourself.

One drawback to using beat-sliced files is that you can sometimes force them to play at a tempo or pitch that is out of their range. For instance, if you were to play a drum loop at 60 BPM whose original tempo was 120 BPM, you may hear glitches between each beat—this is because the file was "stretched" too far. This is why it's a good idea to use loops whose original tempos don't vary too widely from actual tempo of the song that you're creating. Likewise, altering the pitch of a file more than one octave in either direction can sometimes cause playback problems. Similarly, try to use loops that are close to the actual key of the song so that transposing these files won't cause any playback problems.

Another advantage of using beat-sliced files to create audio tracks is that the files use just a small amount of the computer's RAM for playback. For instance, I commonly use about 15 MB of multiple loop files to create audio tracks that would easily consume 400 MB of hard disk space if I were to record them as normal digital audio files. Of course, I eventually have to render those tracks as digital audio data in order to mix down the song to a stereo master file. Until then, though, I can generate a lot of music from a minimal amount of source material. This allows me to save the digital audio tracks for the parts I don't (or can't) loop, such as vocals and instrumental solos.

Naturally, in order to create audio tracks using beat-sliced files, you have to make sure that you have loop files to work with. Fortunately, many programs include a good collection of files to get you started. There is also a wide selection of inexpensive (and even free) loops available in both ReCycle and Acid formats. If they're not already in Acid or ReCycle file formats, they can be easily converted to these types of files.

Most importantly, however, you can make your own loop files out of audio tracks you may have recorded earlier. However, be careful not to use audio loops from copyrighted recordings without getting permission from the copyright holder! Otherwise, the profits you may make from your hit will go towards paying legal fees, punitive damages, and royalties to the copyright holder of the song that you sampled without permission.

As you might guess, creating looped audio tracks from beat-sliced files requires you to keep a fair amount of beat-sliced files on-hand and readily accessible. This means that you're going to need to devote some hard drive space to storing those files. Depending on how much you rely on making music with loop files, you may need to reserve a few gigabytes of hard disk space just for them. In fact, if you plan to rely heavily on creating songs from loops, you may want to consider devoting a separate hard drive just to these types of files. Personally speaking, I use a 40 GB external FireWire drive just for this purpose.

Likewise, keeping a large amount of loop files on-hand requires that they be organized in a way that makes accessing the desired type of file easy. Some organizational categories are pretty easy to create. For example, you can organize loop files by their origin, which works well if you primarily use commercial loop packages. Another way to organize loop files is by type of content—for instance, you can put all of the drum loops in one folder, all of the bass lines in another folder, all of the guitar rhythms in a third folder, and so on. You can even make subfolders for acoustic drum loops; drum machine loops; acoustic bass, electric bass, and synth bass loops; clean and processed guitar rhythm loops; etc. The point is that you should organize your loops so that they can be easily accessed.

CHAPTER 11
EDITING DIGITAL AUDIO TRACKS

Once you've recorded your audio tracks, the next step is to edit them. Most editing tasks are pretty simple and can be performed using the audio editing capabilities of your digital audio sequencer. However, other audio editing tasks may require that you use a separate, more full-featured audio editing program, and perhaps some specialized audio plug-ins as well. A good stereo audio editing program, such as Sonic Foundry's Sound Forge or Steinberg WaveLab (both for Windows) and BIAS's Peak (Mac), are well suited to performing some of the more specialized editing tasks you may need to do. With these applications, you can transfer an audio track from your digital audio sequencer, edit it from within a separate editing program, and then send the edited track back to your sequencer. In fact, most digital audio sequencers have a special link function that allows users to open external audio editing programs from within the digital audio sequencer itself.

Alternatively, a good multitrack audio editing program, such as Magix Samplitude or Adobe Audition (Windows), or BIAS Deck (Mac), will allow you to import *all* of the audio tracks from your digital audio sequencer so that you can use these programs' more extensive native editing capabilities and effects processors. These programs also provide all of the plug-in support plus the mixing and mastering capabilities of digital audio sequencers and then some. In fact, I usually create MIDI and audio tracks in a digital audio sequencer and then export the rendered and recorded audio tracks to a separate multitrack audio editing program for additional processing and mixing. No matter which method you use, though, a good stereo or multitrack audio editing program is a valuable audio production tool. But even if you have only a digital audio sequencer, you can still do most—if not all—of your audio work within it.

Preparing Tracks for Audio Editing

Before you edit your digital audio tracks, there are a few crucial tasks you'll need to perform to prepare them for editing. This preparation work is important because it will determine how easily and accurately you can perform other audio editing tasks and effects processing later. Fortunately, this preparatory work is usually simple and doesn't take long to do. However, I must stress that it is essential that this work be done—after all, it's the foundation upon which you will further edit, mix, and master your digital audio recordings.

Removing the DC Offset

The first step in preparing an audio track for editing is to remove its *DC offset*, which occurs when an audio interface adds direct current (DC) to a recording. The addition of this direct current results in a recorded waveform that is not centered around the baseline, which is sometimes called the *zero-crossing line*. The following screenshot shows a digital audio file (stereo) that has DC offset in its first half, but then none in its second (that dark horizontal line in roughly the middle of each waveform is the baseline). I deliberately created the DC offset in this example so that you could see the difference between perfectly phased and offset audio.

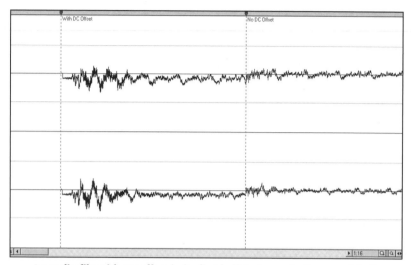

An audio file with DC offset in its first half, but none in its second half

A digital audio file that contains DC offset is not *in phase*; i.e., it doesn't match the compression and rarefaction cycle of what the audio signal should be. This can lead to glitches and other unexpected (and unwanted!) results when effects are applied to these files. Additionally, digital audio files with DC offset are more difficult to edit because there may not be a zero-crossing point available when you need to trim or loop a file (more on this towards the end of this chapter).

If you have a professional-quality audio interface, you shouldn't have any concerns about the possibility of DC offset being introduced into your digital audio recordings. On the other hand, if you have a more consumer-oriented audio interface, chances will be greater that your audio recordings will contain some amount of DC offset. Nevertheless, it doesn't hurt to check to see whether your digital audio tracks contain DC offset, regardless of the quality of your interface. Some audio editors will first scan an audio file, tell you if it contains DC offset, and then tell you the degree to which it is present, whereas others will automatically both scan and process a file to remove offset. In any event, the process of removing DC offset from audio files doesn't take long, and it won't hurt your audio files even if there is no offset present. Check the manual that came with your software for more information.

Noise Reduction

Once you have ensured that your audio files contain no DC offset, the next step is to apply noise reduction to the tracks that need it. The tracks most often in need of noise reduction are those recorded with a microphone, because chances are that you recorded a vocal or acoustic instrument part in the same room as your computer. Even if you took precautions to minimize the possibility of picking up computer and room noise with your microphones, there still may be some computer fan or room noise present in the audio track. Fortunately, eliminating that background noise—or to be more precise, *reducing* it—isn't that difficult if you have the right noise reduction tool. However, to use the right type of tool, you have to know what kind of noise you're dealing with. As you will soon see, there are different types of noise, and each of them must be treated with one or more specific noise reduction tools.

Hiss and Broadband Noise

The two most common types of noise you will encounter as a result of recording your own material are *hiss* and *broadband noise*.

Hiss sounds much like *white noise*, which is the random distribution of all audio frequencies at equal energy. The most common sources of hiss from a recording artist's point of view are from analog tape (as when you transfer audio material from analog tape into a computer-based music production system) and amplifiers with improper *gain staging* (when volume levels aren't properly set from one stage of amplification to the next).

Here's one example of how improper gain staging may occur. During the recording process, the mic *trim* (volume adjustment control) on a mic preamp may be set too low. To compensate for the low signal, the recordist might raise the volume level of the mixer. However, if the mixer channel level is set too high, there is a possibility that hiss from the self-noise of the mixer could be introduced into the signal. Rather than raise the mixer channel level to an extreme setting, it would be better to adjust the mic trim a little higher so that both it and the mixer channel are set to appropriate levels.

Broadband noise, which is related to hiss, comes from sources such as tapes with high noise floors (i.e., cheap cassettes recorded on cheap cassette decks) and HVACs (heating, ventilation, and air conditioning units). HVACs are a particular nuisance due to the noise forced air makes as it comes out of air ducts, plus the operating noise of the HVAC unit itself, which is also conducted through the air ducts. Of equal concern to computer-based music makers is the fan noise generated from the operation of a computer itself. As I mentioned earlier, this noise is difficult if not impossible to avoid when recording in the same room as a computer.

Compared to hiss, broadband noise has more of a roaring sound, and it is usually louder—or at least it often *seems* so. In simplified terms, broadband noise is more like *pink noise*, which is a random distribution of frequencies, but the lower audio frequencies possess more energy than the upper frequencies. This is what gives broadband noise a more roaring sound, like a waterfall.

Hiss can usually be treated with a single-ended processor, like a dehissing program or a plug-in effect (follow the directions included with the software of your choosing). Broadband noise, by contrast, can be treated with a noise reduction plug-in or program that requires a *noise print* to treat the noise. A noise print is just what its name implies: a small sample of the noise that is present in the original recording. Noise reduction applications use these prints as references so that they can distinguish and separate the noise from the desired audio signal. There are also single-ended noise reduction programs that don't use noise prints for removing broadband noise, such as Arboretum Ray Gun and BIAS SoundSoap. By and large, however, most noise reduction applications employ noise prints.

To successfully remove noise using noise prints, make sure that you have recorded some lead-in time and lead-out time on your digital audio tracks. These are the most likely spots for you to get prints of sufficient duration (about one second) for the software to identify the nature of the noise. Other likely spots are sections within the track where there is no audio signal present except for the noise itself. However, don't get a noise print from the *very* beginning of any recorded audio material, especially if the source material has been transferred from tape. Often there is a slight "bump" present at the beginning of an audio signal, and it differs from the rest of the noise that is present. Naturally, you'll want to be sure that you get a noise print that is consistent with what occurs throughout the audio track.

Also, don't make a noise print from the actual audio you recorded (i.e., the audio you *intended* to record), even if there is audible noise mingled in with it. A noise print created from this material will also remove or reduce in volume the audio you want to clean up. Of course, if you want to see what sort of strange effect you can get from working with a noise print from your material, go ahead and try it. Sometimes doing the "wrong" thing can make for some interesting results.

If the noise levels in your tracks are high, you'll find that it's often better to reduce noise in small amounts in multiple passes rather than attempt to remove all of it in one go. That's because attempting to remove a high level of noise or eliminating it altogether in one pass may introduce unwanted phasing effects into the "cleaned-up" audio. On the other hand, removing noise in small increments (–6 dB at a time) can give you more control over the noise reduction process and allow for fewer phasing effects. By the way, don't forget to take a new noise print after every pass! You must always make sure that the print accurately reflects the level of noise present in the *latest* version of the audio file.

As always, be sure to follow the instructions set forth by your software's manufacturer. You should be pretty happy with the results.

Buzz

Another common type of noise that recording artists face is *buzz*, better known to North American musicians as *60-cycle hum* (that's *50-cycle hum* to European musicians). Buzz comes from electrical sources that aren't properly grounded or suffer from RF interference. For instance, electric guitars and basses with single-coil pick-ups often generate buzz. Poorly shielded audio cables can also be a source of buzz, and when combined with instruments with single-coil pick-ups and/or poorly grounded audio devices, you have a recipe for a noise-making nightmare.

Fortunately, most noise reduction applications include a special function for removing buzz. As in the case of broadband noise reduction, you may have to take a noise print of the buzz present in the digital audio track—just follow the same procedure for taking a noise print. Make sure that you set the noise reduction process for removing buzz rather than broadband noise, and note that you may have to reduce your buzz in small amounts in multiple passes.

Clicks and Crackles

If you record tracks or audio loops using vinyl records as your source material, you will probably have two other types of noise to deal with: *clicks* and *crackles*. *Clicks* or *pops* are the result of serious vinyl surface degradation or scratches. *Crackles* are also the result of vinyl surface degradation—their amplitudes are much lower than clicks, but they occur more frequently.

Removing clicks or pops using noise reduction software is pretty much automatic—just set the noise reduction application to remove clicks, and that will usually take care of the problem. However, sometimes the noise reduction software has difficulty identifying every pop or click. If that happens, you may want to reverse the track (all audio editing applications have this feature) and "declick" the track again—sometimes noise reduction software can more easily detect clicks and pops when the audio is reversed. Don't forget to reverse the track again afterwards so that it plays back properly!

Removing crackles from a recording is also an automatic process. You may have to make a noise print of the crackles as well, but if you adhere to the rules of creating prints, you shouldn't have any problems.

By the way, it's *very important* that you perform noise reduction one step at a time and in the following order: declick, decrackle, debuzz, and dehiss. The reasons for this are a bit complicated, but suffice it to say that this order of things will always get you the best results. Naturally, perform only those steps that are necessary. For instance, if a track just contains broadband noise, don't declick, decrackle, or debuzz.

One final note regarding noise removal and reduction: If you have an audio track with low signal levels, avoid increasing its amplitude or normalizing it, especially if comparatively high levels of noise are also present (we'll get into normalizing momentarily). All you'll do is just make the noise louder, which means you will have to use more passes to reduce it. It's better if you first remove as much of the noise as you can and *then* increase the track's amplitude or normalize it. If it's necessary, you can apply noise reduction again after increasing the amplitude, but do so in small increments to prevent phasing from being introduced into the audio material.

Normalizing Audio Tracks

After removing the DC offset and any noise from your digital audio tracks, you may want to perform some form of *normalization* on the tracks. However, there is a right way and a wrong way to normalize tracks. Before we get into how to perform normalization on audio tracks, you must first understand what normalization does and, more importantly, doesn't do.

Normalization is probably the most commonly used digital audio processing tool, but it's also probably the least understood. Beginners and even experienced computer-based musicians believe that normalization ensures that the loudest part of an audio file plays at its maximum level without clipping. However, normalization often has little to do with loudness. Granted, there are some types of normalization that do affect loudness, but you have to be careful as to when and how you apply those forms. Furthermore, there are occasions when you will want to use normalization to *lower* an audio file's maximum amplitude, not raise it.

Normalization is not a simple tool that makes digital audio sound as loud as it can be, and nor does it automatically correct any digital audio that was recorded at too low a level. Like any tool, normalization is better suited for some tasks than others. The trick is to understand when normalization is the right tool for the job. Even then, you need to be aware of the advantages and drawbacks of using normalization in particular circumstances.

Amplitude and Loudness

In order to best comprehend normalization, you should first make sure that you understand two essential concepts and the difference between them: *amplitude* and *loudness*.

What you really see when viewing a digital audio program's waveform display is a collection of individual samples, i.e., representations of sound pressure level at each sampled instance. However, the human ear doesn't follow each change in amplitude (i.e., the peak level of a wave at a sample point as it occurs). Instead, you hear *overall* changes in amplitude that you perceive as *loudness*, which for humans is a subjective experience regarding volume (there are ways to objectively measure perceived loudness, but for now, let's treat loudness as subjective).

To understand the experience of loudness, imagine that you're recording a live stereo performance. The mics have been set up properly, and all of the faders have been set to their ideal levels. You don't have to do anything except hit the Record button and let the musicians perform a perfect take. During the recording session, you notice that the meters consistently peak at –3 dBFS during the recording. As insurance, you record another perfect take. For most of the performance, the meters again peak at –3 dBFS. However, at one point the meters briefly peak at 0 dBFS before dropping back again to the –3 dBFS level. Will people hear that 3 dB difference as a noticeable jump in volume? Does that mean that take two is louder because of this? And is take two more "perfect" because of this difference? The answer to all of these questions is "no," because, again, the ear generally responds to changes in *average* levels of loudness, not peak levels of amplitude. Subjectively, both takes will sound about the same, and both would be considered "perfect" despite the objectively measured differences.

Peak Normalization

Why is it important to understand the difference between amplitude and loudness? To begin with, most digital audio programs feature only *peak normalization*, a process that first looks for the sample with the highest peak amplitude in an audio file and then adjusts it so that its peak is referenced to 0 dBFS. The rest of the audio material is then scaled to this new reference level accordingly. For instance, if the highest sampled peak occurs at 3 dB before normalizing, and the rest of the audio peaks are at –6 dB, the entire file's amplitude will be increased by 3 dB. This brings up the highest peak to 0 dB and the remaining audio to –3 dB.

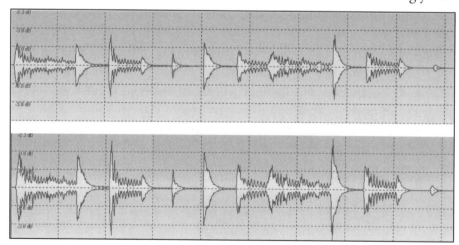

Audio file before (top) and after (bottom) peak normalization

However, it takes only one instance of a sample level of 0 dBFS for an audio file to be considered peak normalized. Also, if there are brief instances wherein the highest peak is close to 0 dB but the majority of the digital audio data is well below that, peak normalization will probably have little effect on the audio's perceived loudness. For example, if the peak is at –1.5 dB and the rest of the material is at –10 dB before normalization, the maximum increase for the entire audio material would be only 1.5 dB. As expected, the other digital audio data would increase to –8.5 dB. You wouldn't hear much of a difference in loudness because the average levels didn't change much. Moreover, you wouldn't see much of a difference in the waveform's display, either. This explains why normalization works well in some cases and seems to have little or no effect in others.

By the same token, peak normalization works well when there is relative consistency in an audio file's amplitude levels. For example, peak normalizing individual tracks in a multitrack digital audio program often increases both the peak level and perceived loudness of each track. That's because most individual tracks don't have wildly fluctuating audio levels that can affect the peak normalization process. Likewise, stereo master tracks with consistent amplitude levels often reap the same benefits from peak normalization as individual tracks.

RMS Normalization

There is a second type of normalization: *RMS normalization*. This form of uses the root mean square (hence, RMS) levels to detect the average level (i.e., loudness) of sound over time, which is more in keeping with the way humans hear sound anyway. Basically, RMS levels are obtained by calculating the sum of the squares of a waveform's positive and negative values to accurately express its average loudness level mathematically. RMS normalization boosts a file's audio signal so that it has the same apparent loudness as a 0 dBFS sine or square wave. Just for the record, by the way, root mean square has nothing to do with the overall shape of the wave.

Normalizing a file to 0 dBFS using RMS levels is going to leave you with an incredibly loud sound file. You might conclude from this that RMS normalization seems like the perfect tool for making your mixes as loud as they can possibly be. Well, I can guarantee you that tracks RMS normalized to 0 dB will indeed be loud. However, that doesn't mean that they will sound good—in fact, I can assure you that they will usually sound bad!

Here's why. As I mentioned earlier, our ears respond to changes in average levels—not peak levels—when judging loudness. To complicate matters further, the ear doesn't hear all frequencies with equal loudness. Fletcher and Munson first investigated this phenomenon, and later Robinson and Dadson developed what are called the *equal loudness contours*, also known as the *Fletcher-Munson curves*. Essentially, the Fletcher-Munson curves show that very low and high frequency material is less audible than mid-range audio. To put it another way, it takes more energy for low and high frequency sounds to be perceived as loud as mid-range sounds.

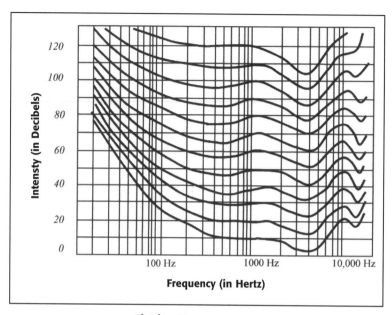

Fletcher-Munson curves

The equal loudness contours flatten out as the decibel level increases. Low and high frequencies become almost as equally loud at the same sound pressure level as mid-frequency content. However, it takes high decibel levels for that to happen. Even if you are willing to make a sound file as loud as it can be, that perfect balance achieved by mixing and equalizing individual tracks to a stereo track prior to normalization will be lost once you perform RMS normalization at 0 dB—the audio file will likely sound distorted.

Even so, audio material with wide fluctuations in peak levels can benefit from RMS normalization. Speech files are a perfect example of this. The peak levels created by consonants (especially plosives and sibilants) are much higher than those created by vowels. Also, because consonants are of brief durations, their energy levels seem even louder than the peaks or average loudness would indicate. Peak normalization to raise overall loudness, then, is out of the question. By contrast, RMS normalization, set at no higher than –10 dB RMS, will often tame speech files quite well. In fact, I usually set the RMS processing level to –12 dB or –14 dB, depending on a variety of factors such as the type of narrated material, whether the speaker is male or female, etc.

Sometimes, though, it's best not to process audio files with wide variations in peak levels using RMS normalization. Even when tracks have wide variances in peak levels, it may be best to leave them as-is because of the type of material they contain.

When to Use Normalization

As mentioned earlier, peak normalization works well when there is relative consistency in an audio file's amplitude levels. Peak normalizing individual tracks in a multitrack recording will often increase both peak levels and overall loudness. The same holds true for stereo master tracks with consistent amplitude levels. However, to maintain consistency without sacrificing dynamics, you may want to employ some gentle compression during the recording phase. Similarly, you can process the audio file with gentle compression or peak limiting afterwards, but before peak normalization (we'll discuss compression and limiting in more detail in "Chapter 13: Advanced Mixing Techniques—EQ and Effects").

Sometimes you need to use normalization to increase the volume level of a track that was recorded at a relatively low level. Most programs will warn you that the normalized material won't have the same quality as if its recording level had been maximized to begin with. For example, it's often said that if the volume level is set to 50% of the possible range, the audio material will be essentially at 15-bit quality in a 16-bit linear recording. Normalizing the material to 100% won't magically change it into 16-bit audio.

However, don't let that bit of information make you paranoid about having audio tracks that weren't recorded at their maximum levels. First of all, stop and think about what a "15-bit" recording really means. A 15-bit recording will have a maximum level of 90 dB, and that's still not shabby. Second, the recorded audio file is still a 16-bit file because the digital audio data was stored in a 16-bit file format! The file size, bit resolution, and sample rate won't fluctuate because of differences in volume levels. Besides, as I mentioned before, you don't necessarily want to record audio tracks at 0 dBFS for a variety of reasons. In fact, it's not a good idea to even *try* to do that. So go ahead and raise audio levels when you have to do so—but do try to record at proper levels first!

On the other hand, there are times when you won't want to normalize an audio file to its maximum peak level. For instance, if you are going to perform further physical processing on an audio file (noise reduction, equalization, compression, filter effects, or reverb) you may actually want to *lower* peak levels to –6 to –3 dBFS. Conversely, if you have to increase peak levels, you won't want to increase them to 0 dB, but rather to –6 to –3 dBFS—this should be enough to avoid clipping during post processing. When I normalize individual audio tracks, I usually peak normalize them to –6 dBFS to –12 dBFS, depending on the number of tracks I have to work with. If I'm handling eight to 12 tracks, I peak normalize them to –6 dB. If there are more than 12 tracks, I usually peak normalize them to 12 dB. The reason for this will become clearer when we discuss mixing and mastering audio tracks a little later on.

Trimming Digital Audio Tracks

If you've recorded some or all of your audio tracks linearly—to recap, from the beginning to the end of your song in an uninterrupted take—you will probably need to trim the silent portions of those tracks. After all, it's likely that at least some of them contain significant sections of silence. Also, these sections of silence, while producing no apparent sound, still generate digital audio data. For example, even if audio levels in sections of a digital audio file are –96 dBFS in a 16-bit system, it still takes 16 bits of data to record that silence. As far as data storage is concerned, recorded silence is the same as audio recorded at 0 dBFS!

So why am I making such a big deal about this? First, it takes a lot of work for your computer and hard drive to stream multiple tracks of digital audio data. Second, recorded silence in digital audio tracks are streamed from the hard drive in the same way as digital audio tracks that contain sound. So why make your computer work harder than it has to by forcing it to stream portions of audio tracks that contain no actual audio? Trim the silence from the tracks and save on system resources that you can use for other types of audio processing! As an additional benefit, you'll also eliminate unnecessary noise from your digital audio recordings. After all, most sections of tracks that contain "silence" may in fact have extremely low levels of background noise that should be eliminated anyway—especially since accumulated noise from several tracks played simultaneously can result in quite a bit of unwanted sound.

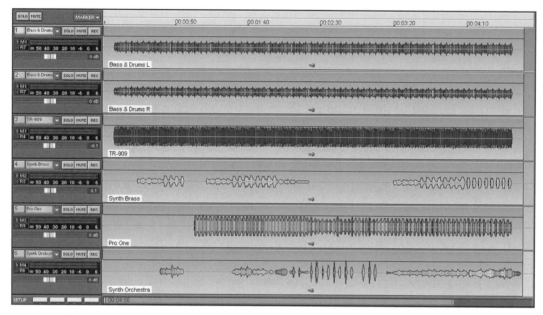

Some linearly recorded digital audio tracks can contain large sections of silence, as shown here.

Digital Audio Data vs. Pointer Information

Before delving into the right way to trim digital audio tracks, let's first go over an important concept in computer-based digital audio production: the difference between *digital audio data* and *pointer information*. Whenever digital audio is recorded—be it in a digital audio sequencer, a stereo audio editing program, or a multitrack audio production application—two types of files are generated. The first type of file is the digital audio data itself, which is usually stored in WAV (Windows) or AIFF (Mac) format. Digital audio data files are often huge, and their size depends on the length of the recorded track, whether it is a mono or stereo file, and the sample rate and resolution of the recording.

The second type of file that is produced from a digital audio recording is a pointer information file. This type of file is much smaller than its associated digital audio data file, and each audio editing application creates a pointer information file in the program's native format. For instance, Cubase saves pointer information as OVW (Overview) files, whereas Sonar saves pointer information as WOV (Wave Overview) files. Simply put, pointer information contains a graphic overview of the data in the larger digital audio file. This graphic overview "points to" and helps the user manipulate the actual digital audio data without physically accessing or altering it.

The advantages of pointer information files are twofold. First, manipulating pointer information allows a program to work much more rapidly than if it were representing any changes in appearance of the actual digital audio data. When I first started working with computer-based digital audio some years ago, many audio editing programs didn't generate pointer information files. If I wanted to resize the audio display, these programs would have to re-read and recalculate the image of the entire audio file first, and then resize it according to the level of detail I indicated. Considering the sizes of many 16-bit stereo audio files, and that computer systems were much slower then than they are now, each change in resizing the audio display meant a minimum five-minute wait! With pointer information file data, any change made in the audio display is nearly instantaneous because the program reads just the pointer information—it doesn't try to read or calculate the digital audio data directly.

Second, manipulating pointer information lets users *non-destructively* edit audio data. For instance, if you were to cut out a section of music via the pointer information, this is what would actually happen: The deleted section of music would no longer be visible onscreen in the digital audio program, but it would not be removed from either the pointer information file or the digital audio file. This means that you could re-insert that deleted section of music back into the audio track if you decided later that you really needed to keep it. After all, you didn't erase the digital audio data itself: You just "masked over" the section of pointer information indicating that the program should play that digital audio data.

You can restore masked over information to a digital audio display by *slip editing*. It's a feature of digital audio programs that allows users to restore "deleted" material by pulling on the edge of an audio file clip and extending it to the point where the deleted material becomes visible again (check with your software manual for specific instructions). By the same token, if you want to remove even more digital audio data from a program's audio track display, you can simply "slip" the edge of the audio clip to a point where the unwanted audio disappears from view on the track. Just as pointer information allows you to manipulate digital audio data without altering it, slip editing allows you to manipulate pointer information without permanently changing it.

Slip Editing

To demonstrate how you can trim audio tracks to remove sections of silence, let's take a simple six-track song and edit it. If you'll look at the individual audio tracks in the screenshot on the previous page, you'll see that the first three tracks have a small amount of silence at the beginning and end of the song. Tracks 4, 5, and 6 (the bottom three) have even larger sections of silence at the beginning. I've already removed the DC offset and noise from each of the tracks, and I've left the audio levels for each track as they are. All I have to do now is trim the silence from the tracks.

To do this, I'd first highlight the first three audio tracks to trim the silence from the beginning of those tracks. If you look at this next screenshot, you'll see that I've also zoomed in on the waveform displays so that I can view them in greater detail. Also, notice the little squares next to the track names on the waveform displays. In this particular program (Samplitude), you can perform slip editing on tracks by click-and-holding on this square and dragging it—click and drag this square to the right to trim silence from the beginning of the track, and click and drag the square at the end of the track to the left to trim silence from the end. If you drag a square on just one of the tracks, all of the highlighted tracks will be trimmed simultaneously. This process is similar in other editing software.

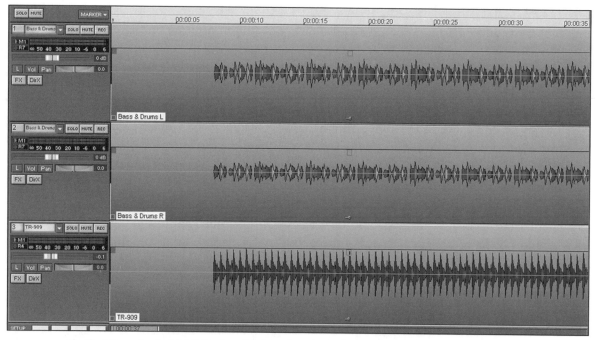

The first three tracks highlighted and enlarged to show the waveform display in greater detail

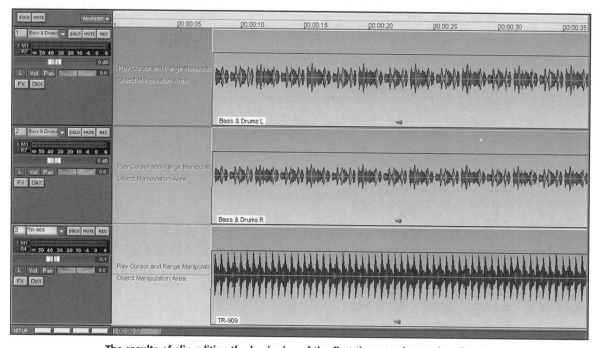

The results of slip editing the beginning of the first three tracks to trim silence

Now, the start and end of each track are bereft of any opening or closing silence. However, in the next screenshot you can see that there are now other problems: It's very obvious that there is a significant amount of "space" (which translates to silence here) before the starts of the tracks themselves, and some tracks have more space than others. Now, you don't want to have to wait through that silence until the audio plays, but you also want to make sure that the audio tracks maintain their relative positions after the elimination of that gap.

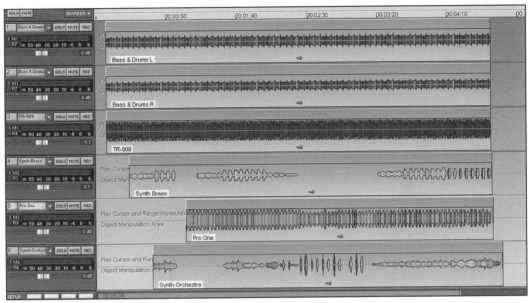

The slip-edited tracks show significant periods of silence that vary from track to track.

Fortunately, it's easy to eliminate unnecessary periods of silence *and* maintain the relative position of each audio track at the same time. In most programs, all you have to do is highlight all of the tracks and then move them all to the left until they're at the very start (or edge) of the audio track window.

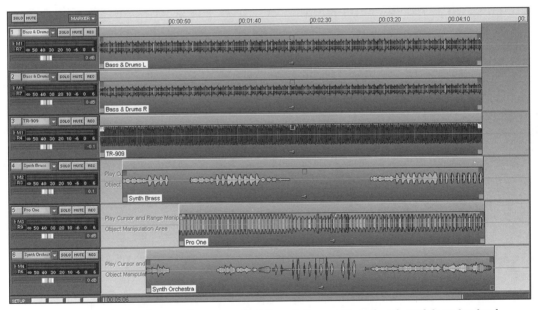

Moving all tracks simultaneously ensures that the relative position of each track is maintained.

Splitting Track Clips

Slip editing works well for removing sections of silence at the beginnings and ends of audio tracks. However, removing silence from the *middle* of a track requires a slightly different approach.

The first thing you need to do is to move the audio editing program's cursor line to the point where the section of silence in a track begins. Now, highlight the track and use the appropriate command to "split" or "cut" or "slice" the track at that point. In most Windows audio editing applications, you simply click and hold down the right mouse button to see and select the proper command. Because Macs don't use two-button mice, you must either access the correct command right from a program menu or hold down the correct keyboard key (Shift, Control, Option, or Command) while using the

mouse in order to do this. In addition, audio editing programs for both Macs and Windows computers usually have keystroke command alternatives for carrying out a program function. Do whatever your software manual tells you to via whatever method works best for you.

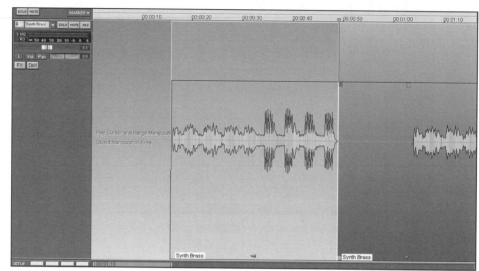

An audio track after splitting

Once you have split a track, you have two options. First, you can drag the edge of the audio clip to the right of the split to hide the silent portion of the track—in other words, slip edit the audio clip. Second, you can move the cursor to the end of the section of silence and perform another split so that you will have three clips: the part before the silence (left), the silent portion (middle), and the part after the silence (right). You can then highlight the silent portion (the middle clip) and delete it. Note that the silence hasn't vanished for good—just drag the edge of the beginning clip to the right (or the edge of the after-silence clip to the left) and the silent section will reappear. All you've done by removing that silence is to tell the program not to play any of the audio data that this silent clip points to in the digital audio file. If you need to play that data again for any reason, you can easily get it back.

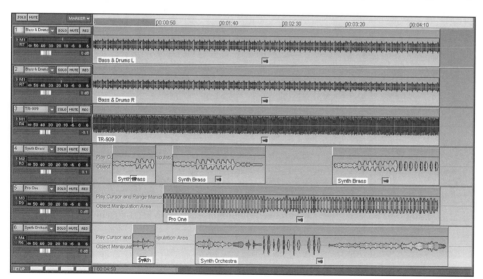

The final result of removing silence by slip editing, splitting, and deleting clips from linear audio tracks

While splitting and deleting silent portions of audio clips can be useful, be careful not to overdo it. Removing smaller blocks of silence, for instance, isn't generally a good idea. For one thing, the time interval of the silent sections may be too small to make it worthwhile to remove them. More importantly, forcing a program to access a hard drive for brief periods of time may actually make the computer work *harder* than it would have if the sections of silence had been allowed to remain in the track. The lesson here is to be attentive to detail, but not obsessive to the point of *causing* what you mean to *avoid*.

Creating Comp Takes

The processes of slip editing and splitting tracks can also be used to create *comp takes*, which is short for "compiled takes" (comp takes can also be thought of as *composite takes*, because you make a composite track from portions of separate takes). In theory, creating a comp take is a pretty simple process—you use only the best portions of all of the takes for a particular part, and then eliminate the unused parts from the audio tracks. However, the process requires some skill on the part of the editor.

Let's say that you have four takes of a vocal track, each of which contains mistakes at different points. Naturally, each take exists on its own separate track, so how do you make a perfect comp take from these four imperfect tracks? Well, the first thing to do is to make sure that all four vocal takes reside on tracks adjacent to each other. If they don't, move them so they do. This will make it easier to splice the individual takes into one composite.

Next, listen to each take separately. Don't forget to mute the other takes or you'll hear them as well. As you're listening to a take, note where the mistakes occur. The easiest way to do this is to drop markers to indicate the approximate location of each mistake (consult your software manual as to how to do this—the process varies from program to program). After you've listened to an entire take, go back to the points where the mistakes occurred, using the markers as guides. Insert a split point into the track just before each mistake—however, don't try to slip edit or delete the portions of the tracks where the mistakes occurred just yet. Remove the markers after going through each take so that you don't get confused.

Now you can begin the process of compiling a take, and note that you should use as few tracks as possible. If you've recorded four takes, for example, use the first two but mute the second two, which can act as reserves if errors exist at the same spot in both of the first two tracks. Use the split points in these first two tracks as markers for slip editing or deleting the unwanted portions of each.

No matter whether you slip edit or delete audio clips, remember that the best way to remove mistakes is to delete naturally occurring sections of material. It's easier and often preferable to remove one note or word in a phrase—after all, these portions will probably have small sections of silence between them, which can make for a smoother edit. Granted, there may be times when you must edit very small portions of audio material, but as a rule, try to avoid doing this. If you must resort to this, however, make certain that you take advantage of the program's ability to find *zero-crossing points* in an audio file—locations in a wave file where the audio crosses the line between the positive and negative cycles of the waveform. To avoid hearing pops and clicks when editing audio files, the start and end of each individual audio clip should occur at a zero-crossing point.

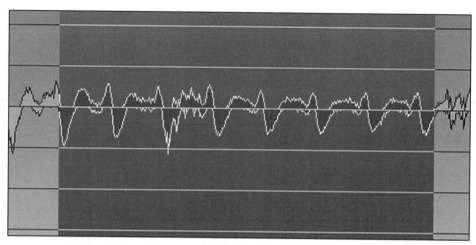

Detail of highlighted audio whose boundaries are at zero-crossing points in the waveform display

Working with multiple takes to create a comp take is useful for more than just creating a perfect track from a series of imperfect tracks. Comp takes can also be used to mix and match different perform-ances to create a unique performance. A perfect example of this is the triple–guitar swapping solo in "The End" on the Beatles' *Abbey Road* recording. George, John, and Paul each performed guitar solos on separate tracks, with each one using different guitars and effects. Then they and their producer switched among different two-bar phrases on those three tracks to create a single solo guitar track. The result was a guitar solo that wouldn't have been so easy to create if a single performer were forced to play it in one pass.

CHAPTER 12
BASIC MIXING TECHNIQUES

After you've recorded your audio tracks and have performed the necessary preparatory digital audio processing as detailed in the previous chapter, the next step is to mix down your audio tracks to a stereo audio file. Inasmuch as this is a beginner's book, we won't discuss mixing for surround sound. Besides, most of you will initially create music that will be burned to a stereo CD.

Part of the discussion on mixing down in "Chapter 9: Creating Digital Audio Tracks" involved the principles of automating MIDI tracks. Fortunately, the same techniques apply for automating audio tracks, but now we'll go into more detail about setting pan positions and volume levels for each audio track. To do that, you'll need to acquire a proper understanding of the stereo field and how to work with it in order to create great mixes.

The Stereo Field

One fact regarding the stereo field is obvious: stereophonic audio requires two speakers in order to be reproduced properly. They may be two "conventional" speakers connected to a home stereo system, a pair of self-powered near-field monitors, or a pair of headphones inserted into the headphone jack of an outboard mixer. The important thing, though, is that there are two audio speakers of some type to which music is output.

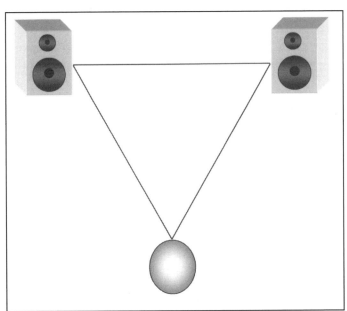

Speakers or monitors should be arranged so that they are at two points of an equilateral triangle, with the listener at the third.

When discussing the stereo field, another fact is also obvious: One speaker is placed to the *left* of the listener, while another speaker should be placed to the *right*. Ideally, the listener and the two speakers should be positioned so that they sit at the three points of an equilateral triangle. In other words, the listener should be sitting at the same distance from each speaker, and the speakers should be set at the same distance from each other as well.

This triangular arrangement describes the first dimension of the stereo field. At its most basic level, the stereo field is a horizontal line, with the left speaker at one end of the line, and the right speaker at the other. Using the pan control knob on your physical or virtual mixer, you can place a sound all the way to the left, all the way to the right, or at any point in between on that line.

In addition to the hard left and hard right pan positions, there is also another important point on the pan line—the center position or *sweet spot*. The reason why this is called the sweet spot is that through it the listener hears an exact reproduction of the mix when the speaker-listener arrangement is properly set up as described. In fact, sounds that are panned dead center (usually the lead vocal) will sound as if they are emanating from a phantom "third speaker" directly in front of the listener. The effect is so startling that you almost look straight ahead for the source of the sound.

In addition to the horizontal dimension of the stereo field, a listener can also experience a blend of different audio frequencies. This range or spectrum of audio frequencies can be visualized on a vertical axis. There's no need to know the frequency measurements stated in Hz or kHz to which these correspond in order to communicate the fact that you want to boost or *cut* (decrease in volume) certain ranges of frequencies. However, it does help to know the measured values of frequency ranges so that one can use EQ properly when mixing or mastering a song. This process of boosting or cutting certain frequencies is known as *equalization,* or EQ for short.

Just as you can set pan positions along a horizontal axis, you can set the relative strengths of frequency levels along a vertical axis of volume. Because different instruments have different frequency ranges, the easiest way to control the strength of their different frequencies is to adjust the individual volume level of each recorded instrument or vocal track. However, sometimes you need to fine-tune the volume of certain frequency ranges. For this, you need to use the equalizer controls of your audio mixer. This is an artform unto itself, and will be discussed in more detail later. For now, be aware that controlling frequency levels is accomplished using both volume and EQ controls.

Finally, there is a third "implied" dimension of the stereo field—*depth*. The reason I say that this dimension is implied is that you really can't create a true three-dimensional listening experience from just a pair of stereo speakers. You have to add the *illusion* of depth to the stereo field, and the way in which this is generally done is by adding reverb effects to any or all audio tracks in a project. As you will see later, you can use reverb to shape the size of the "room" in which the music is being played. Depending on how sophisticated your reverb processor is, you can also control the room's reflective properties for even finer control of the room's sound.

In a sense, you create a "sound painting" when you mix down individual tracks to a stereo master. You place instruments at specific spots on a "canvas," and give the painting balance by blending and contrasting the relative frequencies of each instrument. Finally, you add the perspective of depth with reverb. Small amounts of reverb imply less depth, while larger

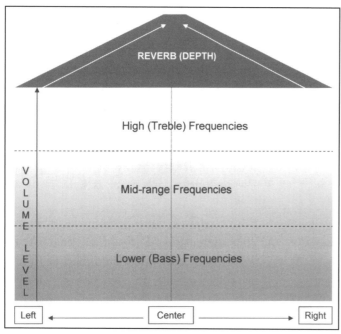

The stereo field can be visualized as a work of art in which the elements are balanced to create a "sound painting."

amounts of reverb imply an aura of spaciousness. In fact, I use this painting analogy to visualize a mix even before I begin the process of mixing down.

Some of you may feel that my description of an audio mix as a sound painting seems a little . . . well, pretentious. However, the concept of a mix as a sound painting is not a totally alien concept. For example, Voyager Sound produces mixing software (GraphiMix) that uses the notion of visually locating pan position and volume level in a stereo field. In fact, the concept of placing sound in a stereo landscape is implicit in the term *panpot*, the name for the knob that controls the pan position of an audio channel—it's short for *panoramic potentiometer*. In essence, the pan control is responsible for determining the location of an audio track in the overall sound picture. Once you start thinking of a mix as a sound picture, the easier it will be to create balanced mixes.

A Short Mixing Primer: Drums, Bass, Guitars, and Vocals

To better understand some basics of mixing, let's mix down a theoretical pop song arrangement of drums, bass, two guitars, and a lead vocal onto a stereo track. Although this may look like a pretty simple arrangement, there is a surprising amount of detail to consider when mixing down even just these five parts. As you read what follows, remember that this is an example of just one way in which these tracks can be mixed—even so, you should find this sample useful to you when you begin to record and mix down tracks of your own.

Drums

The way you mix drums depends partly on how they were recorded in the first place. For example, in a typical recording setup, each drum in the kit is miked individually. The hi-hat is also miked separately, but the crash and ride cymbals are often recorded with a pair of overhead microphones. Each sound in the kit is then panned according to its relative position in the drum kit. For instance, the bass drum is often panned to the center, while the snare is panned slightly right of center. The tom-tom drums are panned from slightly left of center for the highest tom sound, and progressively further left for each lower tom in the kit. The crash and ride cymbals are panned hard left and right because they are recorded in stereo with the overhead mics.

Note that this setup usually applies to MIDI drum machines and modules, too. In some cases, these devices have individual outputs for each sound in its own drum kit. However, MIDI drum machines and modules let users internally set up the pan positions of each percussion sound in a kit before it goes through the instrument's stereo outputs. Unfortunately, users of these devices with "premixed" stereo outputs suffer from one important disadvantage: they lose individual control over key drum sounds (such as the bass drum, snare drum, and hi-hat) when directly monitored. That's one of the reasons why I recommend that MIDI instrument players convert the output of MIDI instruments to separate digital audio tracks that can be individually controlled.

There are other ways to record and mix live drums. In some cases, these alternative methods were designed to save on track space. For instance, recording artists using a four- or eight-track recording deck may mic up a drum kit as detailed previously, but mix all of its sounds into two tracks so that the drums are at least in stereo. In other cases, a specific type of drum kit sound may be wanted. For example, jazz drum kits are often miked with a separate microphone for the bass drum and another mic for the snare drum; a pair of mics is then placed overhead to capture the sound of the rest of the kit. Naturally, this saves on track space because only four tracks are required; nevertheless, the real intent behind this method is to capture the sound of a drum kit played in a particular musical style and setting, not to save space. Note that this jazz recording setup can work with any style of music— just be sure to set up the recording environment so that the drums can be properly recorded in this manner.

Stereo Field Width

In the past, the individual drums in a kit were treated as one instrument recorded to just one track. As production techniques evolved, so did the way in which drums were recorded and mixed to stereo. One way in which to create a stereo drum mix is to exaggerate the relative pan positions of each drum sound in the kit. For example, tom-toms may range from slightly left of center for the highest tom sound to extreme left for the lowest tom sound. Many people are used to hearing drums panned this way on recordings, and may even be under the impression that this is the only right way to record and mix drums. However, listening to a drum kit in a live setting reveals that the drum sounds in a kit have a *tighter* (i.e., narrower) stereo field than what is usually heard on recordings. One decision you have to make is whether you want a narrow or a wide stereo field for your kit; a tighter stereo field will make the drums sound more natural, but a wider stereo field can make the drums sound "bigger."

But what am I talking about when I say a *narrow* as opposed to a *wide* stereo field? As I mentioned earlier, you can think of the stereo field as a horizontal line running from left to right. If you were to position sound sources to the furthest extremes of the left or right channels, you would create a wide stereo field. However, there's no law that says that you have to do this. You could position sound sources close to the center to create a narrower stereo field. The choice to have a wide or narrow stereo field is yours to make, but keep in mind that you should consider the type of material and instrumentation you're working with before deciding how wide the field will be.

Distance and Dimension

Another factor to consider is just how loud the drums should sound in relation to the rest of the mix. Some artists prefer to have the drums sit *in back of the mix*—that is, they're not so prominent in terms of volume. Other artists desire drum sounds that have more presence in the mix. The next screenshot graphically illustrates how two different groups who play similar styles of music decided to mix their drums. The upper waveform display is of Mitch Ryder and the Detroit Wheels' recording of "Sock It to Me-Baby," while the lower waveform display is of Sam and Dave's recording "Hold On, I'm Coming." The top song sacrifices some drum presence in favor of overall volume, which is notable by the lack of sharp peaks in the waveform display. In the bottom song, the drums are much more prominent; in fact, it's easy to see the brief, high peaks of each snare drum hit. The drums don't overpower the other performers in the recording, but it's plain just by looking at the waveform display that the drums are an important part of the overall mix.

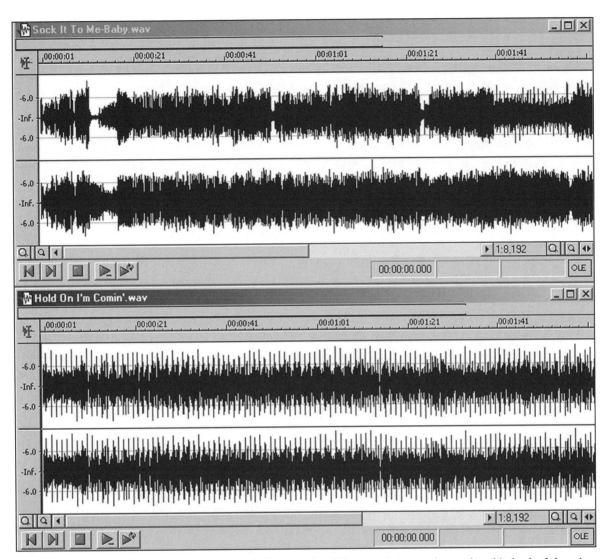

Waveform displays of two songs similar in style illustrate the differences between drums placed in back of the mix (top), and drums placed more to the front of the mix (bottom).

It isn't just volume level that determines the relative strength of drums in a mix. The level and type of reverb applied to the drum tracks influences the perceived volume of the kit in the mix. For instance, little or no reverb in a drum mix can make the drums sound more subdued, even if their volume levels are comparatively high. Larger amounts of reverb can expand the perceived volume of the drum sounds in a mix.

Of course, the size of the room and the wet/dry mix are also important factors. Digital reverbs can recreate the reflective properties of a wide variety of rooms. For example, setting the room size to small and highly reflective makes drums sound very lively. A larger concert hall reverb setting won't make drums sound as lively as a small room would, but it will make the drums sound more "expansive." Even so, the wet/dry balance will finally determine how a kit sounds in the mix. A mix heavily balanced towards dry drum sounds in comparison with the reverb effect will diminish the influence of the reverb setting on the drum sounds. Conversely, a mix weighted towards the sound of the drums as heard through the reverb effect will tend to "wash out" the dry drum sounds. In fact, drum sounds may actually be weakened rather than enhanced if too much reverb is applied. That's why learning how to control the wet/dry balance of effects is an important mixing skill to master.

Bass

By way of transitioning from dealing with drums to dealing with bass, let's dwell a moment on where certain sounds live in terms of frequencies. To begin with, cymbal sounds are present in the upper frequencies of the audio spectrum. Snare drums generate mid-frequency sounds. Tom-toms likewise generate sounds that dwell in the midrange frequencies for the highest-pitched tom to low frequencies for the lowest-pitched. Naturally, bass drums generate low-frequency tones, and this can become a source of trouble once you attempt to mix them with a bass—these instruments generate sounds that reside within the same range of frequencies. To further complicate matters, bass lines are often played in rhythm with the bass drum. The result is that either the bass will *mask* (cover over) a bass drum sound or vice versa, depending on the relative volume levels of each instrument.

Adding to the problem is the fact that low-frequency sounds have little directionality, so they sound best when panned more towards the center of a stereo field. So what can you do to prevent the bass and the bass drum from clashing with each other? For one thing, you shouldn't pan them both to dead center; pan one instrument slightly left of center and the other instrument slightly right of center. This slight separation will give each instrument enough room to be heard without overpowering the other. By the same token, you don't want to pan the bass or the bass drum sounds very far from the center pan position in an attempt to keep the two instruments from struggling with each other for the listener's attention. After all, these instruments sound better when you allow them to naturally fill in the low-frequency area of your "sound painting."

Guitars

You may think that mixing two guitar sounds in an arrangement would be pretty easy to do. After all, the only thing you have to do is pan one guitar to the left and the other to the right so that they stay separated from each other, right? Maybe so, but there's more to mixing similar instruments than simply panning them away from each other. You also need to understand the function of each instrument in the song. For example, one guitar may simply be strumming the song's chord changes, while the other may be playing a combination of short rhythmic passages and single-note phrases as a counterpoint to the lead vocal. Maybe both guitars are playing the same part, with one guitar playing without effects and the other with.

The way in which seemingly similar instruments are used in a song is important in determining how they should be mixed. For instance, if you have one guitar playing just the chord changes and another doing more lead work, you might want to pan the strumming guitar closer to the center and keep its volume relatively low, and then pan the other guitar a little farther from center, but not *too* far either left or right. In another case, with two guitars playing the same part, you might want to place one at the ten o'clock position and the other at two o'clock, as this would keep them separate from each other, but not so far apart so that they wouldn't blend well with each other.

Note that a particular clock position for a sound corresponds to a particular position or setting on a *rotary* (i.e., knob) pan pot control generally found on most outboard mixers. Some virtual mixers contain mimics of rotary pan pots, so setting these "knobs" to specific clock positions shouldn't be difficult. However, many virtual mixers use pan controls with a different appearance (a horizontal slider, for example) and/or other ways of describing pan position. For example, the pan range may be from −50% (hard left) to +50% (hard right), with 0% representing the center position. Naturally, you will have to "translate" the terminology that is used to adjust it to your own specific mixer controls.

Vocals

Most people think that panning the lead vocalist to the center position in the stereo field is the only logical choice. Well, 99.99% of the time it will be. After all, the lead vocalist is usually the center of attention, both literally and figuratively. In fact, properly panning the lead vocalist is rarely a problem. More often, the problem will be that the lead vocalist is either buried in the mix or stands out *too* prominently. When the lead vocalist is buried in the mix, it's usually not because the other instruments are overpowering the lead vocal—it's usually because the volume level of the vocal track is too low. By contrast, lead vocals that stand out too prominently often do so because they *are* overpowering the other instruments in the song—not only is the volume level of the vocal track too high, but the volume levels of the other instrument tracks are often too low as well.

Vocals that are buried in a mix can be fixed by just increasing the vocal track's volume to the point where the vocals can be heard. Handling vocals that are too loud will often require you to lower the volume level of the vocal track *and* raise the relative volume levels of the other instruments in the mix. Unfortunately, there's no magic formula for determining when the lead vocal is properly balanced in the mix—your ears must be the final judges in this matter. However, I can tell you that the best way to mix the lead vocal—and indeed *any* part—is to not become too focused on any one instrument or part. If you pay too much attention to one part, you'll lose the perspective of *all* of the parts as they blend together, and you'll begin to make adjustments based on just that one part. I can tell you from experience that once you start paying too much attention to one part, the rest of the mix will begin to sound bad pretty quickly.

More on Mixing: Additional Instruments

Naturally, adding additional instruments into a mix can complicate matters beyond the issues involved in dealing with just drums, bass, guitars, and vocals. For instance, adding a piano to this arrangement would change the dynamic of the entire mix, and the way in which the piano is used would determine where and how it should be placed in the mix. Although the piano can produce tones that range from low to high frequencies, it's often used for mid-frequency chordal parts in popular song arrangements. This just happens to be the same frequency range in which guitars reside, and the piano often has a similar, chordal function. As you might guess, a guitar part and a piano part could easily end up fighting for the same sonic space if not mixed properly. The best way to make sure that a guitar and a piano don't compete with each other in the same mix is to pan them away from each other. If the guitar is panned more to the left, then pan the piano more to the right, and vice versa. On the other hand, if the piano is deemed to be more "important" than the guitar part, then it should be panned more to the center.

As you add more parts to your mix, you may find that it's easier to treat groups of instruments as single entities rather than to work with each instrument separately. For example, it's easier to work with a horn section consisting of a trumpet, trombone, and saxophone as a unit than it is to work with each instrument separately; however, note that this is true only when these instruments are functioning as a unit. If these three instruments were playing individual parts, as could be the case in a jazz arrangement, then you would want to mix each instrument independently—as always, remember the context in which the parts in your mix operate. One way to handle the situation is to record naturally occurring group entities—like horn sections and background vocals—together on a mono or stereo track to begin with. Another way is to record each instrument in a group on separate tracks and then control their volume as a group. In fact, most virtual and physical mixers include a function designed to let you handle groups of instruments as a single part; it's called *submixing*, and here's how it works.

When each instrument is recorded to its own track, its pan position and volume level are controlled by a corresponding mixer channel. However, you can create a submix of these individual instruments by assigning the mixer channel of each instrument to a mixing *bus*. A bus is a stereo output channel that may be independently routed to another source, such as a multitrack recording device, or to the master stereo output of the mixer itself. For example, you can record each instrument of a horn section onto a separate track and then use their individual channel faders to set the pan position and volume level of each horn part. However, to control the volume level of the horn section as a group, you'll need to assign each horn track to the same bus. For most mixers, this is merely a case of selecting the correct bus button on the individual fader channels. Once each track is assigned to the same mixing bus, you can control the overall volume level of those parts as a single entity. Of course, you can still individually adjust the volume and pan position of these instruments by controlling their channel faders, too. However, that defeats the whole purpose of submixing these instruments to a separate bus, so avoid tampering with individual tracks once they have been assigned to submixes.

Volume

In one sense, volume is a pretty easy concept to understand: you boost the volume of an audio track to make it louder and you cut its volume to make it softer. However, there's really more to it than just that. You need to know how volume levels of separate parts interact to create a final stereo mix.

As I mentioned previously, digital audio represents volume levels using 0 dBFS as the maximum volume level. Any audio levels above that measurement will result in digital distortion, which is a harsh, unpleasant, and definitely unmusical sound. To avoid digital distortion, each track should be set to at least –6 dBFS. After all, you want to make sure that the combined output of all of the tracks to a final stereo mix won't exceed 0 dBFS. To understand why I suggest that you set individual tracks to –6 dBFS, you need to understand a little about decibels and how volume levels of different sound sources combine with each other to create a master volume level. Don't worry—this won't require you to learn all of the technicalities concerning decibels—you'll just come away with a better understanding of how volume works as it relates to them, and you'll also have some easy-to-remember rules of thumb that you can apply when mixing tracks.

Decibels

For our purposes, a *decibel* is defined as a measurement of sound pressure level (note that there are other forms of energy that decibels measure, but ultimately they relate back in some way to the measurement of sound). The human ear can detect an extraordinarily wide range of sound pressure levels. In fact, the range is so great between the threshold of hearing (0 dB) and the threshold of pain (140 dB) that it's expressed logarithmically just to keep the numbers manageable.

Of course, these numbers can sometimes confuse a beginner who is unfamiliar with the decibel scale. For instance, an increase of 6 decibels would make a sound twice as loud (or that a decrease of 6 decibels would make a sound half as loud). But how can this be? After all, if a sound has a decibel level of 88 dB, wouldn't half its volume level be 44 dB? The answer is "no" because the scale of reference is a logarithm, and not a linear scale.

Here are a few settings that you may find useful when working with volume levels. If nothing else, they illustrate the logarithmic nature of decibel measurements.

> An increase of 1dB = approximately a 12% increase in volume
> An increase of 3 dB = approximately a 40% increase in volume
> An increase of 6 dB = approximately a 200% increase in volume (twice as loud)
> An increase of 12 dB = approximately a 400% increase in volume (four times as loud)
> A decrease of 1 dB = approximately a 10% decrease in volume
> A decrease of 3 dB = approximately a 30% decrease in volume
> A decrease of 6 dB = approximately a 50% decrease in volume (half as loud)
> A decrease of 12 dB = approximately a 75% decrease in volume (one-quarter as loud)

Summing Decibels

So far, you've learned about the relationship between decibels and volume as they affect a single sound source. But what happens when you combine two different sound sources? Let's say that you have a bass track set to 90 dB and a guitar part that's also set to 90 dB. Is their combined decibel level 180 dB? No! Decibels are logarithmic measurements, so they just can't be added together like two ordinary numbers. Instead, you have to use a formula to derive the decibel level of two combined sound sources. I won't burden you with the formula itself, but there is something interesting about the result of calculating this formula that beginners can find useful. When combining two different sound sources, the result is never higher than 3 dB above the higher of the two sound levels! In fact, if the two volume levels are the same (as in our case above), the result will always be an increase of 3 dB. Furthermore, the more the two readings differ, the smaller the increase in combined decibel level. This also means that the combined result will be closer to the higher of the two readings. In fact, you can summarize what I've just said with three simple rules of thumb:

1. Combining two different sounds with same decibel level (SPL) will result in an increase of 3 dB.

2. The smaller the difference in dB between two sounds, the greater the increase in their combined SPL to a maximum of 3 dB.

3. The greater the difference in level between two sounds, the smaller the increase in their combined SPL.

However, for every rule there is an exception. These rules apply when you're dealing with two different sound sources, which is almost always the case when you're mixing multitrack recordings. However, if the two sounds are similar enough and are in phase with each other, their actual increase in SPL may be higher than the maximum of 3 dB. In fact, if the two sound sources are the same, the increase in SPL level can be as high as 6 dB.

So, what happens to the combined volume level when you mix several audio sources together? Well, according to the three simple rules of thumb, something like the following should occur. The first two tracks at 90 dB would have a combined SPL of 93 dB. Adding a third track playing at 90 dB would produce a smaller increase in overall SPL because you're calculating the combined SPL of the first two tracks (93 dB) with the SPL of the third track. My rough estimate would be that the combined SPL of all three tracks would be about 94 dB (remember, the greater the difference in level between two sounds, the smaller the increase in their combined SPL). Adding a fourth track with a reading of 90 dB to the combined output of the first three tracks (94 dB) would result in a combined SPL level of about 94.7 dB. As you add more tracks, the overall decibel level would increase at a progressively lower rate. Naturally, you would reach the threshold of 96 dB (or 0 dBFS) at some point. Nevertheless, this example illustrates the principle underlying these rules of thumb so that you can understand what occurs when you mix multiple audio tracks.

Digital Audio Mixing

Of course, you have to remember to convert those values when you apply them to digital audio mixing. For instance, you don't say that a digital audio track has a volume level of 90 dB—rather, you say that the digital audio track has a volume level of –6 dBFS. Even so, what was the point of discussing the relationship between decibels and volume? One important fact you should *always* remember is that you *cannot* exceed 0 dBFS in a digital audio recording system. From the standpoint of recording audio tracks, this means that you can't record a track with a maximum level of 0 dBFS and then record a second track at the same level; the result will mean digital distortion for the output channels and probably for the second recorded track as well. Of course, you can delay this problem by using a multichannel audio interface to record and/or monitor tracks on different pairs of outputs. However, at some point you will run out of audio channels with which to record or monitor tracks. Also, you'll have to control the volume levels of these outputs using an external mixer anyway, and you'll ultimately have to lower the volume levels of each track just to mix them properly without digital distortion. So why not record them at lower, safer levels in the first place?

Likewise, you must also remember that you can't exceed the maximum level of 0 dBFS when *mixing* tracks, either. If the tracks have already been recorded at lower, safer levels, it makes it easier to mix tracks without digital distortion creeping in. As I cautioned earlier, you'll see a lot of advice from experts telling you to record digital audio tracks as hot as possible. The most common reason they give is that you should avoid losing your recording system's effective bit depth. I want to remind you again that this isn't so, and I hope that this discussion about decibels and volume convinces you that it's impossible to record multiple tracks of audio at extremely high settings without quickly introducing digital distortion!

Monitoring the Mix: Headphones or Speakers?

Before you start the mixdown process, you need to decide whether to monitor your mix using headphones or speakers. As I mentioned in "Chapter 1: Before We Begin," a good pair of professional-quality headphones is all you really need to monitor your music. In fact, I use headphones frequently during the mixdown process. Likewise, using a good pair of self-powered near-field monitors to aid in the mixdown process is a good choice, too. Even so, there are differences in what you hear when using headphones as opposed to working with near-field monitors. For instance, when you want to monitor a mix through external speakers, you should set up the monitoring system in the equilateral format. When you use headphones, the audio signal from each speaker goes directly into your ears, and this setup has some far-reaching consequences.

The point in the triangle at which you should sit—the sweet spot—is the optimal listening position at which to determine where sounds are placed in the stereo field. The sweet spot also gives you the sensation that a signal panned dead center sounds as if it is directly in front of you, rather than coming out of two separate speakers with equal energy. But another aspect of the sweet spot is that it is also the ideal location for hearing the reflected sound present in a room. Why is this important? In simplified terms, our heads create an acoustic shadow that blocks out sounds from opposite sources. For example, if you pan a signal hard left, the right ear does not receive a direct signal from the left monitor. Even so, you have no trouble identifying a sound's location because the left ear detects the direct signal while the right ear picks up the reflected sound present in the room. What's more, the signal coming from the left monitor sounds perfectly natural, even though it is coming from just one speaker, because of the reflected sound picked up by the right ear. In short, the combination of direct and reflected sounds provides cues to a sound's location, which the brain uses to "reconstruct" the stereo field.

On the other hand, some of what you can experience while listening through external monitors is absent when you monitor through headphones. For example, you lose that sensation of "seeing" a signal panned dead center "standing" in front of you, even though the audio signal emanates from each headphone speaker with equal energy. Signals that are panned hard left or hard right sound unnatural and lacking in energy because the head, which creates an acoustic shadow in normal listening situations, is now an impenetrable barrier that allows no opportunity for the opposite ear to pick up the reflected sound. Simply put, you lose your sweet spot because headphone speakers cover and directly feed audio into your ears, which is not a natural listening situation.

However, you can recreate in the headphone environment much of what you can experience through external monitors. One way to do this is narrow the stereo field so that no sound is panned hard left or hard right, but rather "almost" hard left or right. The trick is in knowing at what point you should do this in the signal path. For instance, if you use an outboard mixer to mix down tracks, most of the time you will make sure that you don't pan an individual track hard left or right. Likewise, if you use digital audio sequencing or multitrack hard disk recording software to create mixes, you shouldn't pan an individual track hard left or right in the program. However, if you use an outboard mixer for monitoring software-based mixes, set the physical mixer's channel strips hard left or right depending on your computer's audio card outputs. This setup will maintain the accuracy of a stereo field generated from digital audio software.

While the act of narrowing a stereo field is easy, determining the *degree* to which it should be narrowed is a little more difficult—it's often a matter of taste. For example, rather than pan a signal hard left—the seven o'clock position of a panpot—you might want to pan it to the eight o'clock position instead. This setting still places the signal far to the left in the stereo field, but it also ensures that there is also enough signal present in the right channel to make the sound seem more natural in headphones, rather than being fed directly into one ear. Occasionally, though, I set stereo pan settings to the nine o'clock and three o'clock positions respectively. This tighter stereo field is sometimes useful for creating mixes where there is less emphasis on creating a wide stereo panorama, and more on allowing the main elements of a mix to be heard while keeping them as close to the center as possible.

In addition to narrowing the stereo field, an alternative approach is to pan all signals normally, but then insert a *true stereo delay* (i.e., a delay that processes each input channel separately rather than first summing the audio into mono) into the signal path. The most obvious insertion point is in the master output section, although you can use a true stereo delay on specific tracks as an insert effect, too. In either case, the stereo delay must be *cross-delay capable*—in other words, it should be able to send the delayed output to the opposite of its input channel. The delay time should be small (2 to 5 milliseconds), and the wet mix should be small compared to the dry mix (20 percent or less). While this process can give more realism and space to a headphone mix, it may make the mix seem less natural when heard through external monitors. In as much as all mixes are a compromise between absolute fidelity and playability, you have to decide whether this approach is workable or not for a particular project.

Yet another alternative to narrowing the stereo field is to add reverb to recreate a naturally reflective environment. Most people add reverb to mixes anyway, so why not take advantage of the added reverb to make the mix sound more realistic in headphones? Better still, why not insert the previously mentioned true stereo delay just before the reverb to provide the necessary cross delay for stereo image enhancement?

You should take care to avoid drowning your mix in a sea of reverb—or *reverb wash*. While this is noticeable in external monitors, it is even more pronounced in headphones. If it sounds bad in the headphones, it's not going to sound much better through external monitors. Conversely, be prepared for the fact that the reverb that sounds fantastic in your headphones may not sound quite as good through external monitors. This is because headphones create an enclosed, non-reflective environment that loses practically no energy, whereas external monitors are in an open environment and some of their energy is reflected and dissipated in the room. You have to decide for yourself how much to compromise between a good-sounding headphone mix and a good monitor mix.

You can also use a stereo enhancer to make a mix sound more dynamic. Usually, though, most stereo enhancers attempt to spread out a mix that is center-heavy by "scooping out" some of the center channel frequencies and placing them more in the right or left channels. Additionally, stereo enhancing hardware and plug-ins are usually not very good at processing existing hard-panned sounds in a way that reintroduces a more natural sound into a headphone mix. So, use stereo enhancing devices and plug-ins with caution and discretion, if you use them at all.

Even if you prefer to mix your recordings by using external monitors, there are times when listening to a mix through headphones is a better option because of the potential for revealing minute details. For example, I listen to fade-ins and fade-outs exclusively through headphones because I find it's the best way to hear how smooth the fades really are. Unless I turn up my near-fields to high levels, I don't get the same detail that is possible by listening to the headphone output turned up to moderate levels. Likewise, I also perform crucial editing work using headphones as my principal monitors.

In the end, it doesn't matter whether you choose to use headphones or speakers to monitor your mixes, but if you can use both, then do so. Just be aware of the limitations imposed on you by each. No matter what, always make sure that your mixes sound as good through headphones as they do through speakers. After all, many people listen to music primarily through headphones, so it's important that they hear a mix that sounds as if it is being played in a natural environment.

CHAPTER 13

ADVANCED MIXING TECHNIQUES—EQ AND EFFECTS

After you perform your first couple of mixes, you may come to the realization that there will be times when simply panning an instrument to the right spot or raising its volume level won't be enough to ensure that it is properly heard in the mix. Instead, you'll need to enhance or attenuate specific frequencies that an instrument generates via equalization (EQ, for short).

Frequency, Volume, and Overtones

It's easy to think of volume as if it were identical for all instruments in a mix. After all, a bass track with a volume level of 90 dB and a vocal track with a volume level of 90 dB should sound equally loud, correct? Well, actually, no. Our ears are biased towards mid-frequency sounds such as the human voice. Low-frequency sounds such as bass guitars or bass drums require higher sound pressure levels in order to be heard as equally loud as mid-frequency sounds at lower sound pressure levels. At the other end of the frequency spectrum, high-frequency sounds such as cymbals and the highest piano notes also require higher sound pressure levels to be heard with the same loudness as mid-frequency sounds at lower sound pressure levels. As I've mentioned before, two researchers named Fletcher and Munson first investigated this phenomenon. Two other researchers, Robinson and Dadson, further explored this phenomenon and subsequently developed the family of equal loudness contours, also known as the Fletcher-Munson Curves, which show that very low and very high frequency materials are less audible than mid-range audio at the same sound pressure levels.

Here's another item to throw into the mix (so to speak)—instruments produce *overtones*. All instruments produce a range of notes, with each of these notes oscillating at a particular frequency. However, instruments don't produce just one frequency for each note that is played. If that were so, you wouldn't be able to distinguish the difference in *timbre* (tone color—simply put, what makes a saxophone sound like a saxophone and not a flute) among the various instruments. One of the reasons why you can tell the difference between a guitar and a piano (or even between two different guitars) is that each instrument produces several different frequencies at once. For example, playing a note on a guitar will cause its string to vibrate at a particular frequency. The neck of the guitar will vibrate more softly, but at a different frequency. Likewise, the top of the guitar's body will vibrate at a different frequency, and its sides and back will vibrate at yet other frequencies, especially if the woods are of a different material or thickness than the top of the guitar body. Even the other strings will vibrate sympathetically to a degree with a note that's being played and the other vibrations generated by the instrument. The combination and interaction of all of these frequencies create what are called the overtones of an instrument, and these give it its particular timbre.

However, the various frequencies of an instrument don't just blend together equally—some are stronger than others, some frequencies are cancelled out completely, and new frequencies are created from the interaction of existing frequencies. You might think from this description that there is no rhyme or reason to the behavior of interacting frequencies. Certainly, you can't predict the exact interaction of the overtones produced by an individual instrument; however, there are certain underlying principles for overtone creation associated with different types of instruments.

For example, instruments that use a tube or pipe as an *oscillation source* (essentially, a sound generator) behave in similar ways. When the air inside a tube vibrates, a basic frequency or *fundamental* is generated. The overtones that are generated are harmonically related to the fundamental. For example, an instrument playing a note with a fundamental frequency of 440 Hz may generate additional harmonics of 880 Hz, 1320 Hz (or 1.32 kHz), 1.76 kHz, 2.2 kHz, 2.64 kHz, 3.08 kHz, 3.52 kHz, and so on. What I've just described is called a *natural harmonic series*, and each overtone is a multiple of the original frequency.

However, not all instruments generate all of the harmonics in a series. For example, instruments made of closed pipes or tubes will produce only odd-numbered harmonics because the portion of the wave containing the even-numbered harmonics at one end of the pipe are cancelled out by the reflection of the wave at the other end of the pipe. Therefore, only every other harmonic gets heard. Additionally, some instruments produce overtones that don't fall within the natural harmonic series. Cymbals and drums, for instance, produce non-harmonic overtones that are so strong that they drown out the fundamental.

But what do the volume levels of frequencies and the presence of overtones have to do with EQ? Again, there will be occasions when just raising an instrument's volume level won't be enough to ensure that it is properly heard in the mix. Using EQ to enhance or attenuate specific frequencies that an instrument generates lets you alter the volume of just those frequencies that need to be changed. Moreover, EQ allows you to change the tonal characteristics or timbre of an instrument so that you can accentuate or de-emphasize certain frequencies.

Let's take a look at the different types of EQ devices and plug-ins that are commonly used.

EQ Types

Equalization is used to boost or cut the volume level of specific frequencies to improve (hopefully) the sound of an audio mix. How this is done depends on the type of EQ that is used. For instance, the bass and treble controls on your home stereo system are simple forms of EQ. Professional EQ devices and plug-ins, on the other hand, offer a wider variety of EQ forms and effects. For instance, there are *graphic equalizers* with equally spaced fixed frequency bands (usually one-third to two-thirds of an octave from each other). When these fixed bands are boost or cut, their settings look like a graph of a curve or line on the front panel of a device, hence the name "graphic equalizer."

The musically literate among you should be familiar with the term *octave*—it indicates a note that has the same name as another note (e.g., A), but is played at a higher or lower pitch. To describe it more technically, a note that is one octave higher than another note is exactly double its frequency,

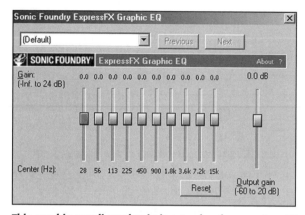

This graphic equalizer plug-in is a ten-band, one-octave EQ because it is divided into ten frequency bands, with each succeeding band being one octave from the previous band.

and a note that is one octave lower than another is half its frequency. For example, for a note with a frequency of 440 Hz, a note one octave higher than would be 880 Hz. The octave of that second note would be 1.76 kHz, the next octave would be 3.52 kHz, and so on.

There are also *parametric equalizers* as well. Although they don't have as many frequency bands as graphic equalizers, they can be more flexible. For one, parametric equalizers don't have fixed (read "unchangeable") frequency bands—you can adjust the frequency band settings to whatever you want. Also, parametric equalizers allow you to adjust the range of frequencies you want to affect. For instance, two-thirds octave band graphic equalizers will affect frequencies one-third of an octave on either side of a fixed frequency, but parametric equalizers will let you adjust the *Q setting* (width of the frequency band) to however narrow or wide you want it to be. In short, a *parametric* equalizer will let you adjust the *parameters* of its EQ settings.

A word of note—graphic and parametric EQs don't affect *all* of the frequencies in a frequency band equally. The shape of an EQ curve is like a bell, with the center frequency representing the highest point in the curve where frequencies are maximally boosted, or the lowest point in the curve where frequencies are maximally cut. For example, if the center frequency is 500 Hz and the Q setting is one octave, the frequencies at the more extreme ranges of the setting (375 Hz and 750 Hz—the 500 Hz being at the midway point between these two frequencies, which are an octave apart) will be only mildly affected, but frequencies closer to the center will be affected more drastically by the EQ setting. How they are affected depends on two factors: the amount of boost or cut of the center frequency and the Q setting. A small boost or cut will affect a smaller range of frequencies, regardless of the Q setting. Conversely, a large boost or cut will affect a wider range of frequencies, and will likely affect them more drastically. Likewise, a small Q setting will affect a narrow range of frequencies, while a larger Q setting will affect a wider range of frequencies. In short, it is both the width and height (or depth) of an EQ curve that determine the range of frequencies that will be affected, and how strongly they will be affected.

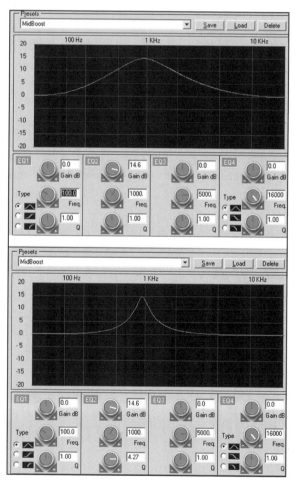

Parametric EQs affect frequencies differently according to the Q settings (as shown here) and/or the amount of boost or cut in the frequency band setting.

There are other types of physical and virtual EQ devices that are essentially variations of graphic and parametric equalizers. For instance, there are *high-pass* (i.e., low-cut) and *low-pass* (i.e., high-cut) filters, whose job it is to confuse beginners with their names and functions.

Of course, I'm kidding, but it's easy to confuse the names of these devices with their actual purposes. A high-pass filter will let frequencies *above* a certain setting pass through its circuitry unchanged—or, to put it another way, it will *reduce* (i.e., cut off) frequencies below a particular setting. A low-pass filter will do just the opposite: Frequencies *below* a certain setting will be allowed to pass through its circuitry unaltered—or, if you prefer, frequencies *above* a particular setting will be cut off.

Shelving EQs, by contrast, raise or lower an entire range of frequencies above or below a fixed frequency setting. For example, a shelving EQ designed to raise or lower bass frequencies might have a fixed frequency setting of 100 Hz. All frequencies below that setting will then be boosted or cut according to the amount of decibels you raise or lower the shelf. Similarly, a shelving EQ designed to raise or lower treble frequencies might have a fixed frequency setting of 10 kHz. Likewise, all frequencies above that setting will be boosted or cut according to the amount of decibels you raise or lower the shelf.

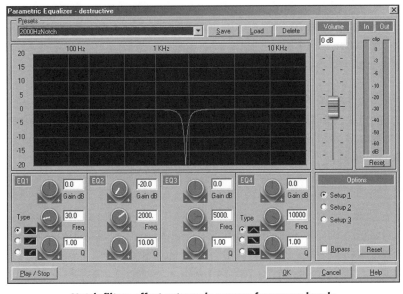

Notch filters affect extremely narrow frequency bands.

Finally, *band pass* and *notch filters* are specific forms of EQ designed to affect an extremely narrow band of frequencies. A band pass filter is like a combination low-pass/high-pass filter that simultaneously cuts frequencies lower than the high-pass setting and higher than the low-pass setting. This allows a specific band of frequencies to pass through. Notch filters are like parametric equalizers with very narrow Q settings (1/12th of an octave, or if you prefer, one half step) and the ability to cut or boost that particular frequency by at least 18 dB.

Using EQ

Now it's time to apply what you've learned so that you can effectively use EQ in the mixdown process. Let's take that theoretical five-part song you started to mix down in the previous chapter and use that to illustrate examples of common EQ problems and their possible solutions. Note that all of these solutions apply to working with individual instrument tracks in a mixdown session—not the final mix in a mastering session.

Bass and Bass Drum

As you've no doubt noticed by now, both the bass and bass drum sounds can cause plenty of trouble. These sounds can quickly go from thin and lifeless to "boomy" and overbearing when controlled by changes in volume level alone. Thankfully, properly applied EQ can give you more precise control over these sounds. For instance, you may have recorded a bass drum that sounds a little thin in the mix, and raising its volume does nothing to change that. To get a little more "thud" in its sound, try using a parametric equalizer on the bass drum's fader channel. Set it to 80 Hz with a Q setting of one octave, and then boost the EQ by a couple of decibels to start with. That should do the job nicely, but if it doesn't, try boosting it one or two decibels more.

Otherwise, you may want to try to narrow the Q setting to focus more on frequencies you're trying to boost—perhaps what you're really trying to accomplish is to give the bass drum a little more presence in the mix. If that's the case, adjust your EQ's frequency setting to around 160 Hz to 320 Hz and boost it a couple of decibels. To hear more of the snap that occurs when the beater hits the head, set a second parametric EQ band to 2.5 kHz and boost its decibel level slightly.

These same settings often work well with bass guitars, too. This shouldn't come as a surprise, since bass drums and bass guitars (and bass synth sounds, too) are all low-frequency instruments. They are likely to suffer from the same types of problems, such as sounding too thin or "boomy." In many circumstances, the EQ setting you use to solve a problem with one bass instrument can be readily applied to other bass instruments with a similar problem.

However, you should avoid extreme EQ levels with parametric EQs. The necessity for a drastic approach like this is often a symptom of another problem—the sound wasn't properly recorded to begin with. Also, you need to watch out so that you're not trying to achieve an effect that can't be accomplished with the settings you're using.

Guitars

Like bass and bass drum sounds, guitar sounds can often be thin and lifeless or too loud and muddy. However, there may be times when that's exactly the effect you're trying to achieve. For example, you may not want to hear the full-bodied sound of an acoustic rhythm guitar, especially if you've got an electric rhythm guitar in the mix as well. Instead, you may want to de-emphasize the lower frequencies without changing the middle and upper frequencies. A shelving EQ with a fixed frequency setting of 500 Hz and *rolled off* (cut, reduced) by at least 6 dB will take away some of an acoustic guitar's punch, leaving you with a lighter, thinner sound. Of course, you can move the frequency setting to the desired point or roll off the frequencies below 500 Hz even more (12 to 18 dB).

Electric guitar solos can often pose a different problem; they often don't punch through a mix when they should. One way to fix this problem is to set a parametric EQ to around 2 kHz with a Q setting of two octaves, and then boost the EQ by a couple of decibels. The wide Q setting will gently raise the frequencies between 1 kHz and 4 kHz, which is where the notes of the guitar solo are likely to be. If this setting seems too harsh or tinny, move the frequency setting down to 1 kHz and raise the Q setting to three octaves. This will still emphasize the range of the notes in the guitar solo without making its sound seem so harsh.

Snare Drums and Cymbals

Many people like to hear the "crack" of the snare drum in a mix; still others prefer a darker tone for their snare drum sound. For those who desire the former, setting the snare drum track's EQ from 2.5 kHz to 4 kHz with a one-octave Q setting and boosting by 2 or 3 dB will give it just the right snap. *Sweep* (that is, move the center point) through the range of these frequencies until you get the effect you're after. For those who want a darker snare sound, setting the EQ from 500 Hz to 800 Hz will do that. If you want a combination of both depth and "snap," use two parametric EQ bands, with each band using one of the previously suggested settings. You may want to further adjust the decibel level of both bands to get the right tonal balance, but remember not to go to extremes in boosting or cutting the sound. You don't want to overpower the rest of the mix with the sound of just the snare drum.

Cymbals are another problem area with beginning recording artists, but not because their sounds are difficult to control—rather, it's because beginners tend to exaggerate the high-frequency sounds of the cymbal to give them more presence than what is usually needed. The result is that the ear gets fatigued quickly by the harsh sound of crash, ride, and hi-hat cymbals that are over-EQ'd. Obviously, the solution is to not over-emphasize the cymbal sounds. If you need to EQ them, set the center frequency to 10 kHz at the most. Don't make the mistake of setting the center frequency to 16 kHz just because you want to add presence to your cymbal sounds. If you set the center frequency to 10 kHz and the Q setting to one octave, you will affect frequencies between 7.5 to 15 kHz—that range is more than enough to add presence to cymbal sounds with just a gentle boost in EQ. On the other hand, moving that frequency range higher (or sharply boosting the EQ of the existing range) will likely do nothing more than add hiss to the cymbal track. Needless to say, that's not the kind of "presence" you need in a mix.

General EQ Considerations

I just gave you a few guidelines as to how EQ can be effectively applied, but there are entire books devoted to the practice of using it properly. However, the bottom line is this: Using EQ is an art, not a science. Certainly, it helps to know some of the acoustic principles that affect it. However, that doesn't mean that you can just follow set recipes to set EQ for different instruments. Ultimately, what I've given you are guidelines, not rules set in stone.

I've stressed again and again that one shouldn't boost or cut EQ settings to extreme levels. This is my own ethic, but it's one that a lot of recording artists share. For one thing, having to use extreme EQ settings often means that the tracks weren't recorded properly in the first place. It is ultimately better and easier for you to record tracks in an optimal fashion than it is to be forced into extreme corrective measures. I've repaired badly recorded tracks on other people's recordings and, believe me, most of them weren't easy fixes.

Another reason that I urge care in avoiding extreme changes in EQ—especially boosting EQ levels— is that it has an effect on the overall decibel level of the individual track and, by extension, the level of the overall mix. For instance, you may be able to boost the bass frequencies by 8 dB without exceeding 0 dBFS, even if the track setting is –6 dBFS (remember the Fletcher-Munson curves), however, doing the same to midrange frequencies will likely cause digital distortion. The combination of safe initial track levels and smaller boosts in EQ can help to prevent digital distortion.

Another common beginner's mistake is to use a bunch of different EQ forms and plug-ins when only one or two will do. Too often I have seen recording artists using several EQ plug-ins to affect the same range of frequencies in a track or a master recording. In my opinion, adding layers of EQ to a track just means that you're taking *guesses* at how to fix the track's problem. Besides, piling EQ upon EQ will ensure that you'll lose control over the very frequencies that you're trying to affect. Before you do anything, listen to the track and then think of the best way to fix the problem—you'll almost certainly conclude that it won't require five or six EQs to do the job.

Also, remember to adjust EQ in the context of the other instruments in the mix. *Soloing* a track (that is, listening to a track by itself) is sometimes helpful when you're trying to isolate a problem in a mix. However, you can only judge how good a track sounds by listening to it in context with the other tracks in the project. One of the surprising things you'll discover is that sometimes tracks that don't seem to sound very good when you listen to them by themselves work perfectly when played in conjunction with the others.

Compressors, Limiters, and Expanders

Another way to control volume is through *compression, limiting,* and *expansion.* The devices and plug-ins that do this are called, logically enough, *compressors, limiters,* and *expanders,* respectively. In fact, these three devices perform interrelated functions that are often combined into one plug-in, since they're each different facets of the same overall process.

Compressors and Limiters

Simply put, a compressor *compresses* the dynamic range of an audio signal. It does this by changing an audio signal's output by a particular ratio. For instance, a setting of 2:1 means that for each 2 dB change in an audio signal's input level, a change of 1 dB will occur at the output. Likewise, a setting of 4:1 means that for each 4 dB change in an audio signal's input level, a change of 1 dB will occur at the output. The compressed audio signal will still have variations in volume—it's just that those changes won't be as drastic because of the compression ratio.

If the compression ratio is high enough, a compressor will then act as a *limiter.* As its name suggests, a limiter limits audio signals from going above a particular decibel level. This is done by setting the *threshold*—that is, the decibel level where limiting will begin to occur. For instance, if the threshold is set to −12 dB, any inputted audio signals above the threshold will be attenuated to that −12-dB setting. Any signals below the threshold will pass through unaffected.

Setting the threshold level is also useful when working with compressors—it gives the user added control over the compression process. For example, you may want to keep most of an audio signal's original dynamic range, but you may want to tame some of the higher audio peaks. In this case, you don't want to use a limiter, because it would squash all audio signals above a certain level. However, a compressor with a ratio of 4:1 and a threshold of –8 dB would smooth out those higher audio peaks without making them all the same level.

The way in which a limiter begins to affect the inputted audio signal is determined by its *hard knee/soft knee* setting. When set to hard knee response, a limiter will clamp down on audio levels exceeding the threshold almost instantaneously. You won't notice much of a variation in the output level because the hard knee response will prevent that from occurring. When set to soft knee, the limiter will progressively limit until it eventually flattens out to full limiting response. This type of action will soften or smooth out an instrument's dynamic range, often making it sound more "musical."

Similarly, you can adjust a compressor's response by setting its attack and release times. A shorter attack time will let a compressor adjust to more frequent changes in an inputted signal, whereas a longer attack time will allow more of an inputted signal's dynamic range to pass through before being affected. This latter situation can allow the track to sound more musical, but the tradeoff is that you'll have less control over quickly changing audio levels.

Release time, on the other hand, determines how long it will take for a compressor effect to stop affecting the inputted signal. With a short release, each change in an inputted signal's volume level will be tracked more closely and processed more quickly. However, this may lead to an undesired effect called *pumping* or *breathing*—unnaturally quick changes in audio levels that sound like someone breathing rapidly. On the other hand, a long release time means that a compressor will affect an inputted signal for a longer period of time. You won't get pumping because the relative dynamics won't be affected quite so much, but the signal may sound "squashed." As you can imagine, it takes some practice to learn how to properly set attack and release times for compressors.

You can also control the output of a compressor/limiter with its own volume control. Think of this as the "volume control of last resort." For instance, if you set the volume level to –6 dB, the outputted signal will never rise above that level. Obviously, this is a useful feature if you want to make sure that the volume of your digital audio tracks never exceeds a certain level, and therefore it's helpful to have a compressor/limiter inserted into an *audio chain* (the series of effects, processors, equipment, etc. through which your audio will run) just before the recorded signal goes into your digital audio sequencer's track. If you don't have an outboard compressor/limiter, you can use a virtual compressor/limiter from within your digital editing software.

Applying Compression Effects

Compressor/limiters are useful for a variety of tasks. For example, they can be used to "even out" the dynamics of a vocalist with a poor mic or vocal technique. Compression can also be used to smooth out bass guitar sounds. One problem with bass guitars is that the varying thicknesses of their strings can make the instrument's sound go from *fat* (rich, full) to *thin* (insubstantial) very quickly, depending on what note is played and what string it's played on—this can make the instrument sound uneven. The best way to tame a bass is to apply some gentle compression to its track so that it's output is at a more consistent level. You can also apply compression after the track has been recorded to smooth out the signal.

Compression and limiting can also each be used to ensure that an inputted signal doesn't exceed a set level. Obviously, the best time to apply compression or limiting in this case is during the recording phase using an outboard compressor/limiter. Some programs also let you use plug-ins during the recording process—if this is possible with your setup, you should definitely use a virtual compressor/limiter to tame your signals on input.

There is one additional form of compression: *frequency-dependent compression*. As its name implies, it's a form of compressor that will compress audio signals within certain frequency bands. In one sense, think of it as compression with built-in EQ. It's generally used in the mastering stage (which we'll cover in the next chapter).

Expanders

As you might guess by the name, an *expander* performs the opposite function of a compressor/limiter: It expands the dynamic range of an inputted audio signal. In other words, the louder portions of an audio track can be made even louder, while the softer parts can be made even softer. When used with analog recorders, expanders can increase the output of an audio track while simultaneously reducing its low-level noise. In fact, expanders are an important part of analog noise reduction circuits. At the recording stage, inputted signals are compressed so that their dynamic range can fit onto the tape. Upon playback, the compressed recorded material is processed through an expander in order to restore the audio to its original dynamics. Coincidentally, this also reduces the noise floor, which can make tape hiss less of a problem.

Expanders aren't used that much in digital audio recording these days. For one thing, digital audio has a wide enough dynamic range and a low enough noise floor that expansion generally isn't needed for most recording processes. However, for those who restore audio using DAWs and editing software, expansion is still an important tool for restoring unnaturally compressed audio tracks.

Effects Processors

So far, the discussion here has been limited to *dynamics processors*—devices or plug-ins whose main purpose is to control the dynamics of an audio signal in a particular manner. Now, let's turn to *effects processors*, whose main function is to apply some sort of effect to a recorded signal. Effects processors include such devices and plug-ins as reverb, digital delay, chorus, and flanging. Below you'll find very basic instruction on how to use these effects properly in the mixdown process, but since procedures and processors vary, you should consult your digital audio sequencer's manual (or audio editing program's manual) to learn more about the specifics of what these effects do.

Insert Effects

One way to use an effects processor is as an *insert effect*. As the name suggests, it is a processor that you insert into a track's mixing channel. The track's signal is then routed through the insert effect, where it is processed before going out to the submix or master mix fader. Also, the wet/dry mix can be adjusted within an effects processor to achieve the right balance between the original and processed signal. Using an effects processor as an insert effect is best done when it is unique in either its type or its settings from track to track. For instance, a filter or flanging effect is usually applied to a specific track in a specific way, so it's best used as an insert effect.

Auxiliary Effects

Unfortunately, many beginners seem to think that each track requires its own effects processor even when it doesn't. Thankfully, it's also possible to use an effects processor as an *auxiliary effect*. Some people also refer to an auxiliary effect as a *send/return effect* because of the way in which they're used in a mixer. You see, most mixers have built-in auxiliary *send* and *return* jacks (which, logically enough, allow the signal to be sent to and from something beyond the mixer). The send jacks should be plugged into the inputs of the effects processor, and the return jacks should be plugged into the outputs of the effects processor (note that this setup applies to virtual mixers as well, even though there are no physical cables plugged into the send/return jacks and the processor inputs/outputs).

The send jacks should be connected to the corresponding auxiliary send faders of each mixer channel. Basically, the send jacks are a separate set of volume controls that determine the volume level of a signal sent from that mixing channel. Naturally, you can send as much (or as little) signal as you would like from a mixing channel to an effects processor's input. The effects processor's wet/dry setting should be set to 100% wet, and all of the various tracks should have their own effects send volume levels set—this is one point where the wet/dry balance is controlled. Most mixers also have a master effects send volume control, which can be used to further control an effects processor's wet/dry balance.

The outputs of an effects processor are then fed into the auxiliary return jacks; a single volume fader subsequently controls the auxiliary return's volume level. This is the third point wherein the wet/dry balance of the processed signal can be modified. When the processed effect is then combined with the signal controlled by the main volume fader, the wet/dry balance is fully under control.

Auxiliary effects are best used when you want to apply the same effect across more than one track. Reverb is a perfect example of this type of effect. Its better to adjust the send/return levels of the tracks you want to affect with reverb than it is to use multiple instances of reverb effects set to different wet/dry settings. For one thing, it's much easier to control reverb as an auxiliary effect than to set and control several independent reverbs simultaneously. Also, using plug-ins as auxiliary effects whenever possible will minimize the amount of processing your computer has to perform to run all of these virtual effects simultaneously. In short, you can play more tracks and use additional effects if you apply auxiliary effects judiciously.

Bus and Master Effects

Bus and master effects are similar in function to insert effects, but with the following differences. *Bus effects* are routed through the inserts of a mixing bus. Few physical mixers have bus effects, but some virtual mixers include this capability as a matter of course. Naturally, effects plugged into a bus insert affect only those tracks that are routed to that mixing bus. *Master effects*, on the other hand, are routed through the inserts of a mixer's final output. Both physical and virtual mixers use master effect inserts, and all tracks are affected by whatever processor is inserted into a master effects chain. Most of the time you will use a master effect insert to connect a dynamics processor (such as a compressor/limiter) to control the overall dynamics of a final mix. However, you can use *any* type of dynamics or effects processor you want to affect the overall mix—it just depends on what you want to do.

A Sampling of Effects—What They Are and What They Do

Reverb adds numerous echoes (or reflections) to an inputted signal to (re)create the illusion of spaciousness. You can adjust various reverb parameters to control the size of the room, which can range from a large concert hall to a small tiled bathroom. You can also adjust the amount of time it takes before the reverb effect starts (*pre-delay*), and the amount of time it takes for the reverb to fade away (*decay time*). Some sophisticated reverb plug-ins will also let you select the materials used in the construction of the "room." I often use reverb as an auxiliary effect, and occasionally as a master effect.

Delay effects (i.e., *delay, chorus,* and *flanging*) are commonly used as insert effects. Even though they are listed as separate effects plug-ins, they're really different facets of a single effect. For example, delay (sometimes called *echo*) generates a series of repeating signals by delaying the original input signal a specified amount of time. Chorus fattens up the audio so that one instrument or voice sounds like many playing or singing together. It does this by mixing the original signal with a briefly delayed copy of it. This process mimics what occurs when people sing or play instruments as a group—each performer is slightly out of tune and off the beat in relation to the other performers, and it is this detuned and delayed sound that makes a group of performers sound richer and fuller.

Related to the chorus effect is the flanging effect, which some people describe as "spacey" or "ethereal," while others describe it as a "whooshy" sound, as if a jet were taking off. Both effects occur because the amount of delay is large enough so that the original and delayed signals are out of phase with each other. The result is that some frequencies in the audio output gain in strength while others are reduced. The major difference between chorus and flanging is that chorus includes a setting that modulates the depth or amplitude of the filter parameter, while flanging contains a setting for modulating the speed of the filter parameter.

The Final Mixdown: Virtual or Physical?

Once you've set your pan and volume positions and applied EQ and effects processing (if wanted or needed) to your individual tracks, then you're ready to mix your tracks down to a stereo digital audio file. At this point, you have a choice as to method: You can either create a virtual mix off-line within your digital audio application, or can create a mix whereby you route your audio tracks to an outboard mixer that then routes its stereo output to a mastering deck or another computer. Both have their advantages and disadvantages and, in each case, you must consult your owner's manuals for specific information on each method as it pertains to your software and hardware setup.

When you perform a virtual mix off-line, the digital audio program calculates the combined results of the volume levels, pan positions, effects processing, and mix automation to produce a stereo mix of your tracks. The advantage is that off-line mixing is a faster-than-real-time process, so you can generate a stereo mix of a song rather quickly. The disadvantage is that sometimes the stereo master won't sound quite the same as the monitored mix because of the program's calculation process. Moreover, you can't make any final adjustments on the fly because the mixing process is virtual, relying on the preset parameters to create the mix in the first place.

A physical mixdown, on the other hand, gives you one last chance to adjust track settings on the fly. However, this method has its own limitations. For one, it's a real-time process, so it will take longer to mix down tracks to a stereo file. Also, physical mixes require you to have an outboard mixer and a mastering device. These add up to additional costs in terms of equipment and space.

Ultimately, the choice between creating virtual or physical mixes is both an aesthetic and financial consideration. There is no right or wrong choice here, except inasmuch as it applies to your personal preference.

CHAPTER 14
MASTERING YOUR CD

Once you've recorded and mixed down a number of songs, you'll want to put your collection of tunes on a CD. This CD can be used either as a master that you will send to a CD replication service, or as a CD that will be duplicated on your own computer system for your personal use. While replication and duplication seem like synonymous terms, they aren't. CDs that are *replicated* are physically stamped out by a machine. A stamper contains a reverse image of the pits and bumps that were burned onto the master CD; it presses (stamps) this image onto a blank CD, producing a copy of the original. The process is fast and can be inexpensive, based on the number of copies you want to produce. However, the preparatory work of making the stamper plates can be expensive, so in order to be cost-effective, use a replication service only if you need 1,000 or more copies of your CD.

CDs that are *duplicated* (or *burned*) are created yourself with a standard CD burner and blank CDs that you can buy at a computer or electronics store. While CD-Rs can burn CDs at extremely fast rates, it still takes some time to produce large quantities. On the other hand, duplicating is the smart choice if you need to knock off just a few copies at a time.

Regardless of whether you create a CD for mastering at a replication service, or duplicate a small number of CDs yourself for limited distribution, there are certain things you have to do to make sure that you'll create a professional-sounding and professional-looking product. There's much more to CD creation than just collecting audio files and burning them to media.

Audio File Preparation

Naturally, the first step in creating an audio CD is to select the stereo audio files that you want to use. In reality, though, preparing an audio CD begins with the recording and mixdown process. As I've mentioned previously, your stereo audio files should be of a sample rate that is a multiple of 44.1 kHz (44.1 kHz, 88.2 kHz, or 176.4 kHz), since you're going to have to downsample audio recorded at a higher rate to the CD rate of 16-bit/44.1 kHz. It's best to use rates that are multiples of 44.1 right from the start. Some of the more sophisticated CD burning programs (and audio editing programs that include this feature) let you work with audio files that have audio sampling rates that are higher than are required for CDs—they can downsample audio recorded at these higher sample rates during the CD burning process.

Likewise, these same CD creation programs can often *dither* 24-bit audio files to 16-bit audio during CD creation. Dithering is a process that converts audio from a high bit rate to a lower one by adding a small amount of low-level noise to the digital audio file. This noise smoothes out the differences in quantization levels that are the result of converting down from over 17 million quantization levels to roughly 65,000. There are different dithering methods available, but the one thing they all have in common is that they use a small amount of low-level noise to scale 24-bit audio down to 16-bit.

Some CD burning programs—notably, the more consumer-oriented software—are unable to work with any audio files that aren't already in 16-bit/44.1 kHz audio format. If you use this type of program for creating CDs, then you will either have to make sure that you mix down your songs to this format beforehand, or convert the stereo audio files to the CD sample rate after mixdown. Most digital audio sequencers will let you convert and export 24-bit audio files as 16-bit audio files, and will perform the downsampling and dithering off-line. However, before you do that, there are a couple of other tasks you may want to perform on your digital audio files.

Adding Master Effects

You probably thought that after you mixed down your songs with all of the EQ, compression, and other effects that you had at your disposal, your stereo audio files would be perfect, right? Well, not necessarily. The truth is that you might have to make a few final tweaks to some of your audio files before you burn them to CD. For instance, you may find that the bass that you thought was perfect in a particular song actually sounds a little thin compared to the bass in the other tracks. Here's your last chance to fix that by using EQ to boost the bass level a little more. Of course, you'll need to make sure that boosting the bass doesn't also boost the bass drum and make it sound too loud. After all, EQs can't tell the difference between instruments in the same frequency range.

To get a little more control over specific frequency ranges, you may need to use a frequency-dependent compressor instead. This will allow you to boost or cut a frequency but also control its output level more precisely so that you can tweak the sound of one instrument while minimizing the effect of this change on other instruments within its frequency range. But be aware that using any type of effect to alter a specific instrument in a stereo mix is extremely difficult. At best, you will be faced with a compromise between the best possible sound for an instrument and the best overall sound for the stereo track.

Compression and EQ

I have had discussions with numerous students and professionals about applying EQ and compression to stereo tracks. Many talk about using compression and EQ as if they were a required part of the CD creation process. There used to be good reasons for this, but for the most part they no longer apply.

Mastering studios used to be the places that performed the specific task of converting stereo analog tape to a format that could be used to make vinyl records. The master analog tapes would be completed at a recording studio and then sent to a mastering studio. The mastering studio was set up with specialized equipment that cut a master lacquer that would be used to make the vinyl records. And when I say "cut," I mean that literally—a mastering lathe would cut a spiral groove into lacquer. The width of the groove was determined by the volume level of the audio material. The louder the audio, the wider the groove. The wider the groove, the less amount of playing time the lacquer (and, ultimately, the vinyl record) would have. To ensure that volume levels had enough *apparent* loudness, and to ensure that there was an adequate amount of time for program material, compression was used.

Compression and high-frequency limiting also ensured that volume levels didn't suddenly peak too loudly or quickly. If either were to happen, the cutting lathe could jump right out of the groove and ruin the master lacquer. And although EQ was used for final corrective purposes, it was also used to roll off frequencies in accordance with RIAA (Record Industry Association of America) standards for creating vinyl records. However, these standards no longer apply—vinyl records aren't nearly as prevalent as they used to be. Yet some people still think that using compression is a *necessary* component of the CD creation process.

Compression can certainly still be used, but it's no longer a necessary component of mastering. Compression and EQ are now used far more for just increasing the apparent loudness of audio for a CD. The reasoning behind this process is often that music has to be loud enough to compete with other music in the marketplace, but the fallacy behind that reasoning is that everyone can make their music just as loud as the next person's, given today's digital audio production tools. You can't get your music noticed just by volume level anymore.

In addition, using compression just to maximize audio levels also has some unintended aesthetic consequences. For one, a well-balanced mix may be obliterated outright by too much compression. You may end up with a CD whose soft ballads sound just as loud as its loudest rock tracks, and you can also easily and unwittingly level out what should be the varying dynamics within a song itself. So, before you mindlessly begin to apply compression at the mastering stage, remember that doing so may have some undesired effects.

Normalization

For some people, the digital audio replacement tool for EQ and compression is normalization. Normalization isn't just for individual audio tracks of instruments in a song—it can be used for stereo audio mixes, too. Just remember that it takes only one instance of a sample level of 0 dBFS for an audio file to be considered peak normalized. If there are brief instances wherein the highest peak is close to 0 dB, but the majority of the digital audio data is well below that, peak normalization will probably have little effect on the audio's perceived loudness.

Moreover, keep in mind that you don't necessarily want to normalize a stereo audio file intended for CD creation to 0 dBFS. Instead, it may be better to normalize to −0.3 dBFS. That's usually enough to ensure that there is no digital distortion when the CD is created or a copy of it is played back on a different audio system.

You should take great care when using RMS normalization on a mix; not only can it make your audio uncomfortably loud, but it will also probably ruin the EQ, volume, and compression balances you set up during the mixdown process. If you're going to go for a loud mix, use compression and EQ instead of RMS normalization at the mastering stage. However, remember what I said about compression for mastering earlier—make sure that you don't ruin the mix with too much compression and EQ.

Cutting Heads and Tails

The songs that you plan to copy to CD probably have noticeable periods of silence at their beginnings and ends. Before you put your tracks in the desired playing order, you should cut the *head* (section of silence at the beginning of the track) and *tail* (section of silence at the end of the track) of each audio file. Cut as closely as possible to the actual audio at each end of a song, but don't make the cuts *too* close. A few samples of silence are needed at the beginning so that CD players and other reading devices can follow the CD's index and table of contents more accurately. Also, make sure that you don't cut off the tail before the song is fully faded out. To avoid both problems, I recommend monitoring your edits through headphones so that you can hear them in great detail.

Fade-Ins and Fade-Outs

A song may also have *hard* starts and ends—in other words, the audio starts and stops abruptly. Most of the time, you'll want your songs to have hard starts, but you'll want the ends to fade-out. You may have to create fade-outs using your audio editing program before you use your CD burning program.

Some programs give you different types of fade curves that you can apply. For instance, you can have a linear curve that fades in a straightforward manner, an exponential fade that progressively doubles or halves the volume level, and a logarithmic fade whose curve is a logarithm between the maximum and zero levels of the curve.

Professional audio CD creation programs let you set fade-ins and fade-outs from within the software. These edits are generally non-destructive—the digital audio tracks are not permanently altered, so you'll have the opportunity to rework a fade if you don't like how it sounds.

Professional audio CD creation programs also include another fade option that often isn't present in consumer-oriented CD burning programs: the ability to *crossfade* tracks. As the term suggests, crossfading fades out one track while simultaneously fading in the next. You generally set up a crossfade by first activating the crossfade tool or function and then overlapping the end of one track with the beginning of the next. The length of a cross fade is determined by how much you overlap the two songs. Some programs are limited to performing *linear crossfades*—that is, a linear fade-out of the first track and a linear fade-in of the following track. However, some programs offer the ability to use the different fade curves mentioned earlier, and in any combination.

Side Sequencing

The next step to perform is *side sequencing*—that is, arranging your songs in the desired order of play. The term is a holdover from the days of vinyl records. Because music is played on both sides of a two-sided vinyl recording, it's necessary to arrange the playing order for each side. This requires both artistic and technical skill because you must make sure that each side has a good mix of songs and the playing time for each side is roughly the same. Nowadays, with CDs, you only have to worry about the order of the songs on *one* side.

Still, you may want to side sequence three or four different playlists so that you can make test copies for comparative purposes. Some songs seem to flow into others naturally, and listening to different playlists can bring this out.

Setting the Index and Gap

A CD player knows the songs and order in a playlist because they are all *indexed* in the CD's table of contents. Most of the time, a CD creation program will automatically index each track when you compile the playlist within that software. Professional CD creation programs may require you to insert indexes by command, but even then, the process is generally very simple (check with your software manual). These programs also allow for *subindexing* so that listeners can go to specific points within a track—but most CD players can't read subindexes, so you may not wish to put forth this sort of effort.

By default, most of these programs also set the time gap between each song in a CD playlist to two seconds. In the past, you couldn't alter this gap using consumer-oriented CD burning programs—however, you can now individually adjust the time gap with many of them. For example, you may want one song to play immediately after the end of another song. So, you just set the time gap to 0 seconds between the two tracks, and the second song will play hot on the heels of the first. Choosing the song order and varying the time gap between songs can be a creative process in itself.

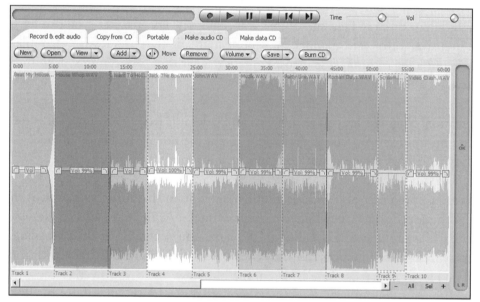

Illustration of a series of songs that's ready to be burned to a CD. The tunes have been side sequenced and checked for differences in volume level, and the time gaps and fades between each song have been set.

Burning the Audio CD

Now you're ready to burn your audio CD. Place the blank CD into your CD-R and begin the burning process according to the instructions of your CD creation program. For the most part, you should have no trouble burning an audio CD using the fastest setting that both your CD-R and the blank media can handle. Some people have told me that they have difficulty burning audio CDs at faster than 2x (i.e., two times faster than the actual playing time of the CD), even with burners and media that are designed to go much faster. While I can't disagree with their experiences, I've never had that problem. For one thing, devices that claim to have high-speed burning capabilities (48x to 52x) don't sustain their highest speeds throughout the burning process. In my experience, their average *sustained* burning speed is 16x to 24x. That's still pretty fast.

There are other factors that may contribute to less-than-ideal CD burning performance. These include the size of the burner's memory buffer, the speed of the computer, the amount of memory it has, the available storage capacity and speed of its hard drive, and so on. If you experience problems while burning CDs, check each of these; usually, the issues stem from system power and maintenance issues.

Packaging the CD

If you're preparing a master for replication, you will probably use the service's package preparation service to produce the artwork for the CD. Even so, you'll need to provide them with the proper information and special artwork (such as a band photo) in the format that they require. Check with the replication service beforehand to find out what they need before you even begin to burn your master CD.

Chances are that you're not going to use a replication service to make a small run of CDs, but that doesn't mean that you should be satisfied with a product with only a handwritten label. You can do much better than that! All of the tools and materials you need to create great-looking CD packages can be found at your local computer or electronics store. For example, you can get blank CD labels and covers that are precut or perforated. Their manufacturers often have blank templates on their websites so you can typeset covers and labels using your favorite word processing, labeling, or illustration program. There are also programs that are entirely dedicated to creating CD/DVD label and cover layouts, and many of the consumer-oriented CD creation programs come bundled with a separate program for CD cover and label design.

In short, there's no reason why you can't create attractive CD labels and covers for your projects. Sure, it takes a little more time to design something and print it, but it will look much better than a handwritten note on the CD itself. You also should bear in mind that CD labels, cards, etc. are promotional material, not unlike the elements of a press kit, so it pays to take the time to create an attractive, professional CD package. If nothing else, it will make you feel good whenever you look at your CD.

Archiving Your Project

Now that you've burned and packaged your CD, you might think that the only thing left to do is erase your audio files and start recording new songs. Well, not so fast, buddy! Before you erase those project files, you should archive them. Fortunately, consumer CD creation programs let you create data CDs and DVDs on which you can store your audio tracks. Some programs will also let you archive across multiple CDs so that you can more efficiently archive large tracks and/or large numbers of tracks.

What should you archive? In a word: everything! Archive all of your audio files, including all of your takes (even the unused ones). Archive the digital audio sequencer's project files, including alternate mixes and their settings. Archive the stereo masters, both the unedited and edited versions. Archive the files and settings you used to create the different playlists for your CD, as well as the settings for the final CD project. Archive the artwork you created, and anything else associated with this CD project.

Finally, make sure that each of the archive CDs is properly labeled and dated so that you can retrieve any or all of the project files if you should need to.

Once you've successfully archived all of your project material, *then* you may erase those files from your hard drive.

And do you know what you can do next?

Begin the process of creating more great music!

EPILOGUE

Thank you for selecting this book and taking the time to read it. Does this mean that you now know everything there is to know about computer-based music production? No way! As I said at the outset, this is a *beginner's guide*. There's not enough space here to teach you everything you need to know about creating music using a personal computer. In fact, no single book can make that claim and be truthful about it. However, I hope that you've been able to use this guide as a starting point for developing your skills regarding all of the different aspects of computer-based music production.

So where do you go from here? Well, there are two things you can do.

First off, you can read as much about music creation as you can. There are a number of great books out there that provide more detailed information about making music, and there are likewise several magazines that can provide a good, constant flow of information and inspiration. The Internet is also a fantastic source for material regarding recording techniques, audio concepts, and product information—don't ignore this vast reservoir of knowledge!

Second off, practice, practice, practice! It's the only way to get good at making music with your computer. All of the reading in the world will be useless if you don't apply this knowledge to real-world situations. Record as often as you can when you can. Listen to other people's recordings to analyze what you like or don't like about them. Try to reproduce things you like that other people have done. But, most importantly, try to develop your own techniques and style of recording.

Remember that computer-based music production—indeed, music production in any form—is both an art and a science. If you're serious about making music, you'll never stop learning about the artistry, the techniques, and the tools involved. In a very literal sense, it's the experience of a lifetime. I hope you enjoy it.

Appendix A
A Hard Disk Primer

It's important that computer-based musicians—and even those who use stand-alone hard disk recorders—understand how hard drives work. After all, this is the media to which all of your audio data is recorded and from which it's played back. Understanding how your computer records and plays back digital audio data from a hard drive is critical. What's more, knowing how to maintain a hard drive is just as important for computer-based musicians as it is for a multitrack tape deck owner to maintain a tape deck for optimal performance. And knowing how to choose the proper hard drive for computer-based music production is vital if you want to get the best possible performance out of your system.

Reading and Writing

The average hard disk drive contains at least one disk (often two or three) or *platter* that is coated with magnetic material on both sides. The surface on each side is divided into concentric circles called *tracks*. These tracks are subdivided into even smaller sections called *sectors*. Your computer's operating system further divides these sectors into a number of *blocks*, each with a set size. Each side of each disk in a hard drive has its own read/write head, whose appearance is reminiscent of a turntable tone arm. The read/write head doesn't read and write data simultaneously—it can do only one or the other at any given moment.

Whenever a computer writes data to a hard disk drive, it ideally stores that information in *contiguous* blocks—that is, blocks that are next to each other. This keeps disk head movement to a minimum so that data can be written to the drive more efficiently. Storing data in contiguous blocks also makes it easier for it to be read back from the hard drive as well. This is important when it comes to dealing with digital audio data, because audio information must be *streamed* to and from a hard drive—in other words, it must be constantly written to or read from a drive—and that takes a lot of work.

In reality, however, computers write data in a less than ideal fashion. Each time you create new files or otherwise change data in existing files, the computer stores that data in the first available space after the point where *all* of the data has been previously written. But how does the computer know where the "end" of the data is? Well, the operating system keeps a record of which blocks are associated with what files on the hard drive itself (it doesn't matter if it's called a file allocation table or a hierarchical file structure system, except as it relates to the operating system being used—it's still the same sort of record). The main function of this record is to keep track of the location of each file's data blocks on the hard drive. This is very important for smooth hard disk operation.

When data is deleted, it leaves behind one or more blocks of free space (i.e., where it was stored). However, a computer won't take advantage of these scattered blocks of free space—it will only write to free space past the end of all existing data. Over time, this continual process of adding, deleting, and altering files will eventually cause a disk to become *fragmented*—i.e., file data is no longer stored in contiguous blocks.

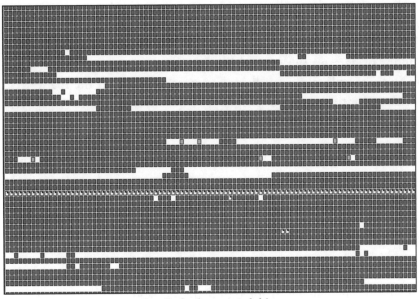

Detail of a fragmented drive

Fragmentation is unavoidable because it happens as a natural part of computer operation. The good news is that a drive's file table keeps track of where all of a file's data blocks are, no matter how scattered those blocks may be. The bad news is that as a drive becomes more fragmented, its read/write heads are forced to move around all the more to locate data. This slows down hard drive performance and increases the chances that a hard drive crash will occur, and your computer may lose data (actually, the data generally doesn't get deleted—it's simply not recoverable because the file table has been broken so it doesn't know where to "pick up the trail").

So why is this a particular problem with digital audio data? Well, digital audio files require a lot of hard drive space: A single audio track recorded at 16-bit/44.1 kHz resolution generates about 5 MB of data per minute, and you can increase that figure to 7.6 MB for tracks at 24-bit/44.1 kHz resolution. Recording digital audio at 24-bit/96 kHz resolution, which is considered the top end for most digital audio recorders and computer-based systems, requires just over 16.5 MB per minute! At this rate, a four-minute 16-track song would require over 1 GB of hard disk space! Obviously, that's a lot of data that has to be streamed to and from a hard drive.

Why a Second Drive?

Again, the most efficient way for a hard drive to read or write data—especially large amounts of data like digital audio—is to make sure that all of the data is stored in contiguous blocks. And the best way to ensure that digital audio data is written and stored that way is to put it on its own drive, away from other files that are accessed and changed more frequently (such as word processing files and so forth). Because main hard drives store more frequently changed files, they tend to fragment sooner, ultimately slowing down hard drive performance. This can adversely affect how smoothly a computer can play back or record digital audio files onto its own hard drive.

Partitioning Drives

Rather than buy a second hard drive for storing digital audio data, you might be tempted to save money and *partition* your existing drive—that is, divide the drive so that it appears as two separate drives on your computer. You can then store programs and frequently changed files on the first partition and digital audio data on the second partition. Of course, this has the same effect as storing digital audio data on a separate drive. However, it's now possible to purchase large-capacity, fast hard drives for about $100–$300, which is a relatively small expense. So, why not just buy a second hard drive devoted exclusively to digital audio data? It's also likely that you'll need all of the available space on the non-partitioned main drive eventually, so why even bother to partition it? After all, some music programs store a large amount of data on the main drive, too—software samplers and some music production packages store audio sample files as well as their program files on the main drive by default, and it's not even uncommon for these types of programs to occupy 500 MB to 3 gigabytes (GB) of hard drive space. And that's before the user even begins to create a project!

At any rate, another reason why it's better to get a second physical drive for digital audio rather than partition the *boot drive* (the drive on which your computer's operating system resides) is that boot drives are not always the fastest drives a computer can use. Some Mac and PC laptops have slow boot drives with slow rotation speeds, making them undesirable for extensive digital audio work. Attaching a second, faster external hard drive can remedy that problem.

Another good reason for using a second physical drive has nothing to do with speed and everything to do with peace of mind. If the main drive becomes corrupted or damaged, you could lose all of your digital audio data, even if it's in a separate partition. Do you really want to take that sort of chance with your music?

The bottom line—it's better all around to have a second hard drive devoted solely to digital audio data.

Hard Disk Maintenance

Knowing how to maintain a hard drive is important because a computer-based musician needs to get the best possible performance from a system. Fortunately, taking care of a hard drive is easy. Windows users have disk utility programs built into their operating system. Mac users don't, but there are inexpensive third-party disk utility programs available (but note that you must use a program designed for the specific operating system on your computer). All of these programs have, among other things, defragmentation and disk-scanning functions. There are several things you can do in conjunction with running these programs in order to obtain the best results.

There are two things that you should do before you begin a defragmentation process. First off, for any files that are in the recycle bin (Windows) or trash (Mac), either formally discard them (i.e., empty the trash or recycle bin) or restore them (i.e., move them out of the trash). When you consign files to the trash, they aren't really thrown away—their contents are still on the drive, but their file allocation information has been moved to a temporary area so that these files aren't "seen" as being on the drive. You should resolve this ambiguity before defragmenting.

Secondly, back up the data on your hard drive before you defragment. Although it's unlikely to happen, rearranging file blocks can sometimes result in data loss.

Simple Defragmentation

Now you can begin to defragment or *optimize* a hard drive. However, there are different ways in which to do this. For instance, there is a simple form of defragmentation that will rearrange individual files so that they aren't scattered around the hard disk, but even so, there will still be gaps between blocks of data between different files because the overall blocks are not grouped contiguously. On the other hand, an individual file's data will be found in one location on the disk, which will make it easier to recover in the event of a hard drive crash.

Space Consolidation

Another form of optimization simply consolidates free space. This method doesn't actually defragment data—it maximizes the amount of contiguous free space remaining at the end of a disk so that it can write new data without causing further fragmentation. This is actually a useful option for computer-based musicians working with digital audio data files, since digital audio programs refer to digital audio data via virtual tracks. These files point to digital audio data that exists on the drive, but changes to them generally don't alter the audio data itself. However, if you delete any digital audio files, they can leave large gaps throughout a drive that won't get refilled because the system will look for the next available space at the end of the drive when it needs to write a file. Consolidating free space closes up those gaps and makes more contiguous space available again for recording.

Full Optimization

Full optimization defragments files and rearranges them in contiguous blocks so that the files are easier to read. This has the added benefit of increasing the amount of available free disk space for recording new data, too. The disk optimization software will usually analyze your file usage and put frequently changed files in a different location than less frequently changed files. This can speed up access to existing files and maximize the speed at which new files are written to a drive.

Disk Scanning

If for some reason you experience a hard drive crash, you may want to do a disk scan to check for improperly named files or folders, find any orphaned data that no longer relates to an existing files on the hard drive, etc. (check with your software manual for more details).

If you suspect that your hard drive has some physical damage (it's not likely, but it is possible with older hard drives), you can instruct the scanning program to check the integrity of the drive's physical surface. Any damaged blocks can then be identified and masked so that the computer won't try to write data to them in the future. However, if you seem to have damaged blocks every time you check the drive, it may just be time to get a new hard drive.

Don't Do That

Disk utility programs offer other features and options that computer-based musicians should avoid using. For example, don't use a real-time data compression program to save on drive space—this will make the computer work harder and slow down the process of smoothly streaming digital audio data to and from the disk.

Also, some disk utility programs will let the user run the program *in the background* (i.e., perhaps unbeknownst to you, and while you're working in another program); for instance, some programs will begin defragmenting drives if they are idle for a specific length of time. Other utilities may begin backing up files if a drive is idle, or if a program is scheduled to begin working at a specific time. However, programs that run in the background take up computer resources, and you don't want something like this to suddenly start defragmenting the boot drive or accessing the hard disk just as you're getting ready to record or play back digital audio data. Remember: Anything that slows down or interrupts hard disk performance is bad when working with a digital audio program.

Hard Drive Specs

As I mentioned in "Chapter 2: Choosing the Right Computer," there are several kinds of hard drives (e.g., ATA, FireWire, SCSI, USB 2.0) that are suitable for multitrack digital audio work. However, a hard drive's specifications are just as important as its type in terms of digital audio work. You need to know what the specs are, and what they really mean. Don't worry—this information is pretty easy to both understand and use.

Data Transfer Speed

Data transfer speeds are supposed to indicate how fast data is transferred from a hard drive into a computer's memory or processor. However, stated data transfer speeds are almost useless when it comes to judging actual hard disk performance. But here are the theoretical transfer speeds for various types of hard drives, just so you'll know.

ATA drives are supposed to transfer data at their designated bus speed. For example, an ATA 66 MHz drive should transfer data at a rate of 66 MB per second. An ATA Ultra 100 MHz drive theoretically transfers data at 100 MB per second. Different types of SCSI drives also transfer data at specific rates, too. For example, SCSI 160 drives transfer data at speeds of 160 MB per second. FireWire hard drives transfer data at roughly 50 MB per second, which at first glance is much slower than ATA and the fastest SCSI drives. However, their sustained data rate is more than sufficient to record and play back multiple tracks of digital audio. USB 2.0 drives transfer data at 480 Mbps, or about 60 MB. Like FireWire drives, their sustained data rate is sufficient enough to record and play back multiple digital audio tracks simultaneously.

Burst Speed vs. Sustained Speed Rates

No matter what type of second drive you decide to buy, keep in mind the following facts. First, nearly all of the advertised data transfer rates are *burst speed* rates, which correspond to how much data a hard drive can transfer over a short period of time. However, for hard disk–based digital audio systems of any kind, the *sustained speed* or data rates are more important because digital audio data gets recorded onto and plays back from a hard drive in a continuous stream. Most manufacturers don't list their hard drives' sustained data rates because they are much lower than their burst speed rates, but most of these drives are capable of sustaining a data stream of at least 12 MB per second, which is sufficient when you consider that playing 24 tracks of 24-bit/96kHz digital audio at once requires a data stream of about 6.6 MB per second.

Rotation Speed

Rotation speed determines how fast a hard drive may be able to access or write data. The faster the drive rotates, the higher its transfer rate will be. Typical rotation speeds for ATA, FireWire, and USB 2.0 hard drives are 5400 to 7200 RPM. Laptop drives often have lower rotation speeds (4500 RPM) but are now beginning to match the rotation speeds of desktop hard drives. Most SCSI drives have rotation speeds of 7200 RPM, but the faster SCSI 160 drives now offer 10,000 RPM rotation speeds. A few SCSI drives even rotate at 15,000 RPM! Naturally, these drives are more expensive, so unless you really need the speed and power that SCSI 160 drives can provide, I would recommend using 7200 RPM drives. They offer the best balance between price and performance, and are superior to less expensive 5400 RPM drives.

Average Seek Time

Average seek time is another factor that indicates how fast a hard drive can transfer data. The reason it's called *average* is that it takes into account information relating to several different types of seek times. One type, *cylinder switch time*, is the average time it takes to move the heads to the next track when reading or writing data. The fastest cylinder switch time occurs when a head moves from one track directly to the next, and that can be as low as 2 ms. The slowest cylinder switch time happens when a head has to jump between the outer and inner tracks, and that can take as long as 20 ms.

Another type of seek time is *head switch time*, which corresponds to the average time the drive takes to switch between the two head functions of reading and writing data. Hard disk heads perform double duty as data readers and writers, and it takes more time to write data than to read it. Head switch time just measures how quickly a hard drive's heads can switch between these two tasks.

After the drive head has been positioned over the desired track, it has to wait for the drive to spin to the exact sector where the data is located or needs to be written. This type of seek time is called *rotational latency*. As you might guess, the faster the drive spins, the shorter the rotational latency time will be. At the very worst, the hard disk needs to turn half way around, and that usually takes about 6 ms for a 5400 RPM drive, and 4 ms for a 7200 RPM drive.

All of these factors combined make up a hard drive's *average seek time*. It's essentially the time that it takes for a drive's heads to go to a random location, and it's a good *general* measure of how quickly a hard drive can transfer data. Naturally, the lower the average seek time, the faster the drive. For digital audio systems, an average seek time of under 10 ms is recommended (8.5 ms or lower is ideal).

Storage Capacity

Finally, get a hard drive that has a large storage capacity. For digital audio work, I recommend nothing less than a 40 GB drive. Digital audio data requires a lot of storage space, and you'd be surprised how quickly it gets used up.

APPENDIX B
MICROPHONE BASICS

Unless you're planning to produce only electronic music, you're going to need to have at least one good microphone for recording vocals and certain types of instrument parts. In the past, a good vocal microphone was easily a four-figure investment. Fortunately for you, you're living in good times, because advances in microphone design and manufacturing techniques have made it possible to buy a good vocal mic for as little as $300 (the average price is between $500 to $700). For instance, you can purchase an AKG C 4000 B, Audio-Technica AT4033, Beyerdynamic MCE90, Røde NT2, or Shure KSM32—all of which are excellent microphones—for a street price of around $500 to $600. Of course, you could still easily spend $1000 or more on a good vocal mic, but if you're just starting out, a good-quality inexpensive mic is all you really need.

While many vocal mics often do double duty as instrument mics, you may want to invest in separate instrument mics as well. You could spend as little as $100 for an instrument mic, or as much as $1000 and up. All of that depends on the type of microphone you need for the recording situation at hand. For example, if you're recording someone who is simultaneously singing and playing an acoustic guitar, you'll often want to mic the singer and guitar separately. Maybe you'll need to mic a singer while recording their electric guitar or bass part from its amplifier. Perhaps you'll even need to record a drum kit or a whole band in one pass. Whatever the recording situation, having one or more mics dedicated to recording instruments is a worthwhile investment.

Microphone Types

As a rule, microphones are classified by their construction—that is, the design of the *transducer* (the part of the microphone that converts sound waves into electrical signals). There are three types of mics that are of interest to the computer-based musician: *dynamic, condenser,* and *ribbon* microphones.

Dynamic Microphones

A dynamic mic consists of a light diaphragm coupled to a small metal (usually aluminum) coil immersed in a strong magnetic field. When sound waves of sufficient strength strike against this diaphragm, it moves in and out in response to the sound wave's cycle of *compression* and *rarefaction* (i.e., high and low pressure). This also moves the metal coil, whose motion in the fixed magnetic field generates voltage levels that are analogous to the changes in sound pressure acting on the diaphragm. If this description of a dynamic mic has a vaguely familiar ring to you, it's because this is just the reverse of the same process that causes speakers—which also contain moving diaphragms—to convert electrical energy back into sound. In fact, some engineers use small speakers as diaphragms for custom-made dynamic mics!

Dynamic mics are the most widely used type of microphone, and there are several good reasons for this. First off, they're inexpensive compared to most other types of microphones. Dynamic mics are also extremely rugged, which makes them suitable for use in abusive environments such as stage settings. What's more, they work well in the studio because they're also able to handle high *sound pressure levels* (SPLs) that emanate from sound sources such as drums, guitar amps cranked up to "11," and screaming death metal vocalists. For instance, the Shure SM57 and the Sennheiser MD421 are two classic workhorse mics most often used for recording drums and guitar amps. Likewise, the AKG D112 is widely used for recording bass drums and bass guitar amps.

Dynamic mics also make good vocal mics for narration. In fact, I know of one voiceover artist who insists on using his own Shure SM7 dynamic mic for all of his voiceover sessions, no matter what other microphones are available at the voiceover studio. I've likewise used the Sennheiser MD421 for narration work with excellent results.

Although dynamic microphones can handle high SPLs well, they don't do such a good job of picking up the high-end detail that gives an "airiness" to some sounds, such as sung vocals and many acoustic instruments. That's not always bad, because you don't want to record some types of high-end detail such as rattles and vibrations in drum hardware and guitar/bass amps. On the other hand, there are times when high-end detail is necessary to the sound of the recording. Fortunately, there are other types of microphones that are better suited to capturing this.

Condenser Microphones

While condenser mics have diaphragms just like dynamic mics, they differ in that they have a fixed backplate that is positioned near the diaphragm. A fixed electrical polarizing charge is maintained between the backplate and diaphragm, and when sound waves cause the diaphragm to move, the voltage between the diaphragm and backplate changes accordingly. Compare that to a dynamic mic, whose diaphragm is attached to a coil that *generates* variable voltage whenever the diaphragm moves.

All condenser microphones have a preamplifier located next to the diaphragm. The preamp's job is to convert the very high electrical impedance of the condenser element into a low enough voltage value so that the signal can be easily transmitted down a standard microphone cable. Some microphones are prepolarized with power provided by an internal battery. This type of condenser mic is often referred to as an *electret* mic. Most condenser mics, however, don't have prepolarized backplates, and instead the polarity is generated by an external 48-volt direct current power source that travels through the mic cable from a power source provided by a mixer or mic preamp. This power source is known as *phantom power*, and it's an important feature to have in a mixer, mic preamp, or even an audio interface.

Condenser mics are more sensitive to high frequencies than dynamic mics, and respond better to transient signals such as the short, initial attacks of notes. Small-diaphragm condenser mics are especially good at capturing transients and higher frequencies because it takes less energy to move the mass of their diaphragms—this is why they're often used as instrument mics. On the other hand, small-diaphragm mics don't do so well at capturing the warmth of complex low-end frequencies, such as those generated by the sound of a human singing voice. Large-diaphragm condenser mics are better suited to this task.

Ribbon Microphones

Ribbon mics are constructed with a very thin metal ribbon suspended between the poles of a powerful fixed magnet. When the ribbon moves in response to sound waves, it causes changes in the magnetic field that produces an electrical current. The low-voltage output it generates is usually fed into a step-up transformer and then sent down the mic cable.

Because of the extreme thinness of its ribbon, this type of mic is the most sensitive of the three, especially at picking up very low sound levels. Ribbon mics are most often used in close-miking situations where detail is important, such as recording violins, acoustic guitars, hammered dulcimers, and similar instruments. Ribbon mics also handle high sound pressure levels well, so they're also great for recording brass, saxes, and other woodwinds. You can even use them to record snare drums and cymbals.

However, ribbon mics are physically the most fragile of the three microphone types. They need to be handled gently and with great care, and they should only be used in very controlled recording conditions. Ribbon mics also tend to have low output levels, which often means that you have to apply more gain to the signal than you would with other types of mics. For that reason, it's important that ribbon mics be paired with high-quality mic preamps to prevent unwanted noise from occurring in the final output.

As a beginning computer-based musician, you probably won't use ribbon mics. However, as your recording skills develop and improve and your equipment base expands, you may want to consider getting one if you plan on recording the types of acoustic instruments mentioned earlier.

Polar Patterns

A microphone's *polar pattern* describes how it detects incoming sound waves. Knowing a mic's polar pattern is as important as understanding its type of construction, since this will also determine how a mic should be used. In fact, some mics have selectable polar patterns so that you can adapt them to different recording situations, not to mention get even more use out of the mics themselves.

Cardioid Pattern

The most common polar pattern found in microphones is the *cardioid* pattern, and it gets its name from its resemblance to a heart shape. Cardioid mics are *unidirectional*—that is, they pick up sound mainly from the front of the microphone capsule while the back of the capsule rejects sound. Cardioid mics allow a recordist to isolate a signal source from other signal sources or background noise. This is helpful when you need to mic band members or individual drums in a kit while simultaneously minimizing noise from other sources that could bleed through into the track.

Cardioid mics come in three varieties: *standard cardioid*, *supercardioid*, and *hypercardioid*. The standard cardioid mic picks up signals mainly from the front of the mic, but also picks up signals to a lesser degree from the sides of the mic. A supercardioid mic will reject more of the signals that are to either side of the mic, while a hypercardioid mic will reject even more of the side signals present.

Supercardioid and hypercardioid mics are more often used on stage, where their greater "focus" ensures superior signal isolation and reduces the chance of feedback. However, any type of cardioid mic can be used where signal isolation is a crucial consideration.

Omni Pattern

Microphones with an *omni* (short for *omnidirectional*) polar pattern pick up sound equally well from all directions. This type of microphone is best used when you want to capture room ambience along with a source sound. It's an excellent technique for capturing the full flavor of an acoustic instrument in a good acoustic space. Omnidirectional mics are also great for recording groups of singers: just gather them around the mic and let them naturally blend their voices together. This technique often yields better results than attempting to mic each singer with a separate cardioid vocal mic.

Omni mics, unlike cardioid mics, are relatively immune to *proximity effect*—as the proximity (i.e., nearness) of the source material to the cardioid mic gets shorter, the low and mid frequencies increase. At the right distance, you can achieve a great, full sound. However, if the mic is positioned too close to the source signal, the resulting sound can be boomy and muddled. For example, many vocalists have a tendency to sing very close to the microphone, often placing their lips right on the microphone itself! This almost always forces the engineer to roll off low-end frequencies to compensate for any resulting boominess in the vocalist's sound. One way that recordists (myself included) avoid this problem is by using an omni condenser mic in a controlled acoustic environment for recording vocals. The problems of proximity effect are then negligible, yet vocalists feel that the full range of their vocal sound is captured well. It's a lot easier to do that than to remind the vocalist every two minutes to stand a couple of inches back from the mic!

Bidirectional (Figure 8) Pattern

Microphones with a *bidirectional* polar pattern (sometimes called a *figure 8* pattern) detect sound with equal sensitivity on two opposite faces and reject sound from the sides. This kind of mic is great for capturing duets: just position the singers so they're facing each other with the bidirectional mic between them.

Figure 8 mics exhibit the same characteristics of the proximity effect as do cardioid mics. This shouldn't be too surprising if you realize that bidirectional mics can be made by wiring two cardioid mic capsules back-to-back out of phase with each other. Similarly, omnidirectional mics can be built by wiring two cardioid mic capsules back-to-back *in* phase with each other. As a matter of fact, that's how many multipattern microphones are made. The other way is to create removable capsules for each polar pattern type, which is more expensive to manufacture and, therefore, to buy.

Other Microphone Features

There's more to selecting microphones than just recognizing types of mics and polar patterns. For one, it helps to know whether a microphone is a *side-address* or a *top-address* mic. Basically, a side-address mic has a diaphragm oriented to the side of the mic, while a top-address mic has a diaphragm oriented to the top of the mic. In other words, you either sing or play into the side or top of the mic, respectively, depending on its construction.

Both types of mic designs have their advantages. For instance, top-address mics are usually unidirectional mics that can be "aimed" at sound sources and fit into tighter spots (such as between drums). Because of the inherent nature of their design, side-address mics often have *multipattern capability*, so you can use them as unidirectional, omnidirectional, or figure-8 mics with the flip of a switch, as your recording situation dictates.

A *roll-off switch* can also be an important microphone feature as well for a variety of reasons. As I mentioned earlier, using a cardioid mic can introduce the problem of proximity effect. A roll-off switch on a mic can act as a *high-pass filter*—that is, a filter that allows frequencies higher than a cut-off point to pass through. One common high-pass setting for roll-off switches is 80 Hz; this is a good setting because it not only handles common proximity effect problems, but it usually eliminates *room rumble* (the noise present in a room because of random air molecular movement) as well. Depending on the make of the mic, it may have other roll-off settings besides 80 Hz. My Sennheiser MD421, for example, has a roll-off setting of 500 Hz. Moreover, it has five discrete roll-off steps that further *attenuate* (reduce) the decibel level at which the microphone starts to roll off the lower frequencies.

A *pad switch* that reduces a mic's sensitivity to high sound pressure levels can be a useful feature, too. Sometimes you want to reduce a mic's output without necessarily turning down the sound source's or the mic's preamp. A mic with a pad switch that can reduce its sensitivity to signal levels is perfect for this type of situation. Most pad switches attenuate mic sensitivity by 10 or 20 dB, although that's not a hard and fast rule. Check the mic's specs to see if it has this feature and, if so, how much it reduces its sensitivity.

Roll-off and pad switches mean little, though, unless you also know the mic's frequency response—however, there's more to knowing about a mic's frequency response besides its frequency range. For example, many mic manufacturers can state that their microphones have a frequency response of 20 Hz to 20 kHz, which sounds outstanding on the face of it. However, microphones don't respond to all frequencies equally, and neither do they exhibit the same polar response pattern at all frequencies.

You don't necessarily want a mic that responds to all frequencies equally. For example, you may want a vocal mic to respond better to higher frequencies than to low frequencies. Conversely, you may want a mic for bass guitars and bass drums to record lower frequencies better than high frequencies.

This all just scratches the surface on the topic of proper mic selection. If you want to learn more about choosing mics for recording work and how to set them up for various recording situations, I suggest that you check out the web pages of the various microphone manufacturers. Shure Incorporated (www.shure.com) and Audio-Technica (www.audio-technica.com) have excellent information online, as well as PDF files of instructional materials complete with illustrations. As of this writing, M-Audio (www.m-audio.com) has on their site an excellent PDF file of a booklet called "A Quick-Start Guide to Choosing & Using Microphones."

Microphone Accessories

While the selection of a microphone should be done with due care and diligence, it's also important to make sure that you have the right accessories for your new mic. These important accessories will ensure that your newly acquired mics give you many years of useful service.

Mic Stand

I know it sounds as though I'm belaboring the obvious, but many a beginning recording musician buys mic stands based on price and appearance rather than true functionality. One of the more common mistakes is to buy a mic stand that doesn't adequately support the weight of the microphone that's attached to it. Basically, a light boom stand and a heavy large-diaphragm condenser mic is an unstable combination that will probably fall over or easily get knocked down, most likely damaging the mic in the process. At the very least, the weight of the mic will often force the boom arm down, eventually causing the mic stand to be unusable after repeated attempts to readjust and tighten the boom. Save yourself the headache (not to mention potential disaster) by getting a mic stand that's able to properly support your mic.

Shockmount

Condenser and ribbon mics are delicate pieces of equipment, and should be protected from physical shock. Never allow them to be hand-held while in use! Rather, use a mic stand that provides proper support, and be sure to attach a *shockmount* to the stand and then place the mic *inside* of that. A shockmount suspends a microphone in an elastic web that prevents vibrations from the floor and any light physical shock from reaching it. This will not only protect your condenser or ribbon mic from harm, it will also ensure that the sounds of these unwanted vibrations and bumps won't make their way into the recording.

Some microphone manufacturers include shockmounts with the mics they sell, but most sell shockmounts as optional equipment. An optional shockmount is usually designed for a specific microphone model, so it will hold that particularly mic perfectly. So even though it may cost extra, it's worth getting the shockmount, considering that it helps to protect a valuable mic.

Pop Filter

As I mentioned earlier, many vocalists have a tendency to stand extremely close to a mic when singing. Besides the problems with the previously mentioned proximity effect, this also causes issues with *plosives* and *sibilants*. Plosives include the hard "p" sounds and, to a lesser extent, the "b" sounds in speech production. Producing these sounds projects a lot of extra energy compared to other sounds made by vocalizations. "T" sounds, which are technically called *dentals*, project extra energy as well. This extra energy often creates unwanted "pops," which are not only unpleasant to hear, but are hard on the mic as well.

Sibilants, or "s" sounds in speech, can also pack a lot of energy, depending on how a vocalist or narrator enunciates. A high amount of sibilance in a recording is unpleasant and potentially damaging to the mic, and it's such a common problem that there is a piece of equipment made to handle this specific problem—the *de-esser*. As you may have guessed from the name, a de-esser minimizes the effects of hard "s" sounds in recordings. However, de-essers can cost hundreds of dollars, and many recordists misuse them so that all of the "s" sounds disappear from a recording—which sounds just as unnatural as too much sibilance.

The more cost-effective (and often more natural-sounding) solution to this problem is to use a *pop filter* between a mic and a vocalist. A pop filter consists of a piece of nylon mesh stretched over a circular frame, which is then usually attached to a small gooseneck stand and a clamp that attaches to a mic stand. Pop filters are adjustable, so you can position them in such a way as to keep a singer at a proper distance from a mic. This can help to tame the plosives and sibilants mentioned earlier while still maintaining the natural enunciation of words. A pop filter can also have an additional benefit: It can prevent a singer's saliva from reaching a microphone, and thereby further protect it from damage.

APPENDIX C
GENERAL MIDI AND STANDARD MIDI FILES

Understanding the differences between General MIDI (GM) files and Standard MIDI Files (SMF) is one of the most common sources of confusion for beginning MIDI musicians. The best way to illustrate the differences between the two is to explain how these two standards developed in the first place.

Before there were digital audio sequencers, there were simply MIDI sequencing programs. Then, as now, each program stored sequence files in its own, or *native* format. The problem was that different programs couldn't share the same information because they weren't in a standard file format. Sometimes, even different computer platforms couldn't share the same information generated by a cross-platform version of the same program! Gradually, a Standard MIDI File format was developed so that MIDI information could be shared, regardless of what program or computer one used.

Even so, that didn't solve the other problem that occurred when trying to share MIDI file data—matching the patches or sounds that the author of the MIDI file used. For instance, the program number I used with my synthesizer to play a piano sound might be a trumpet sound in your synthesizer. In other words, MIDI files had been standardized, but not MIDI sound patches.

The General MIDI standard was developed in response to this problem. A standard list of 128 different sounds, as well as a set of percussion sounds mapped to specific MIDI notes and played on MIDI Channel 10, ensured that sounds would resemble each other from program to program. Note that I said *resemble*, because even though the sound patches are standardized, this doesn't guarantee that each General MIDI instrument sounds exactly the same on every piece of hardware. The quality of a General MIDI instrument's sounds depends on its samples.

Shortly after the development of General MIDI, Roland developed the GS format for its instruments. It's based on the GM format, but includes extra sounds and percussion sets that are variations on this sound set. These sounds and percussion sets can be accessed using Bank Select control change messages (digital audio sequencers access these sounds automatically). Yamaha likewise developed the XG format for its own instruments, which is its own extended version of the GM sound set. Now, there is a new General MIDI format called General MIDI 2 (GM2), which has variations on the basic 128 GM and the original percussion sound set. Basically, it is similar to the GS sound set found in the original Roland SC-55 SoundCanvas module

So as you can see, it's possible to have Standard MIDI Files that don't use the GM, GS, or XG sound sets. It's also possible to use GM, GS, and XG sound sets in native file formats. But if you want to author MIDI files that can be easily shared by all, it's best to use the GM or GM2 sound set, and save the MIDI sequences in Standard MIDI File format.

Patch #	Sound	Patch #	Sound	Patch #	Sound	Patch #	Sound
1	Piano 1	33	Acoustic Bass	65	Soprano Sax	97	Ice Rain
2	Piano 2	34	Fingered Bass	66	Alto Sax	98	Soundtrack
3	Piano 3	35	Picked Bass	67	Tenor Sax	99	Crystal
4	Honky-tonk Piano	36	Fretless Bass	68	Baritone Sax	100	Atmosphere
5	Electric Piano 1	37	Slap Bass 1	69	Oboe	101	Brightness
6	Electric Piano 2	38	Slap Bass 2	70	English Horn	102	Goblin
7	Harpsichord	39	Synth Bass 1	71	Bassoon	103	Echo Drops
8	Clavinet	40	Synth Bass 2	72	Clarinet	104	Star Theme
9	Celesta	41	Violin	73	Piccolo	105	Sitar
10	Glockenspiel	42	Viola	74	Flute	106	Banjo
11	Music Box	43	Cello	75	Recorder	107	Shamisen
12	Vibraphone	44	Contrabass	76	Pan Flute	108	Koto
13	Marimba	45	Tremolo Strings	77	Blown Bottle	109	Kalimba
14	Xylophone	46	Pizzicato Strings	78	Shakuhachi	110	Bagpipe
15	Tubular Bells	47	Harp	79	Whistle	111	Fiddle
16	Santur	48	Timpani	80	Ocarina	112	Shenai
17	Organ 1	49	Strings	81	Square Wave	113	Tinkle Bell
18	Organ 2	50	Slow Strings	82	Saw Wave	114	Agogo
19	Organ 3	51	Synth Strings 1	83	Synth Calliope	115	Steel Drums
20	Church Organ	52	Synth Strings 2	84	Chiffer Lead	116	Woodblock
21	Reed Organ	53	Choir Aahs	85	Charang	117	Taiko
22	Accordian	54	Voice Oohs	86	Solo Vox	118	Melodic Tom
23	Harmonica	55	Syn Vox	87	Saw Wave 5th	119	Synth Drum
24	Bandoneon	56	Orchestra Hit	88	Bass & Lead	120	Reverse Cymbal
25	Nylon-String Guitar	57	Trumpet	89	Fantasia	121	Guitar Fret Noise
26	Steel-String Guitar	58	Trombone	90	Warm Pad	122	Breath Noise
27	Jazz Guitar	59	Tuba	91	Poly Synth	123	Seashore
28	Clean Guitar	60	Muted Trumpet	92	Space Voice	124	Birds
29	Muted Guitar	61	French Horn	93	Bowed Glass	125	Telephone
30	Overdrive Guitar	62	Brass	94	Metal Pad	126	Helicopter
31	Distortion Guitar	63	Synth Brass 1	95	Halo Pad	127	Applause
32	Guitar Harmonics	64	Synth Brass 2	96	Sweep Pad	128	Gunshot

Note: Patch changes on Channel 10 will call up different drumsets, depending on the capabilities of the MIDI module being used.

A typical General MIDI patch list

ABOUT THE AUTHOR

Zack Price has been a recording artist since 1984, and a computer-based musician since 1986. He has regularly contributed features, reviews, columns, and editorials to music magazines such as *Electronic Musician, Guitar Player, Home Recording,* and *Mix.* Currently, he is the editor of *Home & Project Studio,* a downloadable digital magazine.

Zack Price

ACKNOWLEDGMENTS

Many people have been helpful to me in writing this book, and I would like to recognize their contributions.

Rusty Cutchin, for recommending that I do this project in the first place.

Jim Cooper (Mark of the Unicorn), Brian McConnon (Steinberg), David Poncet and Vanessa Giraudet (Arturia), Steve Thomas (Cakewalk), Marsha Vdovin (Propellerhead Software), Tom Sailor (Synthax), and Clint Ward (Emagic) for contributing music software.

Susan Poliniak and John Stix at Cherry Lane Music Publishing, for maintaining their calm and poise while I regularly taxed their patience.

Finally, to my wife Susan, for proofreading the text, keeping me supplied with homemade oatmeal raisin cookies, and just being there in general for the last 20 years and counting.